W9-DIT-495

Ernest Hemingway and the arts

"I can make a landscape like Paul Cézanne."

—ERNEST HEMINGWAY TO LILLIAN ROSS (1950)

Paul Cézanne, "Mont Sainte Victoire." Oil on canvas, 25¾ x 32⅛ in. The Metropolitan Museum of Art, bequest of Mrs. H. O. Havemeyer, 1929. The H. O. Havemeyer Collection.

Ernest Hemingway and the arts

EMILY STIPES WATTS

University of Illinois Press

URBANA CHICAGO LONDON

Manufactured in the United States of America
Library of Congress Catalog Card No. 77–146456
252 00169 9

For BEN, NED, *and* TOM

Contents

Illustrations

Preface

"A number of people are beginning to attribute to Ernest interests and activities in which they themselves are interested and I find it shameful," Mary Hemingway wrote me, but she did not object when I suggested this study of her husband's work. Ernest Hemingway had more than a passing interest in painting, sculpture, and architecture. This book is about Hemingway and his special interest in these arts. It is also a book about just how the poetry and prose of Hemingway might have been enriched and deepened by the paintings and sculpture and architecture which he saw being created around him, which he owned, and which he had viewed in museums or in prints or on location.

The interrelationship of literature, painting, and sculpture is not a new topic. Art historians, following the pioneering work of Erwin Panofsky, have searched literature for iconographic motifs with which to elucidate paintings. These scholars, however, concentrated their attention upon the painting and not upon the literature. More encompassing works, such as the intellectual histories of Wylie Sypher or the sociologically based examinations from Jacob Burkhardt to Roy McMullen, have been directed at unifying all the arts under one or two general concepts. There are practically no studies of literature and, for example, the pictorial arts which concentrate upon the literature or which are, in a sense, a reversal of Panofsky's iconography. One exception is Helmut A. Hatzfeld's *Literature through Art: A New Approach to French Literature*, which attempts to "elucidate French literature with the help of pictorial art" from 1100 to 1940. Clearly, Hatzfeld does not concentrate upon any one author in an extended examination. Two other exceptions are Clara Marburg Kirk's *William Dean Howells and Art in His Time*, a study which examines contemporary artistic and critical milieus as reflected in Howells's novels and journalism, and Viola Hopkins Winner's *Henry James and the Visual Arts*, a work which explores James's aesthetic theories with reference to literature and the pictorial arts. My concern is with one author and his special interests in painting, sculpture, and architecture, as well as upon the actual borrowing which a writer of prose might have done from other art forms.

Hemingway was not primarily a literary critic or an art historian, nor was he an interpreter of intellectual and social history. He was a man who liked certain paintings, sculptures, and buildings. He was also an artist. His response to another art form was not limited to any specific approach or by a predetermined standard. His was an individual response which reached across the boundaries of any one discipline. Thus my methods of examination will vary as Hemingway's own interpretation or response to any specific work varies.

As I investigated Hemingway's use of another art form, I found that elements of literature and painting had, at times, become blended in such a way as to suggest a single idea of art. Hemingway seemed, in a sense, to be working toward a single art. A definition of art, or of what constitutes a unitary sense of art, is admittedly a controversial subject. Even today, for example, such prominent aestheticians as Jacques Maritain and Etienne Gilson steadfastly refuse to consider any novels, except those written by James Joyce, as art. Joyce's novels are generally examined in such studies as poetry rather than prose. Maritain consistently speaks of "creative intuition" only in terms of painting and sculpture and poetry. Gilson is more specific: in his *Forms and Substances in the Arts*, for example, he states that the novel, or prose fiction, is not "an art of the beautiful," because the ultimate aim of prose fiction is "factivity," not "beauty." Such philosophers (and they have a broad historical basis) have established not only an ideal definition of art but also a set of ideal types or forms of art which must be understood and studied as separate entities.

Yet the concept of a single art implies that such ideal categories are perhaps not as strictly delineated as one might suppose. At least in the works of Hemingway, there has been a fusing of art forms—not just in the sense of theme or motif, which is obvious, but even, to a certain extent, in form or in technique. Hemingway expressed himself in words, and his favorite painters expressed themselves in paint; to this extent, the ideal categories of the Maritains and the Gilsons are valid. Just how closely, however, can words approach paint?

Panofsky has shown how the reverse is true, at least in terms of motifs, images, and symbols. Others, such as Sypher, have at least attempted to show generally parallel technical expressions in all the arts. On certain levels, therefore, it is clear that paint can approach words. But the question remains, how closely can words approach paint? Thus, for Hemingway and his contemporaries, could words and paint be made to act in the same way? Specifically, can a writer of prose fiction borrow profoundly from another art form? Can he utilize in language the techniques of a painter, techniques originally developed for and expressed with paint?

The result of any such crossing-over of categories is not just the creation of hybrid art forms, such as those originating notably in baroque Europe. Hybrid forms, such as the collage, do appear among the works of many of Hemingway's contemporaries, but not in any of Hemingway's works. It seems to me that the kind of "borrowing" which a novelist can do in an original and creative fashion implies that "ideal categories," like so much else in the twentieth century, are no longer viable and that the prose fiction of Hemingway is representative of this change. In his experimentation with techniques and motifs from other art forms, Hemingway was not monotypal, like the duck-billed platypus;

his merging of art forms is indicative of a significant development in the twentieth century.

In the development of this study, many valuable suggestions were offered by my colleagues at the University of Illinois at Urbana, especially John T. Flanagan and Edward H. Betts. Part of my research was funded by the Research Committee of the Department of English of the University of Illinois at Urbana. Ann Lowry of the University of Illinois Press has closely read this manuscript and has aided in other ways. I am also indebted to Henry Strater, who kindly granted me interviews in 1968, and to Mary Hemingway, who has generously allowed me to use reproductions of paintings from her personal collection. Primarily, however, I must thank my husband, who has always encouraged me.

A note on texts

For the texts of Hemingway's major works, I have cited the following editions, all published by Charles Scribner's Sons:

Torrents of Spring in *The Hemingway Reader* (1953), originally published in 1926
The Sun Also Rises (1954), originally published in 1926
A Farewell to Arms (1949), originally published in 1929
Death in the Afternoon (1955), originally published in 1932
Green Hills of Africa (1935)
To Have and Have Not (1937)
For Whom the Bell Tolls (1940)
Across the River and into the Trees (1950)
The Old Man and the Sea (1952)
A Moveable Feast (1964)
By-Line: Ernest Hemingway, ed. William White (1967)
The Fifth Column and Four Stories of the Spanish Civil War (1969)
Islands in the Stream (1970)

Citations from the following short stories are to *The Short Stories of Ernest Hemingway* (New York: Modern Library, n.d.). The dates of original publication are indicated in parentheses:

"Up in Michigan" (1923)
the vignettes (1923–24)
"The Revolutionist" (1923–24)
"The End of Something" (1925)
"Indian Camp" (1925)
"Big Two-Hearted River," Parts I–II (1925)
"The Undefeated" (1925–26)
"Today Is Friday" (1926)
"Now I Lay Me" (1927)
"A Canary for One" (1927)
"Ten Indians" (1927)
"Che Ti Dice la Patria?" (1927)
"Hills Like White Elephants" (1927)
"On the Quai at Smyrna" (1930)
"Wine of Wyoming" (1930)
"A Natural History of the Dead" (1932)
"A Clean, Well-Lighted Place" (1933)
"The Gambler, the Nun, and the Radio" (1933)
"A Way You'll Never Be" (1933)
"The Short Happy Life of Francis Macomber" (1936)
"The Snows of Kilimanjaro" (1936)

Ernest Hemingway and the arts

I

Toward a single art

> "I put in painters [in a list of "literary forbears"], or started to, because I learn as much from painters about how to write as from writers. You ask how this is done? It would take another day of explaining. I should think what one learns from composers and from the study of harmony and counterpoint would be obvious."[1]

What could be more explicit? Hemingway claims that he has learned from both painting and music. As Baudelaire observed, "The arts inspire, if not to complement one another, at least to lend one another new energies."[2] Hemingway, however, seems to indicate that he gained more than "new energies" from painters and musicians. And what of Hemingway's friends in Paris in the 1920's, the years of his literary experimentation and then of his artistic maturity? There was certainly a great deal of artistic energy in evidence, and most of it was being expressed in a variety of artistic directions.

In the Paris of the lost generation, creative minds in all areas of art met and exchanged ideas; all of art participated, or at least aspired to participate, so to speak, in a single art. It was a time when poets became librettists, painters became poets, musicians became painters. A creative genius like E. E. Cummings was painting and writing poetry and prose at the same time. Articles con-

1 Quoted in George Plimpton, "An Interview with Ernest Hemingway," *Hemingway and His Critics: An International Anthology*, ed. Carlos Baker (New York, 1961), pp. 27–28.

2 Quoted in Marcel Raymond, *From Baudelaire to Surrealism* (New York, 1950), epigraph.

cerning music, the pictorial arts, and literature appeared in the same periodicals (and there were many "little magazines"), and these were read by writers, painters, and musicians. Such an atmosphere is clearly reflected in Hemingway's posthumous *Islands in the Stream*, in which painter Thomas Hudson's friend Roger is both a painter and a writer.

Obviously, close personal relationships developed among all the artists. In his early years in Paris, Hemingway himself formed what was to be a lifelong relationship with Joan Miró. One of Hemingway's favorite paintings was Miró's "The Farm," which Hemingway borrowed money to buy in 1925. It was one of Miró's last realistic paintings before he reached the surrealistic symbolic expression for which he is best known. Miró purposely sought out writers as friends because he "felt that it was necessary to go beyond the strictly plastic and bring some poetry into painting."[3] Herbert Read has analyzed the "poetic" in Miró's paintings in this way: "images, for the painter as for the poet, are things as real objects–he does not distinguish between perceptual images and hallucinatory images–all are equally real, equally the material of art."[4] Hemingway, of course, must be included among the friends whom Miró termed poets, for much of Hemingway's earliest work in Paris, at the time he became friends with Miró, was poetry.

Others of Hemingway's friends at this time, both writers and painters, formed close relationships. Hemingway's friendship with and interest in Pablo Picasso and Gertrude Stein have been documented both by Hemingway and by his biographers and critics. He owned two paintings by Gris and was friends with Picasso at least through the 1940's. And, despite the bitter portrait of Miss Stein in *A Moveable Feast*, Hemingway spent many happy and profitable hours at Miss Stein's, surrounded by the paintings of Picasso, Gris, and other contemporaries. "It is easy to see how

3 Quoted in Miró's "I Dream of a Large Studio," *XX Siècle* (Paris, May–June 1938), in *Picasso, Gris, and Miró* (San Francisco: San Francisco Museum of Art, 1948), p. 95.
4 Herbert Read, "Joan Miró," *Picasso, Gris, and Miró*, p. 92.

"It has in it all that you feel about Spain when you are there and all that you feel when you are away and you cannot go there."
—ERNEST HEMINGWAY IN *Cahiers d'Art* (1934)

Joan Miró, "The Farm." 1923. Oil on canvas, 47½ x 54¾ in. Hemingway Private Collection, courtesy of Mary Hemingway.

stimulating such a give-and-take atmosphere, filled as it was with tremendous enthusiasm and energy, must have been to the development of the artist. And . . . Gertrude Stein herself drew upon Picasso and Gris to such an extent that it becomes almost impossible to conceive of her work as existing independently of theirs."[5] In fact, according to Hemingway's friend, Henry (Mike) Strater, who is himself an artist, it was at Miss Stein's that Hemingway "learned to like abstract art."[6]

Although Herbert Read was speaking primarily of the pictorial arts, this statement indicates just how far the ideal categories were breaking down: "Nowhere, in the [modern] psychology of art, will you find any justification for the notion that art is primarily an intellectual activity concerned with the formulation of absolute or ideal types."[7] That is, painting and sculpture were no longer separate types, but could be and actually were mixed. The appearance of such hybrid forms as the collage or the prose-poem, for example, indicates, at least to a certain extent, the breakdown, or, from a different perspective, the bastard cross-breeding of artistic types.

Much of the spirit and philosophy of this time is reflected in the introduction to Cummings's *The Enormous Room*, which was originally published in 1922 with the introduction added in 1934. The introduction is in the form of an imaginary dialogue between Cummings and another unspecified, but obviously Philistine, voice:

> [other voice:] . . . what do you call yourself? painter? poet? playwright? satirist? essayist? novelist?
> [Cummings:] Artist.
> But not a successful artist, in the popular sense?
> Don't be silly.
> Yet you probably consider your art of vital consequence—
> Improbably.
> —To the world?

5 Donald Gallup, "Picasso, Gris, and Gertrude Stein," *Picasso, Gris, and Miró*, p. 23.
6 Personal interview, Ogunquit, Maine, August 24, 1968.
7 Herbert Read, *Art Now* (London, 1948), p. 52.

What about the world, Mr. Cummings?
I live in so many: which one do you mean?
I mean the everyday humdrum world, which includes me and you and millions upon millions of men and women.
So?
Did it ever occur to you that people in this socalled world of ours are not interesed in art?
Da da.[8]

There was thus an ambitious and conscious attempt for men to become artists, an attempt to transcend any categorization of arts. It is, of course, always difficult to specify the beginnings of a movement or development. Clearly, however, the unitary sense of art which asserted itself in the 1920's was a continuation of the theories of certain artists before World War I. In fact, by 1912, the painters and writers had already joined in cooperative artistic efforts: "The poets and critics had played a considerable part in stimulating and organizing the first manifestations of the Cubists, but the connections between Orphism and contemporary literature were stronger and more direct. Apollinaire . . . at that time was fascinated by the interrelationship of the arts, and was exploring the visual possibilities of poetry in *Calligrammes*."[9] A review entitled *Montjoie*, founded in 1913 by Apollinaire's friend Canudo, had as its object the discovery of "the link between various arts" and the investigation of their "common tendencies."[10] Perhaps, however, it is more important to examine just exactly what was happening in Paris in the 1920's, because this was when and where Hemingway reached artistic maturity.

When Hemingway arrived in Paris in late 1921, Dadaism, at least by one account,[11] was already dead in theory. And yet Tris-

8 E. E. Cummings, *The Enormous Room* (New York: Modern Library, n.d.), pp. viii–ix.
9 John Golding, *Cubism: A History and an Analysis, 1907–1914* (London, 1968), p. 37.
10 Ibid.
11 ". . . it may be said that after 1920 Dada no longer existed," stated Georges Hugnet in "The Dada Spirit in Painting" (written 1932–34), trans. Ralph Manheim, *The Dada Painters and Poets: An Anthology*, ed. Robert Motherwell (New York, 1951), p. 152.

tan Tzara was a major figure in Paris, and the Parisian Dadaists were continuing their public festivals and demonstrations in the early 1920's. Dadaism had originally been formed by a group of writers, painters, and musicians in Switzerland before and during World War I. After the war, it had divided into the quite separate German and Parisian movements with Tzara, who was not quite a member of the original group, the leader of the Paris Dadaists.

Philosophically, Dada was a destructive movement. Its advocates attacked all traditional values and institutions; it was "a state of mind"[12] which offered nothing really constructive: "dada is death of the spirit."[13] The implications of nihilism are clear. In Germany, it disintegrated into a Marxian political movement. In Paris, however, Dadaism affected more particularly the arts—all the arts.

The original advocates of Dada developed three parallel and interrelated art "forms." The term "form" is used with reservation here, because of course there were no rules for Dadaists. They practiced "simultaniety"[14] in poetry, bruit music, and the unnamed "new painting medium." The essence of each was total freedom for the individual artist in the expression of creative intuition and innovation. For example, bruit music might employ typewriters or pot covers; simultaneity "presupposes a heightened sensitivity to the passage of things in time, it turns the sequence a=b=c=d into a–b–c–d and attempts to transform the problem of the ear to the problem of the face."[15] The "new painting medium" was most undefined, but at the Galerie Dada, Tzara ex-

12 Ibid., p. 167.

13 Tristan Tzara, "manifesto on feeble love and bitter love," tr. Ralph Manheim, ibid., p. 94.

14 The term "simultaneity" was used to denote in painting the technique of presenting different perspectives of a single object in a picture. Thus a teacup might be painted simultaneously with the perspective from above, from back or front, and from right or left. As the Dada poets borrowed this term from the painters, so they also depicted in words the technique of multiple perspective, the "simultaneous" quality of paintings which used this type of perspective. Such paintings were, of course, primarily those of the cubists.

15 Richard Huelsenbeck, "En Avant Dada: A History of Dadaism," in Motherwell, ed., *Dada Painters and Poets*, p. 35.

hibited cubist, expressionistic, and futurist paintings, all three of which actually preceded Dada.

These three art "forms" were usually performed at the same time during the Dada festivals and demonstrations. One Dadaist, Kurt Schwitters, based his *merz* drama upon a concept of the basic unity of all the forms. Schwitters consciously attempted to display and mingle each form in a dramatic production. Apollinaire was still active at this time and was still writing poems, which were intended not only to be read, but also to be seen and heard. Although his simultaneist poems, such as "Zone," are totally "free," it is clear that he wishes his readers to study the actual make-up of the poem on the page–its pictorial composition. Moreover, Apollinaire's poems and others like them are often designated with the same terms used to describe the plastic arts of the period–expressionist and cubist: "the influence of painting on the poetry of Apollinaire is most apparent, his images being almost entirely visual."[16] Throughout his life, Apollinaire was the literary spokesman for certain groups of painters. Like Harold Rosenberg, who explained abstract expressionism in the 1950's, Apollinaire mediated between the artist and his public beginning in 1913 with his now-classic *The Cubist Painters; Aesthetic Meditations.*

As confused and chaotic, as nihilistic and destructive, as the Dadaist movement was in Paris, it presented the young artists with more than just discussion: "Those who refuse to see in the Dada movement anything but a Parisian scandal characterized by violence and buffoonery, will never understand the intense moral crisis of the 1920's and the current of anarchistic individualism, the refusal to be useful, that upset so many age-old slogans and age-old beliefs."[17] It was not simply the search of the Dadaists for anarchistic individualism and challenge of old orders and values, however, which brought about their assertion of a single art. To

16 Amédeé Ozenfant, *Foundations of Modern Art,* trans. John Rodker (New York, 1931), p. 18.

17 Raymond, *From Baudelaire to Surrealism,* p. 269.

be sure, the Dadaists did not create cubism and expressionism in painting, nor were they the first, even in the immediate past, to demand individualistic freedom and originality. Their single art, it seems to me, was the direct result of their attempts to involve all the senses in both artistic expression and response. Their festivals and demonstrations involving all of the art forms were directed toward a total response in the audience: music, poetry and prose, painting—a single art. Moreover, each Dadaist form demanded a multiple sensual creation and response. Note, for example, that simultaneist poems were to be "not the problem of the ear," but "the problem of the face"—that is, the problem of man's complex and total sensual responses.

Perhaps the Dadaists came to their aesthetic of sensuality as a result of the anti-intellectualism inherent in their kind of rebellion. Or perhaps it was the Dadaist celebration of "LIFE" which ultimately led to the artistic involvement of the senses: "Freedom: Dada Dada Dada, a roaring of tense colors, and interlacing of opposites and of all contradictions, grotesques, and inconsistencies: LIFE."[18] Or perhaps it was the Dada insistence upon activity which led to such an emphasis upon mixed sensual involvement: "the Dadaist should be a man who has fully understood that one is entitled to have ideas only if one can transform them into life—the completely active type, who lives only through action, because it holds the possibility of his achieving knowledge."[19] There was also an attempt to make poetry, for example, "an activity of the mind," to give it "a profound force aside from the text."[20]

Marshall McLuhan would undoubtedly observe, at this point, that the Dadaist interest in the artistic establishment of a total sensual response occurred at this time because of the influence of electronics. According to McLuhan, the printing press and the domination of the phonetic alphabet caused Western man to separate and isolate his sensual responses; radio (extremely popular

18 Tristan Tzara, "Dada Manifesto" (1918), tr. Ralph Manheim, in Motherwell, ed., *Dada Painters and Poets*, p. 82.
19 Huelsenbeck, "En Avant Dada," ibid., p. 28.
20 Hugnet, "The Dada Spirit in Painting," ibid., p. 129.

in the 1920's) and television, however, have caused the essentially visual modern man to alter and unify his sensual responses. It is particularly significant that McLuhan distinguished certain artists as important early advocates of "synaesthesia" or the "interplay of the senses":[21] most especially Rimbaud and Baudelaire, both precursors of the Dada and surrealist movements, and Paul Cézanne, who exerted great influence upon the cubists as well as upon Hemingway.

Yet whether or not this new interest in a total sensual involvement in the arts was the result of electronics generally or the radio specifically, the artists had bound themselves to an expression of sensual wholeness. The result was not only new forms of art but also a parallel breakdown of the ideal artistic categories. For these categories, on one level, represented an older order—a part of the order which Dada proposed to destroy. This order was restrictive and, worst of all for the Dadaists, it had rules!

Moreover, these orders also represented a shattering or splintering of man's own creative, as well as sensual, expressions. There could be no freedom for "LIFE" when only the visual *or* audile *or* tactile sense could be exercised in any artistic creation or in any response. This is not to say that painters did not use paint, writers words, and composers music. They did employ the traditional modes of expression. Painters, however, also used words; writers used methods generally associated with the plastic arts, such as artistic arrangement of type or images which were pictures in themselves; composers attempted to juxtapose painting and poetry with their music. In short, boundaries were crossed, and modes were mixed.

This new search for the synaesthesia was not just on an artistic level. The rebellion of Dada, as expressed by the Parisian group, with all its foolishness and nihilism, was indeed "a [total] state of mind," a total response and participation. And by the time Hemingway got to Paris, the "state of mind" had become one of total freedom, of individualism, and of total sensual commitment to

21 Marshall McLuhan, *The Gutenberg Galaxy* (Toronto, 1962), pp. 41–42, 65, and 182.

"LIFE." Certainly Hemingway arrived at a time when the creative and moral atmosphere was one of artistic anarchy. And yet this anarchy, which led on one level to a breakdown of formal types of literary expression, eventually pointed to a more profound order for the arts: the demand that art must stimulate a full sensual, as well as intellectual, response. Perhaps the only area of the human experience which Dada did not fully exploit was that of dreams and the subconscious. To be sure, the Dadaists recognized and examined the Freudian subconscious, and many, like Max Jacob and Apollinaire, suggested "the presence of an irrational element in the heart of reality, a disquieting aura."[22] It was the surrealists, however, who were to explore most fully the world of dreams and the subconscious.

André Breton signaled his break from the Dada movement and the ultimate formation of the surrealists with an essay, "Lâchez tout," which appeared in the April, 1922, number of *Littérature*. It was followed by his first *Manifesto of Surrealism* in 1924. The surrealists recognized the lack of constructive aims in Dada and wished to develop some more meaningful and definite philosophy: "when literature lost its ancient meaning, saw its function as servant to God and crown disappear, its continued existence was called into question. For some, no class, no group or ideal merited their allegiance: hence the bacchanale that was Dada. The Surrealists, however, recognized early the pointless and ultimately dreary circularity of spoofing the ridiculous, of parodying the pompous, of mocking society, themselves included."[23]

While they continued the Dadaists' search for the involvement of the senses in art, the surrealists added another mode—the examination of the inward sense. With Freud as a springboard, they examined the subconscious and dreams—that inward, sensual world which Freud had described for them. They were forced to adapt and create new symbols, usually quite personal, to describe this inner world of the sense or the subconscious. For ex-

22 Raymond, *From Baudelaire to Surrealism*, p. 261.

23 Herbert S. Gershman, *The Surrealist Revolution in France* (Ann Arbor, 1969), p. 13.

ample, the static and often deserted villages of de Chirico, Miró's circles and triangles, and Masson's fish all represent visual and sensual images of inner psychic reality.

Their art forms were as overlapping and intertwined as were those of the Dadaists: "The arts are conceived to exist not in and of themselves, but as a function of desire, of pleasure, of the need for a change—which change must be social as well as aesthetic."[24] The surrealists thus based their concept of art on no traditional or ideal types. Moreover, they saw the nature of art as functional —as an examination of individual desire, pleasure, and need for a change. The non-rational, and in fact non-intellectual, quality of their art is indicated by the two nouns, "desire" and "pleasure." Finally, their very general concept of art makes especially clear their unconventional, non-traditional vision of a unity of the arts —or of a single art.

Thus the surrealist writers, painters, and musicians moved as freely from one art "form" to another as had the Dadaists. The Freudian psychology, however, gave these artists more specific direction and unity than there had been for Tzara's Dadaists. And yet the surrealists, in effect, innovated very little. Many of them, such as Breton and Picabia, had been Dadaists and then became surrealists; "there is nothing in their [the surrealists'] work that is substantially new, nothing that had not previously been tried in the so-called Dada period."[25] It is true, however, that the surrealist movement produced more influential and recognized artists than did Dada: of the painters and sculptors, Salvador Dali, Yves Tanguy, Max Ernst, Giorgio de Chirico, Alberto Giacometti, and Hemingway's friends, Miró and André Masson, who were associated with them for a time. Among the poets: Breton, Louis Aragon, Paul Éluard, and Robert Desnos. Among the novelists: Desnos, de Chirico, Joyce Mansour, Maurice Fourre, and Alain Jouffroy. Of these groups, the painters and sculptors are more universally known and have had the most profound influence.

Such was the intellectual, social, and ethical atmosphere of

24 Ibid., p. 18.
25 Ibid., p. 25.

Paris in the 1920's when Hemingway arrived and as he struggled to artistic maturity. Standing outside the Dada and surrealist movements were many artists in all fields, such as Picasso and Hemingway himself. For although Hemingway was no Dadaist or surrealist, this Paris of the 1920's, this "moveable feast," had a profound influence upon him.

Before Hemingway reached Paris in 1921, there is no real indication that he had any deep interest in the pictorial arts, sculpture, and architecture. His mother had taken him to Chicago's Art Institute when he was a child, and he had written a feature article for the *Toronto Star Weekly* concerning a ladies' art-lending library,[26] in which his major concern was not so much the paintings themselves, but rather the ladies and their different activity. Just before Ernest and Hadley Hemingway went to Paris, their group in Chicago seems to have discussed paintings, but there is no evidence from this period that Hemingway himself had any special interest in painting. From the time of Hemingway's arrival in Paris, however, he manifested a profound interest in the arts.

It is important to remember that Hemingway thought of himself as both a poet and a writer of prose. His first published writings, after his arrival in Paris, were a poem and a fable in *Double Dealer* in 1922. The influence of the imagist poets at this time in his career has already been noted in other studies. The early poems, however, are not totally imagist. This influence actually became more important later—in Hemingway's prose: "The Imagists vowed to use the language of ordinary speech, and always the exact word; to present an image and to render particulars exactly, with no 'vague generalities'; to be 'hard and clear' and concentrated; and to demand a complete freedom of subject. In his prose, Hemingway stuck by these principles as fast as any of the poets who formulated them—faster."[27]

26 "Circulating Pictures a New High-Art in Toronto," *The Toronto Star Weekly* (Feb. 14, 1920), reprinted in *By-Line: Ernest Hemingway*, pp. 3–4.

27 Philip Young, *Ernest Hemingway: A Reconsideration* (University Park, Pa., 1966), p. 184.

Much of the early verse does clearly use imagist techniques, of course. In certain poems, such as "Riparto d'Assalto," Hemingway carefully tried to describe a scene as faithfully as possible, with an emphasis upon physical detail and fact. That is, he tried to re-create the image of a truckload of Italian soldiers riding to a battle in which they were to die, with such phrases as "Hob-nailed boots," "Bristly faces, dirty hides," and "splintered pines."[28]

The emphasis of the imagists upon the *exact* physical image clearly suggests the attempts of the Dadaists to express artistically a mosaic of sensual response. T. S. Eliot's "objective correlative," for example, indicates a search for a broadening of the aesthetic and sensual expression, on the part of the writer, and of the response, on the part of the reader. By concentration upon the physical reality, the imagists hoped to suggest a new mental reality or awareness. The means of suggestion, however, were no longer strictly intellectual or even emotional. Nor is only the visual sense required to relay the image to the reader. Depending upon the image, all of man's senses must be incorporated into the experience of the image. Hence the imagists, contemporaries with the Dada and surrealist movements, were also working to expand the sensual consciousness. Indeed, the imagists traced their beginnings to Baudelaire, as did the Dadaists and surrealists, although the imagists emerged before the other two movements and found a different perspective in their art.

It is also significant that imagist poetry employed images of physical detail as the means of intellectual, symbolic, and emotional communication and artistic expression. In other words, the imagists were attempting to paint a picture, so to speak, with words. The word, in such poetry, was clearly the message, but a very special kind of message. The word must be as true as a painter's color. Moreover, the arrangement and juxtaposition of words and word images are as significant as the arrangement of pears and apples and guitars in a cubist painting. Perhaps it is

28 Originally published in *Poetry* (January 1923), "Riparto d'Assalto" was later included in Hemingway's first book-length work, *Three Stories and Ten Poems* (Paris, 1923), p. 55.

only coincidence, but long before Eliot employed the phrase "objective correlative" to describe the visual and physical nature of his images, the American painter Washington Allston had also used the term with reference to the pictorial arts.[29] In short, it should be no surprise than an imagist poet, or a poet who uses certain imagist devices, might turn to the pictorial arts for suggestion, even instruction, in technique.

One American poet who visited Paris in the 1920's saw such a relationship between poetry and painting, as well as the unity of all art forms, at this time: "the poem, like every other art form, as an object . . . in itself formally presents its case and its meaning by the very form it assumes. Therefore, being an object, it should be so treated and controlled. . . . The poem being an object (like a symphony or a cubist painting) it must be the purpose of the poet to make of his words a new form: to invent, that is, an object consonant with his own day."[30] The emphasis upon art as an object, as an empirical object which must be understood through the senses, represented a profound departure from traditional poetry for William Carlos Williams and his friends, such as Ezra Pound and Hilda Doolittle.

Williams also specifically understood this new art as a departure from the old in terms of sensual experience:

> the [poetic] progression from the sentiment, the thought (philosophy) or the concept to the poem itself—from the concern with Hamlet to *Hamlet*, the place: That was the secret inside the term "transition" during the years when the painters following Cézanne began to talk of sheer paint: a picture a matter of pigments upon a cloth stretched on a frame. . . .
>
> It is the making of that step, to come over into the tactile qualities, the words themselves beyond the mere thought expressed, that distinguishes the modern, or distinguished the

29 See Nathalia Wright, "A Source for T. S. Eliot's 'Objective Correlative'?" *American Literature* 41, no. 4 (January 1970): 589–91.

30 William Carlos Williams, *The Autobiography of William Carlos Williams* (New York, 1951), p. 264.

> modern from the period before the turn of the century. And it is the reason why painting and the poem became so closely allied at that time. It was the work of the painters following Cézanne and the Impressionists that, critically, opened up the age of Stein, Joyce, and a good many others.[31]

No longer could a poem be merely visual; it must be tactile; it must have the quality of a painting.

Although Hemingway employed certain imagist techniques in his poetry, he also used techniques most often associated with the Dada poems of simultaneity. In a long poem, "The Soul of Spain with McAlmon and Bird the Publishers,"[32] Hemingway rather crudely and directly struck out at such diverse subjects as democracy, dictators, H. L. Mencken, and even Dada. Yet, in Part II, Hemingway "exploits the technical innovations of Dada": "both the 'black' wit of the verbal play and the expressionistic element of symbol-making, akin to Imagism, reveal the pastiche of Dada."[33] Thus Hemingway's early poems represent a curious and interesting reflection of the two dominant poetic styles of the 1920's, imagism and Dada.

Yet Hemingway was not a Dadaist. He personally disliked Tzara and even wrote a rather stinging "newsletter" attacking Tzara in the August, 1924, issue of *The Transatlantic Review.* Moreover, as Nicholas Joost has pointed out, "At bottom Hemingway was opposed to the sweeping destructiveness of Dada; he was too traditional in attitude."[34]

It was in prose, of course, that Hemingway found his most satisfactory means of artistic expression, although he continued to write occasional poems for most of the rest of his life. Here those particular Dadaist techniques which were evident in his poems disappeared, but the techniques of imagism remained. In transferring the imagist elements to prose, Hemingway had only

31 Ibid., p. 380.

32 Originally published in *Der Querschnitt* (Part I, October 1924; Parts II–VI, November 1924).

33 Nicholas Joost, *Ernest Hemingway and the Little Magazines: The Paris Years* (Barre, Mass., 1968), p. 137.

34 Ibid., p. 100.

"to drop the rhymes of poetry and the strongly emphasized musical rhythms of the new poetry of Imagism; he would carry over into prose the new freedom of choice in subject . . . and would insist, in prose, on the exact, not merely the decorative, word, in order to avoid the cliche and the trite."[35] He would also carry over into his prose the image, the tactile quality.

Hemingway was a man whose senses were quite alert and who seemed to work consciously to increase their receptivity. His eye for physical detail was developed early, as is manifest in those poems most closely influenced by the imagists. Hemingway was also acute in audile response. Henry Strater believes Hemingway to have been even more audile than visual: "Hem was audio. He had a wonderful ear for language."[36] But Hemingway's ear extended beyond an ability to produce nuances of spoken language. Even before he had come to Paris, he had advocated a total sensual submersion before the creative process could even begin; he told a group of friends in Chicago, "You've got to see it, feel it, smell it, hear it."[37] And in the creative process itself, Hemingway indicated a total physical involvement: "anything to be read by the eye . . . must be written out by hand and checked by the eye and ear in the process."[38] Thus, even in the creative process, three specific sensual faculties must be involved: tactile ("written out by hand"), visual ("checked by the eye"), and audile ("checked by the . . . ear").

Furthermore, Hemingway indicates a revolution in prose fiction when he consciously asserts the audile quality of his own prose. In the past, at least before Joyce, poetry had been the written art which commanded both the eye and the ear—if only the "inner ear." Hemingway, however, demands that his prose have both visual and audile relevance. He demands that his prose be read and responded to, in a sense, like poetry. Such a concern is

35 Ibid., p. 37.
36 Personal interview, Ogunquit, Maine, August 24, 1968.
37 Quoted in Charles Fenton, *The Apprenticeship of Ernest Hemingway: The Early Years* (New York, 1954), p. 103.
38 Quoted in Carlos Baker, *Ernest Hemingway: A Life Story* (New York, 1969), p. 217.

not really original. Hemingway had learned from both Dada and imagism of the necessity of audile-visual, even tactile, responses. Dadaists such as Apollinaire and Tzara had already carried these poetic principles into prose. It is no wonder that Philip Young remarked, concerning *The Sun Also Rises*, that "Hemingway's wide-awake senses fully evoke an American's Paris, a vacationer's Spain."[39] In short, Hemingway, as an artist, was involved in sensation. The artist must first "see it, feel it, smell it, hear it." Then he must create with his senses fully alert, checking with both the eye and the ear while writing by hand. As a result, his prose will manifest and evoke sensations—that synaesthesia which, it seems to me, lies at the basis of that single art which Hemingway and his friends sought.

In his creative work, Hemingway gave us only one intimate portrait of an artist actually at work or gathering perceptions for his art. In the posthumously published *Islands in the Stream*, Hemingway intersperses scenes of action with the play of Thomas Hudson's consciousness. More often than not, Hudson is allowed to savor his drinks more than any other Hemingway character is: "Thomas Hudson took a sip of the ice-cold drink that tasted of the fresh green lime juice mixed with the tasteless coconut water, strong with the real Gordon's gin that made it alive to his tongue and rewarding to swallow, and all of it tautened by the bitters that gave it color" (244). And when Lil asks Hudson to tell her of his "happiest time," she especially requests that he tell it "not with smells." Hudson responds, "It has to have smells" (285). In short, like Hemingway, Hudson had to "see it, feel it, smell it, hear it."

One means of expanding the sensual quality of his prose, Hemingway discovered, was an examination of the fine arts, paintings especially. Paris abounded with painters; contemporary paintings were exhibited continually; the Louvre and Luxembourg galleries offered not only *objets d'art* but also warmth on cold winter days; and besides, Gertrude Stein had urged Hemingway to study the

39 Young, *Hemingway: A Reconsideration*, p. 85.

paintings. "Everybody in Paris seemed to paint, and in store windows in strange little streets you would see reproductions of Matisse, Derain, Rouault, Chirico, Modigliani, Picasso, Utrillo, and in the Quarter the surrealists Picabia and Miró were famous names."[40]

Hemingway quickly and naturally learned and responded to paintings; despite continuing eye problems, "Hem had uncommonly good eyesight, the hunter's cold acuity. . . . He had the same shrewd eye for painting. Maybe Gertrude Stein, who was no bungler in that direction either, helped him develop the knack. He would take in excellence of color and design at a glance."[41] Hemingway was, however, more than simply a judge of "color and design." He also learned specific technique: according to Strater, Hemingway "learned the technical part of [painting] from Miró and me."[42] Thus Hemingway attempted to perfect his knowledge of painting as thoroughly as he later did his understanding of bullfighting.

It is well known that Hemingway visited art galleries and museums throughout his life. His favorites were the Louvre and the Luxembourg (which later became the Jeu de Paume Annex to the Louvre) in Paris, and the Prado in Madrid. Other museums of special interest to Hemingway were the museums in Milan and the Accademia, Scuola di San Rocco, and the Ducal Palace in Venice. At the Louvre, of course, he saw a wide-ranging collection of great paintings and sculptures, but it was at the Luxembourg where he viewed the impressionists and post-impressionists and where he found Cézanne. Although the Prado also has a broad collection of art, its greatest treasures are works of Spanish artists, especially of Goya, Velázquez, and El Greco. The Venetian museums specialize in Italian paintings. Of American museums, Hemingway mentioned only two: the Art Institute in Chicago, which has a major collection of impressionist and post-impressionist paintings among its wide holdings, and the New York Metropoli-

40 Morley Callaghan, *That Summer in Paris* (New York, 1963), p. 147.
41 John Dos Passos, *The Best Times* (New York, 1966), pp. 143–44.
42 Personal interview, Ogunquit, Maine, August 24, 1968.

tan Museum of Art, again a museum with a large general collection of European and American paintings. Despite his knowledge of these museums, Hemingway did not seem to be a habitué of galleries. He simply kept returning to those he most enjoyed.

He could lead a group through a museum with a running commentary which was both intelligent and personal.[43] It was the paintings which held his interest; he liked very little sculpture. Perhaps Frederic Henry's remarks concerning his dislike of sculpture are indicative of Hemingway's own opinions of this art form. In *A Farewell to Arms*, Henry observed, "There were many marble busts on painted wooden pillars along the walls of the room. . . . The hall too . . . was lined with them. They had the complete marble quality of all looking alike. Sculpture had always seemed a dull business–still, bronzes looked like something. But marble busts all looked like a cemetery" (29).

Hemingway himself owned works by Gris, Paul Klee, Miró, Masson, and Roberto Domingo and was friends with many contemporary painters. To George Plimpton, he specifically mentioned that he "had respect" for Gris, Picasso, Braque, and Monet, "who was still alive then."[44] In *A Moveable Feast*, Hemingway even devotes part of a chapter to a chance meeting with the Bulgarian-born Jules Pascin (101–4). The only sculptor for whom Hemingway showed any respect was another contemporary, the Romanian Constantin Brancusi. Yet most of the references to painting which occur in Hemingway's works, whether creative, expository, or critical writings, are primarily to older, pre-twentieth-century artists. The painters who had some special significance for Hemingway are an oddly assorted group, but nearly all are Europeans; few are American. In his creative works, Hemingway only briefly mentions his friend Peirce and has Thomas Hudson compare a group of bathing men to a painting by Thomas Eakins. He also, at one time, indicated admiration

43 See Lillian Ross, *Portrait of Hemingway* (New York, 1961), originally published as "Profile of Hemingway," *The New Yorker* (May 13, 1950), pp. 36–66.

44 Plimpton, "An Interview with Ernest Hemingway," p. 26.

for Winslow Homer and for the "cowboy artist," "C. W. Russell."[45] Beyond Strater's remark that Hemingway had learned technique from him, there is little indication that Hemingway *used* or was influenced by the paintings of any American artist.

The painters whom Hemingway mentions or by whom he can be shown to have been influenced generally represent three European schools: Spanish, Northern, and Italian. The Spanish artists most cited or used by Hemingway compose the great triad of Spanish art: Diego de Velázquez (1599–1660), Domenicos Theotocopoulos, "El Greco" (ca. 1541–1614), and Francisco de Goya (1746–1828). Hemingway's interest in El Greco is, of course, indicative of his general interest in Spanish art, but it is also a reflection of the renewed interest in El Greco's paintings in Paris in the 1920's. He was a favorite of both the Dadaists and the surrealists: "The Moderns liked his distortions, but they were, ironically, only distortions to avoid distortions as to their position in a church, above an altar."[46] According to Strater, "El Greco [was] in style. . . . They liked El Greco because of his light and shade and his religious intensity."[47]

The Northern painters whom Hemingway mentions specifically are Peter Paul Rubens (1577–1640), Pieter Brueghel the elder (ca. 1525–69), and Hieronymous Bosch (c. 1450–1516), all Flemish and all well represented in the Prado. Among this group, Hemingway's references to Bosch are also perhaps indicative of Dada and surrealistic influence. Both groups considered him as a sort of precursor, with his fantasy, monsters, and sensual expressions of love and anti-love. The surrealists especially found relevance in Bosch's paintings: "Puns and eroticism, play and love—surrealistic art is a Garden of Eden, a modern Garden of Delights by a collective Hieronymous Bosch, lacking only in transcendental implications."[48]

One other Northern artist whom Hemingway mentions by

45 Baker, *Hemingway: A Life Story*, pp. 197 and 218. Undoubtedly, Hemingway meant Charles Marion Russell.
46 Ozenfant, *Foundations of Modern Art*, p. 58.
47 Personal interview, Ogunquit, Maine, August 24, 1968.
48 Gershman, *The Surrealist Revolution in France*, pp. 22–23.

name primarily in his expository writings and interviews is the Frenchman Paul Cézanne (1839–1906). The influence of Cézanne is, of course, definitive. Nearly all modern schools of painting trace their beginnings to Cézanne: cubist, Dadaist, surrealist, and expressionist. Ozenfant defines cubism as "super-Cézannism."[49] The poet Williams obviously saw Cézanne as the precursor of *all* modern art, that special catalyst for the single art of the moderns. Three other post-impressionist painters with whom Hemingway indicated familiarity are Edgar Degas (1834–1917; French), Vincent van Gogh (1853–90; Dutch) and Paul Gauguin (1848–1903; French).

The Italian painters most often specifically cited by Hemingway outnumber either the Spanish or Northern painters; the Italian painters, as a group, however, are least influential in Hemingway's works. They are the traditionally most-respected Italian painters: Giotto di Bordone (ca. 1266–ca. 1337; Florentine), Piero della Francesca (ca. 1420–92; Umbrian), Andrea Mantegna (1431–1506; Paduan), Leonardo da Vinci (1459–1519; Florentine), Michelangelo Buonarroti (1472–1564; Roman), Tiziano Vechellio, "Titian" (1477–1576; Venetian), and Jacobo Robusti, "Tintoretto" (1518–94; Venetian). Of these painters, the references to Mantegna are most numerous. The works of one other Italian artist, Sandro Botticelli (ca. 1444–1510; Florentine) are certainly suggested, though not specifically mentioned by Hemingway in any published work.

Hemingway's interest in art continued throughout his life. He also took a personal interest in certain contemporary painters—an interest which extended beyond friendships. Particularly in the 1930's, he befriended young artists, such as Luis Quintanilla and Antonio Gattorno. He helped Gattorno, a Cuban painter whom he met in 1934, by buying some of his paintings. He met Quintanilla in 1931 when they had a very special mutual interest, the Spanish Revolution. When Quintanilla was imprisoned in Spain in 1934 for conspiring against the Spanish government, Heming-

49 Ozenfant, *Foundations of Modern Art,* p. 51.

way was one of the sponsors of a New York showing of the artist's etchings. He also signed and helped circulate a petition to free Quintanilla: "Luis, said he [Hemingway], was not only a damned fine artist but one of the 'best guys' he had ever known."[50]

Hemingway also wrote commentaries on art and artists. He composed articles or pamphlets for his friends Gattorno and Quintanilla.[51] He also wrote an article concerning his purchase of Miró's painting "The Farm."[52] Yet his most perceptive criticism occurs elsewhere, primarily in *Death in the Afternoon.* In the articles or prefaces for painter-friends, Hemingway tends to praise too highly without documentation or illustration. He can compare Quintanilla and Peirce[53] to Goya and Miró to Joyce, but only in very general adjectives. Moreover, much of his criticism is of the "I feel" or affective school; for example, this comment concerning Miró's "The Farm": "It has in it all that you feel about Spain when you are there and all that you feel when you are away and you cannot go there."

On the other hand, when Hemingway is writing for himself (not in articles or prefaces), his criticism is more specific and revealing. He tends not to use the terms used by professional art critics and does not elaborate upon each point. His critical intentions, however, are clear. Consider this passage concerning Goya from *Death in the Afternoon*: "Goya did not believe in costume but he did believe in blacks and in grays, in dust and in light, in high places rising from plains, in the country around Madrid, in movement, in his own cojones, in painting, in etching, and in what he had seen, felt, touched, handled, smelled, enjoyed, drunk, mounted, suffered, spewed-up, lain-with, suspected, observed, loved, hated, lusted, feared, detested, admired, loathed, and destroyed. Naturally no painter has been able to paint all that but

50 Baker, *Hemingway: A Life Story*, p. 267.

51 *Gattorno* (Havana, 1935), pp. 11–16; reprinted in *Esquire* 5 (May 1936): 111, 141; "Quintanilla," *Exhibition of Drawings and Paintings by Luis Quintanilla* (New York: Pierre Matisse Gallery, 1934), reprinted in *Esquire* 3 (February 1935):22–27. Hemingway also wrote a preface for Quintanilla's *All the Brave* (New York, 1939), pp. 7–11.

52 *Cahiers d'Art* (1934), pp. 28–29.

53 Harry Salpeter, "Rabelais in a Smock," *Esquire* 5 (July 1936):121.

he tried" (205). The build-up of nouns and then verbs in this long sentence is closer in form to one of Hemingway's poems than to his prose; this sentence, however, reveals a great deal about Hemingway's interpretation and understanding of Goya's paintings and etchings.

Goya's refusal to "believe in costume" is a reference to the sentence preceding this one in which Hemingway states that Velázquez did believe in costume. In just these few words are indicated not only Goya's preference for depicting people rather than artificial trappings, but also his desire to paint the common man rather than the royalty whom he did not really "believe in." The immediately juxtaposed phrases, "in blacks and in grays," emphasize not only Goya's preference for somber colors, but also the contrast with the reds and golds of the costumes which Velázquez preferred. "In dust and in light" suggests both the chiaroscuro effects of Goya's etchings and also his rather unusual and peculiar use of light such as in "The Third of May" (Prado). The next two phrases, "in high places rising from plains, in the country around Madrid," give a further indication of the subject of some of Goya's paintings, especially the early cartoons for tapestries.

That gushing, bumping list of verbs, however, is the most interesting element in this passage. Here Hemingway is emphasizing the emotional content of Goya's work; it is, however, a very *physical* emotional quality. That is, Hemingway is not content to use such verbs as "loved" and "hated." The verbs call up nearly all of the senses ("seen, felt, touched . . . smelled . . . drunk"); only the sense of hearing is omitted. Yet Hemingway is not content with these verbs, either; he becomes more specific with verbs like "spewed-up." Goya's erotic paintings, such as "The Maja Clothed" and "The Maja Nude" (Prado), are sensually called forth with the two verbs "mounted" and "lain-with." For Hemingway at least, Goya's paintings and etchings were not simply visual representations, but rather complete sensual experiences. Nearly every sense was involved—and involved dynamically. This involvement of the senses—the synaesthesia—is just that quality which led the artists of the 1920's toward the single art. That Hemingway should so expressly delineate the synaesthetic quality of Goya's art indicates Hemingway's own response to art.

With this long list of verbs, however, Hemingway might appear to be criticizing too affectively. And yet he is clearly defining some very special and recognized qualities of Goya. The first is his realism, not only with reference to his emotional reality, but also with reference to a more physical reality, such as "the country around Madrid." Yet in almost direct contrast, the rushing list of verbs suggests Goya's interest in the irrational and the unreal, as for example in the etchings of "The Caprices" (Prado). The burst of verbs ends with "feared, detested, admired, loathed, and destroyed"—all verbs denoting deep emotional involvement, except for "destroyed." Yet in context, the implication of this final verb "destroyed" is one of mental violence, not physical destruction. Furthermore, Hemingway's references to color (blacks and grays) and to Goya's chiaroscuro (light and shade) indicate his understanding of certain technical qualities of Goya's art. Thus Hemingway commented upon the emotional as well as the technical qualities of Goya's paintings and etchings. The reader who has only a little knowledge of Goya's work can easily comprehend the essence of Hemingway's criticism.

Not all of Hemingway's artistic references are this complete. Some are quite brief and even superficial. In the fictional works, some specific allusions are only incidental and not always integral in the scene or action. For example, in *A Farewell to Arms*, Catherine Barkley's elementary and superficial identification of Rubens, Mantegna, and Titian serves only as a preparatory examination before she must meet Swiss customs officials in her new role as an artist. Some references, however, are integral for an understanding of both theme and structure, such as those in "The Revolutionist." Some allusions, such as those in *Across the River and into the Trees*, are necessary for a complete understanding of character. And, of course, the protagonist of *Islands in the Stream* is himself a painter.

Hemingway only briefly indicated what he meant by learning

from painting. He told George Plimpton that "they [the painters] were a part of learning to see, to hear, to think, to feel and not feel, and to write."[54] A study of painting was thus one means of expanding Hemingway's sensibilities and sensual responses: the paintings helped him "to see, to hear . . . to feel." On the other hand, the painters also suggested ways of thinking and even of writing to Hemingway. Clearly, he affirmed that not just his thoughts and his life experience, but even his writings, were influenced by painting.

Elsewhere, Hemingway also indicated that part of learning is imitation. In *Death in the Afternoon*, he states that "Cézanne's discoveries" were "used by . . . imitators" (99). A "great artist," like Cézanne, bases his own art on the art of all times: "The individual, the great artist when he comes, uses everything that has been discovered or known about his art up to that point, being able to accept or reject in a time so short it seems that the knowledge was born with him, rather than that he takes instantly what it takes the ordinary man a lifetime to know, and then the great artist goes beyond what has been done or known and makes something of his own" (100). Thus the "great artist" must learn from others before he can reach his full expression.

The aesthetic leap from one art form to another, or the incorporation of elements and techniques of one art form into another, is a difficult one. The individual artist is wandering both ethically and artistically into a new world. This struggle was part of the moral and artistic chaos and confusion of the 1920's. It was the demonstrations of the Dadaists; it was the experimentation of the surrealists; and it was the hard, physical lines of an imagist poem.

It should be clear at this point that the overlapping of art forms took place on several levels. Certainly these artists had a common interest in similar themes. Yet it is not just this interest in specific themes which indicates the breakdown of ideal artistic types. The treatment of theme, the actual artistic expression, whether presented in words, paint, stone, or music, is a more significant indica-

54 Plimpton, "An Interview with Ernest Hemingway," p. 29.

tor of this overlapping of art forms. That is, the cacophonies of Stravinsky's symphonies, the lack of color harmony in the painting of the Fauves, the free association and irrationalities of Dada and surrealist poetry and prose, might all be considered parallel technical means of examining the same theme. More important, however, is that certain technical means were not just parallel, but identical. Apollinaire's cubist poems could be read as poems, but they could also be viewed as cubist paintings. E. E. Cummings' elaborate experimentations[55] with the typographical page can be seen as an attempt to break up the flat, visual surface, much as, for example, the collage enriched the flat surface of the canvas. Such borrowing could and did involve nearly any element of technique.

For a writer of prose, however, the traditional lines had been more sharply drawn; hence his task was most difficult. In an indirect manner, Hemingway himself indicated his own problems in broadening the sensual scope of his prose. The painter Thomas Hudson admits, "It is luckier to be a painter [than a writer] . . . because you have more things to work with. We have the advantage of working with our hands and the metier we have mastered is an actual tangible thing" (103). To create in prose, not even in poetry, the single art—the synaesthesia or interplay of the senses —with black letters printed on a white page was nearly an impossible task. James Joyce had found one means of accomplishing this in prose, but his novels tend to approximate poetry. Although Hemingway admired Joyce's prose, this was not the method Hemingway was to choose. To create a landscape like Cézanne, to embody the world of dreams and the irrational like the surrealists, to create a poetic image in an extended prose work, could be the way to this single art. To paraphrase Hemingway's final sentence concerning Goya, "Naturally no writer has ever been able to write all that but he tried."

55 Cummings was not the first writer to experiment with such devices; other writers from the English metaphysical poets to Victor Hugo had tried the same types of innovations. From the perspective of 1971, it is easy to see that all these experimental poets are precursors of such modern forms as "concrete" poetry.

II

Landscapes

> "I can make a landscape like Paul Cézanne. I learned how to make a landscape from Mr. Paul Cézanne by walking through the Luxembourg museum a thousand times."[1]

Hemingway was always careful at least to sketch background landscapes or city landscapes for the reader. He was a man who himself had spent much time outdoors wherever he was–Michigan, Spain, Africa, Switzerland, France, Cuba. His stories and novels set in these places clearly and consciously reflect their locales.

Hemingway often sketched in only enough landscape so that the reader is aware of the immediate physical relationship between nature and the fictional character. Thus, for example, in "The Short Happy Life of Francis Macomber," the thicket from which the lion springs is carefully described as it would appear to Macomber but not to a botanist. Or in any of the many fishing scenes scattered throughout Hemingway's works, such as "Out of Season," the stream itself is often described only with reference to the possibility of trout living in it, and the bank is important only insofar as it provides trees for shade and a smooth area for lunch. In descriptions such as these, Hemingway is interested in nature as it immediately appears and physically affects the fic-

1 Quoted in Lillian Ross, *Portrait of Hemingway* (New York, 1961), p. 60. I first conceived the central ideas of this chapter in 1959, and I wrote the chapter itself, in the main, in 1968. I did not read until the summer of 1969 Robert L. Lair's article, "Hemingway and Cézanne: An Indebtedness," *Modern Fiction Studies*, 6, no. 2 (Summer 1960): 165–68. Moreover, Mr. Lair and I clearly see a different sort of relationship between Hemingway and Cézanne.

tional character; the depiction of these specific aspects of nature is to provide texture.[2]

Another type of landscape description used by Hemingway indicates a mental relationship between the character and the land. Such a relationship is not really a type of pathetic fallacy, but a projection of the fictive consciousness upon nature itself. More often than not, these descriptions take the form of a metaphor or simile. For Sordo, in *For Whom the Bell Tolls*, the hill on which he is to die "is truly like a chancre . . . and we are the very pus of it" (310). At other times, this fictive projection takes form in a mythic or religious significance, as with the beaches which Santiago dreams of in *The Old Man and the Sea.*

There is, however, another type of description of nature to be found in Hemingway's works—that of the landscape or city landscape. Hemingway's characters often stop the movement of the novel and simply view the land surrounding them, gaining a broad and comprehensive view of nature, a panoramic view perhaps not limited to the consciousness of the character. This vista or expanded view of the land is often set into the fabric of the novel; that is, the description itself is, in a way, set apart from the rest of the novel. Movement of some sort precedes it, and movement follows it, but the action stands still for the description itself. Clearly, such landscapes are significant. It is with these special views of the land that this chapter is primarily concerned.

Like any writer or artist describing a landscape, Hemingway chose specific details or elements for emphasis; an artist or writer cannot present the whole of a landscape, but must necessarily emphasize some areas and neglect or ignore other areas within his vision. Hence there is an element of abstraction manifested in the very conception of the landscape itself. Hemingway, however, abstracted the details of the landscape further than the initial

2 "As he [Hemingway] well knew total effect depends upon placing figures in a context—verbal, schematic, and scenic—and in this respect he is as good a 'contextualist' as T. S. Eliot, who adopted if he did not invent this special application of the term." Carlos Baker, *Hemingway: The Writer as Artist* (Princeton, N.J., 1963), p. 68.

conception might have demanded. The nature and manner of this abstraction indicate the importance of the influence of Cézanne's paintings upon Hemingway's verbal landscapes.

Cézanne was no longer a neglected painter by the time Hemingway reached Paris after World War I. He had died in obscurity in 1906, but shortly afterward Picasso, Braque, and other artists "discovered" Cézanne and quickly borrowed some of his techniques for their new movement, cubism. Like others in Paris in the 1920's, Hemingway was aware of the new artistic movements and the general influence of Cézanne on modern art. By 1922, when Hemingway viewed the French landscape east of Paris, he commented, "I began to understand Cubist painting."[3] Hemingway, however, was not so interested in Cézanne's technique as applied to the abstraction of a guitar as he was in Cézanne's aesthetics and techniques as applied to landscape. During the last twenty years of his life, Cézanne had produced a number of paintings depicting the hills, woods, and fields near his home in Aix-en-Provence. Many of his landscapes are dominated by Mont Sainte-Victoire, which becomes a recurring image in the vistas.

That Hemingway knew, admired, and studied Cézanne's paintings is clear from any number of sources. In the epigraph to this chapter, he rather explicitly stated his debt to Cézanne; he also acknowledged the influence of Cézanne to George Plimpton.[4] In a letter to Gertrude Stein in August, 1924, Hemingway described a recently completed short story, "the long one I worked on before I went to Spain where I'm trying to do the country like Cézanne."[5] Miss Stein had "explained [to Hemingway] that he must look at his material, and at each new experience, as certain painters

3 "A Paris-to-Strasbourg Flight," *The Toronto Daily Star*, September 9, 1922, reprinted in *By-Line: Ernest Hemingway*, p. 43.

4 George Plimpton, "An Interview with Ernest Hemingway," *Hemingway and His Critics: An International Anthology*, ed. Carlos Baker (New York, 1961), p. 27.

5 Ernest Hemingway to Gertrude Stein, August 15 [1924], *The Flowers of Friendship: Letters Written to Gertrude Stein*, ed. Donald Gallup (New York, 1953), p. 164.

–Cézanne, in particular–looked at their own compositions."[6] One of Hemingway's close friends in the early years, Morley Callaghan, remarked that the landscapes in *A Farewell to Arms* were not influenced by Cézanne: "The landscape was done with his painter's eye, not Cézanne's eye, his own, and I recalled that back in Toronto he had told me that he wished sometimes he had been a painter."[7] Moreover, Hemingway was quite capable of isolating and recognizing artistic techniques. Is it possible that he borrowed certain of Cézanne's techniques for his own verbal landscapes? Hemingway himself thought so. It can be shown, in fact, that Hemingway's special views of the land, primarily his mountain landscapes, are composed by means of certain of Cézanne's own techniques.

There are at least four methods of the painter which Hemingway was able to transpose into words. The first of these is the use of a series of planes for depth and structural development. Particularly in his later pictures, which include the landscapes Hemingway studied, Cézanne often used planes parallel to the surface of the canvas, mounting one upon another, or one behind another, or simply scattered throughout the picture, all usually interjoining and interpenetrating.

Hemingway's series of planes is not so complex as Cézanne's; his landscapes are more simply drawn and do not contain the series of smaller planes. Hemingway preferred to use a series of larger planes united by a diagonal line. Most often, these are landscapes of which the viewer has a very wide vista, as in Jake's view of Burguete from *The Sun Also Rises*: "Looking back we saw Burguete, white houses and red roofs, and the white road with a truck going along it. . . . Ahead the road came out of the forest and went along the shoulder of the ridge of the hills. The hills ahead were not wooded, and there were great fields of yellow gorse. Way off we could see the steep bluffs dark with trees and

6 Charles Fenton, *The Apprenticeship of Ernest Hemingway: The Early Years* (New York, 1954), p. 154.

7 Morley Callaghan, *That Summer in Paris* (New York, 1963), p. 107.

jutting with gray stone that marked the course of the Irati River..." (117).

There are four planes clearly marked in this passage: the village, the forest, the hill, and the bluffs. The first three are cut across and through by the diagonal line of the road. Compare this verbal landscape to any one of Cézanne's works which are primarily landscapes, such as the Mont Sainte-Victoire paintings. In nearly all of these, Cézanne has developed his landscapes by a series of planes cut across and through by a road, river, line of trees, or simply color modulations. The viewer is taken back into the depth of the vista by the diagonal line.

Furthermore, both Hemingway and Cézanne concluded or topped these series of spatial planes by a heavy mass of rock: in Cézanne's paintings, Mont Sainte-Victoire itself, and in Hemingway's description, "the steep bluffs . . . jutting with gray rocks." The series of smaller planes have been leading to this mass of rock, and, with the added emphasis of the diagonal line, the reader/viewer must focus on the pyramid of Mont Sainte-Victoire or upon the rectangular "steep bluffs." Thus both artists have used these planes not only to designate landscape elements and create depth but also to form the basic structure of the vista itself.

A second technique which Hemingway apparently borrowed from Cézanne can also be illustrated by this passage from *The Sun Also Rises*. As Erle Loran has pointed out,[8] Cézanne never allowed his distant mountains to become lost in space by blurring the peaks and horizons. By using planes and outline, Cézanne was able to create and maintain the solidity of mountains and ridges and also to clarify their positions in space. Such a technique separates Cézanne from, for example, the impressionists, with whom he studied for a time and who usually created a feeling of endless space by letting their mountains and horizons become lost in haze. Hemingway, like Cézanne, was also careful not to let the mountains and ridges become lost in space. Note that the ridges

8 Erle Loran, *Cézanne's Composition* (Berkeley and Los Angeles, 1944), pp. 12ff.

are "dark with trees" and "jutting with gray rocks." And despite Callaghan's observation that Hemingway had used "his own" eye, rather than Cézanne's, the ever-reappearing mountains of *A Farewell to Arms* are generally[9] not allowed to vanish: "The mountains were sharp and steep on the other side of the lake and down at the end of the lake was the Rhone Valley flat between the two ranges of mountains; and up the valley where the mountains cut it off was the Dent du Midi. It was a high snowy mountain and it dominated the valley but it was so far away that it did not make a shadow" (300). Thus even a faraway mountain maintains its position in space; moreover, like Cézanne's Mont Sainte-Victoire, it is shadowless. A writer cannot outline a ridge or a mountain peak as a painter might, but Hemingway's use of the dark trees, gray rocks, and snow—all specific colors which contrast with the surrounding scene—is as close to Cézanne's outline technique as is possible.

A third technique common to both Cézanne and Hemingway is the emphasis upon volumes of space with the use of simple geometrical forms as the basis of definition. In a letter to Emile Bernard, dated April 15, 1904, Cézanne commented that "natural forms all tend to the sphere, the cone and the cylinder."[10] Although the philosophical implications of this statement are uncertain, it is clear that Cézanne's oranges, cups, mountains, trees, and rocks all appear to be painted as spheres, cones, and cylinders, with endless variations upon the basic form. Rather than painting the top of a tree as an uneven texture of varying shape, Cézanne painted a sphere on top of a cylinder. This is not to say that his trees resemble large lollipops. The geometrical forms do not often appear in an absolutely pure shape; Cézanne "always seemed to imply that he is at home thinking in terms of extremely simple geometrical forms, and allowing those to be infinitely and infinitesimally modified at each point by his visual sensations."[11] Finally,

9 In the rain, the mountains do become realistically "lost."
10 Roger Fry, *Cézanne: A Study of His Development* (New York, 1927), p. 52.
11 Ibid., p. 53.

Cézanne's interest in the volume and solidity of objects is clearly implied by his use of these geometrical forms.

For Hemingway, too, the solidity and volume of objects was of primary importance in his landscapes. For example, in "Big Two-Hearted River," Nick sees the area near the river in terms of its solidity and simple geometrical forms: "[He] kept on through the pine plain, mounting the small rises to see other rises ahead of him and sometimes from the top of a rise a great solid island of pines . . ." (310). Or again, from *The Sun Also Rises*: "We climbed up and up and crossed another high Col and turned along it, and the road ran down to the right, and we saw a whole new range of mountains off to the south, all brown and baked-looking and furrowed into strange shapes" (93).

Despite the fact that this passage is part of Harry's death dream in "The Snows of Kilimanjaro," the landscape itself is clearly representative of Hemingway's interest in volume and shape: "the plain [extended] as far as you could see, gray-yellow now . . . then they were over the mountains with the sudden depths of green-rising forest and the solid bamboo shoots, and then the heavy rain-forest again, sculptured into peaks and hollows as they crossed and hills sloped down and then another plain, hot now, and purple-brown, bumpy with heat" (174). In this passage, even the plain, which might usually be described only as a plane, is given volume—"bumpy with heat." Further, the trees of the rain forest are "sculptured into peaks and hollows," perhaps a series of tops of cones. Here Hemingway has given solidity to the forest, as seen from above, making it appear a mass of molded form rather than fragile leaves and branches. The word "sculptured" also suggests the outlines which Cézanne often used to differentiate major objects, such as a mountain or important trees.

Hemingway himself saw nature in terms of solidity and geometrical form. He was impressed by the Rocky Mountains: ". . . and you sat in the sun and marvelled at the formal clean-lined shape mountains can have at a distance so that you remember them in the shapes they show from far away, and not as the broken rock slides you crossed, the jagged edges you pulled up by, and the narrow shelves you sweated along, afraid to look down, to round that peak that looked so smooth and geometrical."[12] Hemingway's own view of nature corresponded with the ranges which his fictional characters observe. Thus there is a very realistic basis for his descriptions of the mountains.

Finally, there is one other technique quite basic to Cézanne that Hemingway occasionally attempted to use. Cézanne did not use color "as an adjunct to form, as something imposed from without, but as itself a direct exponent of form."[13] That is, Cézanne modulated his colors in such a way that they themselves defined the form. He ignored the traditional restrictions of light and shade and used the colors themselves for molding. Such a technique demands a very great amount of modulation and sophisticated handling of color, obviously impossible for a writer to imitate.

Yet at times, and almost only when describing nature, Hemingway seems to have been attempting to modulate with a mixture of color, not with the more natural light and shade. Consider again the passage from "The Snows of Kilimanjaro." Hemingway did not use pure colors. The first plain is gray-yellow, the second purple-brown. These are, in fact, exactly the type of color modulations Cézanne employs; examine the Mont Sainte-Victoire paintings, or nearly any of his other landscapes. Further, both of Hemingway's modulations are juxtaposed to the pure green of the rain forest. Green is composed of yellow (juxtaposed to the gray-yellow modulation) and also of blue (juxtaposed to the modulation of purple [blue and red]-brown). Cézanne, of course, used such color variation within a single object; and although Hemingway has here altered his tones for different objects, the

12 "The Clark's Fork Valley, Wyoming," *Vogue* (February 1939), reprinted in *By-Line: Ernest Hemingway*, p. 298. *Green Hills of Africa* contains many such passages; for example, "we came to a sort of amphitheatre, a bowl-like valley" (171), or "there were steep, rounded, wooded hills" (250). Even elephant dung is "conical" (10).

13 Fry, *Cézanne: A Study of His Development*, p. 13.

basic nature of the modulation itself is the same. Such a carefully considered blending of colors is indeed rare in Hemingway, and one must wonder if even these rare passages would have occurred had Hemingway not studied Cézanne carefully.

Moreover, Hemingway's landscapes are very seldom described in terms of the traditional values of light and shade. Shade is mentioned only when a weary fisherman wishes to nap or a tired hiker wishes to rest. The landscape descriptions themselves are seldom concerned with the sun as a source of light or with shade as a means of contrasting or giving form. In this sense, Hemingway is closely related to Cézanne and the artists of the twentieth century: "Cézanne achieved light in the sense that modern painters give to the word, namely the creation of an inner light that emanates from the color relations in the picture itself, without regard for the mere copying of realistic effects of light and shade."[14] Light, as such, is not important in the passages from *The Sun Also Rises* and "Big Two-Hearted River," but in the passage from "The Snows of Kilimanjaro," the light does seem to emanate "from the color relations."

Thus one can validly state that Hemingway was able to transpose certain Cézanne-like techniques of landscape painting into verbal descriptions. The correspondences are not always exact; that is impossible. There is, however, enough specific evidence to indicate that the writer could and probably did borrow from the painter.

What do such correspondences mean? Why did Hemingway turn to Cézanne for techniques of describing landscapes? What was it that attracted Hemingway to Cézanne? It is clear why he was *not* thus interested in the two groups of painters who dominated the Parisian world of fine arts in the 1920's. The cubists were too abstract; besides, they did not paint landscapes. The surrealists did paint landscapes, but their symbolic dreamscapes could not have been meaningful to the realistic vision of nature which Hemingway, at least in part, wished to express. For Hem-

14 Loran, *Cézanne's Composition*, p. 29.

ingway wanted to depict "a great solid island of pines," not the wilted clock which never existed in any natural, physical form.

Both Hemingway and Cézanne wished, on one level, to produce reality. They both attempted to describe a landscape so that any reader or viewer might recognize it, should he actually visit it. Thus their landscapes are imitative or mimetic. It is, in fact, this quality which separates Cézanne from the artists of the twentieth century who studied and used his techniques, such as the cubists. Erle Loran has pointed out that Cézanne's landscapes are recognizably real: "To one who knows the country around Aix-en-Provence, Cézanne's color expresses the very essence of that sun-baked land. In fact, Cézanne's landscapes are, in my estimation, among the first produced that re-create and express nature in its true atmosphere."[15]

Hemingway also produced recognizably real landscapes. Constance Chappel Montgomery had little trouble finding the fields, fences, and groves of trees near Petoskey, Michigan, which Hemingway depicted in "Up in Michigan" and in other short stories set in Michigan.[16] Hemingway also recognized the realistic qualities of Cézanne's landscapes. With reference to "Rocks of the Forest" (New York Metropolitan Museum), Hemingway stated, "This is what we try to do in writing, this and this, and the woods, and the rocks we have to climb over."[17] Thus both artists recreated the characteristics of an actual landscape precisely and realistically. Their concrete vision of the land itself was thus realized.

Yet I have said that Hemingway abstracted, that his landscapes are carefully contrived rather than wholly real, and that he borrowed techniques which were also used by many artists of the twentieth century who produced abstract, symbolic, or expressionistic paintings. The use of these techniques should indicate some deeper significance in Hemingway's imitation, some deeper

15 Ibid., p. 28.
16 Constance Chappel Montgomery, *Hemingway in Michigan* (New York, 1966).
17 Quoted in Ross, *Portrait of Hemingway*, p. 60.

"This is what we try to do in writing, this and this, and the woods, and the rocks we have to climb over."

—ERNEST HEMINGWAY TO LILLIAN ROSS (1950)

Paul Cézanne, "Rocks of the Forest." Oil on canvas, 28⅞ x 36⅜ in. The Metropolitan Museum of Art, bequest of Mrs. H. O. Havemeyer, 1929. The H. O. Havemeyer Collection.

conceptual relationship between the painter and the writer. Hemingway did not study and learn from Cézanne simply because he liked his paintings or because Miss Stein had told him to; there are more significant relationships between the two, of which the techniques themselves are only a manifestation of method. This relationship lies in the meaning of the land for each man.

Let us reexamine the techniques themselves. I have said that Hemingway probably borrowed at least four methods from Cézanne for landscape descriptions: the use of a series of planes often cut across by a diagonal line, the careful delineation of even the most distant mountains and ridges, the emphasis upon volumes of space with the use of simple geometrical forms as the basis of definition, and the occasional use of color modulation. The first three techniques, I believe, indicate most clearly certain values and implications concerning the concept of land for both Cézanne and Hemingway.

With the planes, the delineation, and the simple geometrical forms, both men asserted the existence or presence of form and organization in nature. These techniques represent a breaking-up of natural forms into simple shapes; the complexity of nature has been reduced to a series of planes or geometrical forms. Mountains become pyramids, ridges become rectangles, trees become "solid islands" or "sculptured." Both Cézanne and Hemingway have used this means to assert that there is order in the chaos. This is not, it seems to me, necessarily a subjective imposition of order upon the diversity of nature.[18] It is not necessarily certain that Cézanne and Hemingway simply used these forms in the same way that a child is taught to draw a head by beginning with a circle or a lamb by outlining first an oval and then a circle which is placed precariously on one end of the oval. It is clear from the passage quoted above that Hemingway actually *saw* at least one peak of the Rocky Mountains as geometrical.

The geometrical shapes and forms push themselves out and

18 In *Cézanne: A Study of His Development,* Fry doubts whether Cézanne saw this ordering "as something like a law of nature" and adds that "he found these forms convenient as a kind of intellectual scaffolding" (52–53).

through the texture of variation and color modulation. In any landscape of Cézanne, the tree trunks may be leaning diagonally across the canvas and the color modulation may be infinite, but the basic cylindrical form asserts itself. Or consider Hemingway again, this time *For Whom the Bell Tolls*: "El Sordo was thinking: It [the hill] is shaped like a chancre. Or the breast of a young girl with no nipple. Or the top cone of a volcano" (309). Although El Sordo's metaphors of the hill are dominated by his own despair and frustration, the geometrical forms still assert themselves. Such an assertion of geometrical form is indicative, it seems to me, of a vision of reality common to both Cézanne and Hemingway. Nature has order; it has form; it is not chaos. The reduction to these simple forms, therefore, is an imperative, not a choice.

The emphasis on volume and the delineation of the distant mountains indicate, at the same time, an assertion of solidity and substance in nature. The "lost in space" technique leaves the viewer or reader wandering in the haze of distance; the technique of delineation maintains the position of the distant mountain solidly and clearly in space. Even the leaves of trees were given a solid form by Cézanne and Hemingway. There is a permanence implied in this solidity—a permanence unrelated to man. Curiously enough, neither Hemingway nor Cézanne often depicted people as part of their landscapes—houses and villages and even trucks, perhaps, but not people. In Cézanne's paintings, Fritz Novotny has noted that "there is one characteristic of Cézanne's mode of representation which one may describe superficially as aloofness from life, or, more profoundly and comprehensively, aloofness from mankind. . . ."[19] Hemingway is not aloof from mankind. Other than the fictional character himself, and perhaps his friends, who merely view the vista, the presence of people is seldom noted within the area of his landscapes. Hemingway and Cézanne generally isolated man from the landscape vision. They sought a pure vision of the land, unrelated to the human being. They

19 Fritz Novotny, *Cézanne* (Vienna, n.d.), p. 8.

found order, solidity, and permanence not only in the volumes of the land and delineation of mountains, but also in the series of planes and geometrical forms.

There are, therefore, two concepts underlying the use of these techniques: an assertion of form and orderliness in nature, and a view of nature as substantial and solid. Art historians and critics have long realized that the real and subjective have been thus combined in Cézanne's paintings. Jacques Maritain has observed: "More, to be sure, than Manet or any other, he [Cézanne] has been the liberating figure in contemporary art: precisely because he was so totally, he seemed so obdurately and desperately intent on that bound, buried significance of visible things, which he felt perpetually escaping him as he took hold of it. . . . Hence . . . his longing for a consubstantial order and harmony emerging from the brute universe of the eye in the act of seeing, and that quality of emotion, echoing both being and man, which the least landscape or still life painted by him awakes in us."[20] Thus, although Cézanne could depict a landscape realistically, there are very subjective and emotional concepts expressed in and communicated by his paintings.

When Cézanne retreated from Paris to Aix-en-Provence, his paintings had been rejected and he himself had been humiliated and jeered. It was at this time that he turned primarily to nature, although he also did portraits and still life. It was particularly in nature that he sought the order from the chaos, the absolute from the relative, the solid from the fragmentary. In the Mont Sainte-Victoire paintings, the pyramid of the mountain looms solidly and substantially behind the small planes of the surrounding landscape. The realistic vision has thus been both maintained and modified by the metaphysical vision of the artist.

With Hemingway, a similar process occurred. In the same way, the landscape, although realistically described, still represents something more, some metaphysical or emotional or symbolic

20 Jacques Maritain, *Creative Intuition in Art and Poetry*, Bollingen Series, xxxv.1 (New York, 1955), p. 29.

expression of the artist himself. Carlos Baker has maintained that it is this double vision, combining both the realistic and the symbolic, which "is the chief of many reasons why his work is likely to last when that of most of his contemporaries in fiction and poetry has been forgotten."[21] Clearly, it is through the use of the techniques which he might well have found in Cézanne's paintings that he was able to express this double vision.

On the other hand, unlike other critics, I believe that the role of the land in Hemingway's works is not always simply a part of the texture of the novel, nor is it just a reflection of a fictional character's state of mind.[22] One does not need to state that any reproduction of nature, whether by artist or writer or any other means, involves a subjective element; nature, to be reproduced, must necessarily be filtered through a human mind which is unique in itself. It is possible, however, to see nature per se—to examine it not simply as a reflection of a human's mind, but in and of itself. It seems to me, in fact, that Hemingway's nature has been described and examined for itself; it is not simply part of the context or simply a reflection of a human's mind, although it may, at the same time, also be either one or both of these.

The essence of the land, especially of the mountains, is too consistent in Hemingway's works to be understood only as a part of the texture or as a further means of understanding the human mind. Nature, in the broad sense, is the same throughout Hemingway's works; the fictional characters who view this nature are not. Consider how many of Hemingway's works are either set in nature or have major scenes set in nature: clearly a majority

21 Baker, *Hemingway: The Writer as Artist*, p. 292.

22 In *Hemingway: The Writer as Artist*, Baker has observed that "Hemingway was very rarely interested in the passing show of the non-human universe unless it could serve him in some way to gain further understanding of one of nature's more complex phenomena, the human mind" (290). Mark Spilka has stated, "For, with Hemingway, the great outdoors is chiefly a state of mind, a projection of moral and emotional attitudes onto physical arenas, so that a clear account of surface action will reproduce these attitudes in the reader" ("Death of Love in *The Sun Also Rises*," in Baker, ed., *Hemingway and His Critics*, p. 85).

of his works, both short stories and novels. And in each of these, the land[23] is solid, substantial, and orderly. It is a kind of idyll in the midst of confusion and chaos in "Big Two-Hearted River" and *For Whom the Bell Tolls*; the mountains are the home concept in *A Farewell to Arms*.[24]

And yet phrases like "idyll" and "home concept" are meaningless unless the very essence of nature in Hemingway is understood. The fictional characters in these works retreat from the cities and from other people and are alone, or alone together. It is, however, more than isolation that creates the idyllic mood or the home concept. There must be some basic quality of nature—of the land—to which these characters can respond. The solid, substantial, nearly primitive qualities of the land draw these characters to it and create the idyllic or home mood. The prefatory quotation from Ecclesiastes to *The Sun Also Rises* indicates the significance of the land for Hemingway: "One generation passeth away, and another generation cometh; but the earth abideth forever. . . . The sun also riseth, and the sun goeth down, and hasteth to the place where he arose. . . ." Or, as Hemingway later told A. E. Hotchner, "The characters in *The Sun Also Rises* were tragic, but the real hero was the earth and you get the sense of its triumph in abiding forever."[25] It is the land, therefore, with its mountains and ridges and planes, which is solid, substantial, and orderly.

The land in Hemingway's works remains a constant, an element of eternity in the midst of man's relativity and transitoriness. The mountains of Switzerland (*A Farewell to Arms*) or the hills of Spain (*The Sun Also Rises*) are Cézanne's Mont Sainte-Victoire in literary form. The careful delineation of the distant mountains, hills, and ridges, which places them clearly and certainly in space, and the emphasis on volume, which points to a

23 I am obviously not dealing here with his short stories and novels set near or upon the sea. The sea will be discussed in Ch. IV. Cézanne himself never painted seascapes as such, although he did paint a few shorelines which were dominated by cliffs and mountains.

24 Baker, *Hemingway: The Writer as Artist*, pp. 101ff. and 257.

25 A. E. Hotchner, *Papa Hemingway* (New York, 1966), p. 50.

solidity and substantial quality of nature, are the means by which both have expressed this vision.

Furthermore, there is a suggestion of the primitive, the elemental, in the landscapes. The simple geometrical forms through which nature is represented are a manifestation of the basic form and order of the land. The forms are pure, simple, and thrust through the sophistications of color and detail. Moreover, these basic geometrical forms are repeated in nature. In Cézanne's paintings, the pyramid of Mont Sainte-Victoire is often echoed by the roof of a house or the top of a tree. In Hemingway, El Sordo can find at least three other objects, from the very small to the very large, with which to describe the hill on which he was to die. There is, therefore, an assertion of the essence, the most elemental, of physical form. And this elemental form has been found to be orderly: not only orderly in the sense of balance and proportion, but orderly also in the sense of universality.

Indeed, the land is the only element of consistency in Hemingway's universe. People are inconsistent, to say the least. Even bullfights can sometimes offer only weak bulls and poor or ruined bullfighters. God is too distant, if he is there at all. Only the land remains the same in Hemingway's works; this land is primarily the mountains or the hills, whether they be in Switzerland, Spain, Wyoming, Michigan, or Africa. It is this land to which Nick returns in "Big Two-Hearted River" and to which Jake escapes in *The Sun Also Rises*. The mountains, the hills, and the ridges have become a major symbol in Hemingway's works—a symbol of permanence, security, solidity, perhaps even of eternity. As a symbol, they are invested with emotional and metaphysical connotations.

This is not to say that the land cannot be hostile or, perhaps more significantly, cannot be altered by man. Especially in *The Sun Also Rises* and *A Farewell to Arms*, the plain represents corruption, prostitutes, dust, and death. In both of these novels, on the other hand, the mountains are juxtaposed. The unalterable domes or pyramids or ridges represent the only stability and consistency on earth. Even the Fascist bombers in *For Whom the Bell Tolls* cannot destroy the mountains; the people hiding on the mountains may be killed, the trees may be burned, but the mountains remain. In *A Farewell to Arms*, Catherine Barkley must leave the mountains and go to the valley where she dies in childbirth.

It should be noted that most of the fictional characters do not "communicate" with the land; that is, there is no spiritual or mental or mystical union with the land. Frederic Henry, Jake Barnes, and Nick Adams are not Thoreaus. No pine needle quivers in sympathy with a Hemingway protagonist. Only Robert Jordan seems to have an undefinable special relationship with nature, especially in the final pages of the novel. Yet there is no communion as such involved. In short, man must come to the mountains not to commune with nature, but simply to be in nature.[26]

The mountain is a symbol, therefore, which is related to man only insofar as it points up man's instability and tenuousness. Literally, as well as symbolically, the mountain stands above man. It stands apart from man. No wonder people do not often appear in Hemingway's landscape vistas. Hemingway, however, does allow the symbol to affect the actions of his fictional characters to a certain extent. And different characters respond in different ways to the symbol. The ritual of fishing in "Big Two-Hearted River" can thus be seen not only as a ritual cleansing and healing for the young Nick, but also as a sort of ritual in the cathedral of the hills.

26 Mary McCarthy feels that Hemingway's protagonists do not "communicate" with nature in any special sense, and that, for them, "Nature is not a reference point, outside man, giving the scale, but something inseparable from the viewer and his cognitive processes, themselves in doubt." Furthermore, "what betrays the bad faith in Hemingway is the invariable intrusion of the social into a natural context: hierarchies, exclusions, competitive *brio*." That Hemingway did allow the social to intrude upon the natural is generally true with reference to actions set upon the plains or lowlands or, to a certain extent, in scenes set in the mountains (such as the bombing of El Sordo's hill). On the other hand, in those people-less vistas which Hemingway seems to have created with the help of Cézanne's techniques, nature does indeed become a reference point. In these vistas, as I have shown, "Nature is not just the circumambient ensemble of non-human life but history on a grand scale —duration"—the type of nature which Miss McCarthy has found primarily in nineteenth-century writers and painters. See "One Touch of Nature," *The New Yorker*, January 24, 1970, pp. 39–57.

Frederic Henry and Catherine Barkley must leave the mountain when it is time for their baby to be born—dead. On the other hand, Robert Cohn sleeps on the ride to Pamplona in *The Sun Also Rises*. Other characters, such as the captain in Chapter II of *A Farewell to Arms*, do not even wish to go to the mountains. The mountains are there for everyone, but only special ones can appreciate or find meaning in them.

Yet the mountains are obviously something other than symbol. They are also very much a reality: the mountains and the hills—the land—still appear as they are. Thus we have returned to the double vision of nature which Hemingway shared with Cézanne, a vision which led Hemingway to examine and study Cézanne's paintings and which manifested itself in use of at least four techniques similar to Cézanne's. Furthermore, the three techniques which dominate and are repeated in the structuring of Hemingway's landscapes are those for which Cézanne was particularly noted and which were, in fact, just those techniques which Hemingway's artistic contemporaries had been imitating. Indeed, the manner in which Hemingway set apart his landscape descriptions from the narrative flow is a means of "framing" his picture. In this way, he has attempted to prepare the reader for the important description to follow.

Finally, one cannot forget the corresponding and merging views of nature which both Hemingway and Cézanne expressed. The quality of realism, inextricably intertwined with symbolism, is common to both. The metaphysical significance of the enduring, orderly, and solid land, most especially of the mountain, is manifest in the works of each artist. The looming pyramid of Mont Sainte-Victoire has found the new form in Hemingway's prose.

Indeed, it is rather surprising to note just how closely Hemingway was able to repeat in prose the techniques of a painter—to realize just how much like paint words can be made to act. For even if one can never finally prove Cézanne's influence upon Hemingway, at least one can observe how very intimate the writer's technique and the painter's technique have become. Hemingway's special landscape vistas are very nearly Cézanne's paintings in words.

On one level, Hemingway was employing a technique of imagist poetry in creating these scenes. That is, he was isolating and describing a specific image as precisely as possible. The carefully chosen words of physical description are made to stand for the emotional or intellectual significance (Eliot's "objective correlative"). The fictive consciousness viewing these vistas does not consciously reflect upon the stability or consistency or orderliness of the landscapes; the narrator simply describes the physical image. Note further that these special views of the land (and mountains) are carefully set into the framework of the action. It is almost as if Hemingway had embedded an imagist poem in the context of a novel.

On another level, Hemingway attempted to use methods from another art form. He moved at least one step closer to that single art. It is significant, too, that, at least for his landscapes, he chose to use the techniques of Cézanne, who was so influential in the formation of modern art. It is Cézanne who is viewed as the immediate precursor of those who desired and sought a synaesthesia or interplay of the senses in the arts. Cézanne helped to break down the visual, linear perspective, and it appears that Hemingway attempted to use certain of Cézanne's techniques to avoid a strictly linear, visual prose. Both were attempting to make art "an affair of the face."

On still another level, the affinity of the painter and writer is affirmed by their similar symbolic responses to landscape, especially to mountains. While adamantly realistic in the main, each had a common vision of the land. Under their tense statements, whether in paint or in print, lie the profound emotional and intellectual concepts of the land and the mountains as orderly, constant, and stable. It seems especially significant that they both sought to express this vision in a highly organized and intellectualized mass of physical detail. They have used very nearly the same techniques to express their visions.

It was perhaps this dual realistic-symbolic concept, as well as a mutual interest in Cézanne, which drew Hemingway to Miró in the early 1920's. Today Miró is best known for his paintings of fantasy, which often use only simple outlines of symbols or symbolic figures. When Hemingway first met Miró, however, the artist was painting in a far different style. Quite early, Miró had been a follower of Cézanne; his landscapes before 1918, for example, were clearly influenced by Cézanne. In "The Path, Ciurana" (1917), no human is present, the mountains are clearly outlined and situated in space, and there is a careful build-up of a series of planes, as well as the use of geometrical forms. By 1921–22, when he painted "The Farm," which Hemingway was later to own, Miró had shifted in tendency toward "poetic realism."[27] Yet the series of planes and the geometrical forms, handled in a more realistic manner, are still evident. In Miró's later paintings, these realistically handled geometrical forms were to be reduced to the symbolic line-images of his best-known work.

Moreover, Miró also shared a special vision of the land with Hemingway and Cézanne. The landscapes painted before 1923 reflect certain specific, recognizable places; in this sense, they are realistic. On the other hand, Miró also responded emotionally and symbolically to the earth, much as Hemingway and Cézanne did:

> It is to the propitious earth of Montroig [Miró's home in Spain] that he owes his telluric imagination, the power of his lyricism, his visionary conviction, and his ability to be at once restrained in his boldness and precise in his delirium. For the earth does not only inspire, it also corrects; it supplies energy and stimulates movement, but it dictates direction and imposes order as well. Nature's superabundance is not a squandering of energies, but an ordered profusion, subject to cycles, governed by rhythms. The peasant and the painter know this, and when to be guided by it.
>
> It is above all in his art, at the level of the creative instinct, that Miró incarnates this harmony between man and the earth.

27 Jacques Dupin, *Joan Miró: Life and Work* (New York, 1962), pp. 82–83.

> The rhythm of his paintings, the organic development of his forms, the successive stages of his art have all been governed by natural laws. . . .[28]

Perhaps this is what Hemingway meant when he stated that his painting by Miró, "The Farm," expresses "all that you feel about Spain when you are there and all that you feel when you are away and cannot go there." And, conversely, this statement concerning the art of Hemingway's friend Miró says something of Hemingway's own art.

Obviously, Cézanne had a profound effect upon Hemingway, just as he had on so many artists who were Hemingway's contemporaries. And like the other artists, such as, for example, Miró, Picasso, or the surrealists, Hemingway borrowed from Cézanne just what he needed. He had studied the painter's works for himself; he did not assume these techniques secondhand. His choice of techniques to be repeated in words are Cézanne's own. Certainly, too, the dual vision of the land (both realistic and symbolic) which is expressed by these techniques represents Hemingway's own special response to the painter's works. The surrealists, for example, did not find the same special significance in Cézanne. Hemingway's use of Cézanne thus represents how one writer of prose fiction was able to borrow from another art form—how one writer refused to accept artistic "forms" as static and restrictive.

28 Ibid., p. 34.

III

Iconography and technical expression: the agony of man

> The numbers of broken-legged mules and horses drowning in the shallow water called for a Goya to depict them. Although, speaking literally, one can hardly say that they called for a Goya since there has only been one Goya, long dead, and it is extremely doubtful if these animals, were they able to call, would call for pictorial representation of their plight.[1]

> We will lay it on the line once more and the hell with it, and with its ugly face that old Hieronymous Bosch really painted. But you can sheath your scythe, old brother death, if you have got a sheath for it.[2]

The term "iconography" specifically implies an examination of similar and recurring motifs, images, and symbols which appear during a particular historical period. Following Panofsky, art historians have used iconographic means to examine the source and relationship of such motifs, images, and symbols, as ultimately expressed in paintings. In the discussion of a particular motif, the historian generally draws upon all evidence of its appearance, whether in literature, or in other paintings, or in any other art form. Thus far the methods of iconography have been almost exclusively used to illuminate and elucidate particular paintings. Surely it is possible to apply iconography to literature—that is, to

1 "A Natural History of the Dead," *The Short Stories of Ernest Hemingway*, p. 539, originally a section of *Death in the Afternoon.*
2 *Across the River and into the Trees*, p. 254.

examine motifs, images, and symbols of painters or artistic movements in order to illuminate and elucidate literature.

In a purely iconographic study, no attention is paid to the actual technique of expression. An art historian who is tracing an iconographic motif is not concerned with whether the paintings have been done in oil or in pastel, or whether the artist made short strokes or long strokes with his brush. The historian is concerned strictly with the motif, the image, or the symbol. In the next two chapters, however, I shall be discussing, along with iconography, particular artistic techniques which seem to appear and reappear in the expression of motif, image, or symbol; for, as was evident in the last chapter, technique and content are often closely associated in Hemingway. Since Hemingway apparently borrowed technique from Cézanne in order to express a vision of the land which he shared with the painter, the iconographic images which Hemingway shared with particular painters will often be examined along with certain specific techniques which are associated with these same painters.

"The Agony of Man" is, of course, a rather broad theme, encompassing and offering all sorts of pessimistic potentialities from Aeschylus to Beckett. It is a theme which certainly characterizes much of the art of the 1920's, whether relevant to Dada nihilism, Eliot's "The Waste Land," or Miss Stein's now-classic observation, "You are all a lost generation"—a statement which Hemingway, by the way, rejected. It is obvious that Hemingway's disillusionment, his preoccupation with violence, his theme of *nada*, and his concern for war are all at least generally related to the social, moral, and artistic confusion of the 1920's. What is curious about the motifs and symbols, as well as their technical expression, in the works of Hemingway is that they can be related not so closely to the poetry and prose of the 1920's as to the paintings. Moreover, certain motifs and techniques, although examined and perhaps used by Hemingway's contemporaries, are often found in Hemingway's own prose to be much closer in expression to those older painters who were influencing his contemporaries. As with landscape, it is entirely possible to imagine that Hemingway used the interests of his age as a springboard for his own personal examination of artists who had already expressed such motifs sometimes even centuries before. Thus one must continually keep in mind not only the themes and techniques of Hemingway's contemporaries, but also those of artists in whom Hemingway was especially interested.

Hemingway's major and minor themes have a way of recurring. That is not to say that his works are composed of dull variations of similar motifs; his novels and short stories are, rather, supremely individual and unique entities, much like the individual canvases of Cézanne's series of Mont Sainte-Victoire paintings or the individual thematic interpretations of Brahms's "Variations on a Theme of Haydn." Hemingway's images of certain motifs are transplanted from continent to continent; they alter, develop, and become more symbolically dominated as the author himself matures both artistically and personally. The motifs, however, remain variations of recurring themes. Some motifs which might be treated individually by other writers are often closely associated in Hemingway's works, as, for example, violence/war/death. Other motifs, such as love, are often treated in conjunction with a variety of others, such as war/death or sports or religion. It is rather remarkable that each of these recurring themes and certain specific motifs can be related in one way or another to at least one of Hemingway's favorite painters or to artistic movements which are more closely linked with the plastic arts.

"The Agony of Man" is indicative of the type of experience which the Hemingway protagonist was forced to suffer. The Jake Barneses, Frederic Henrys, and Nick Adamses all had to live in a generally hostile world in which innocence had to be destroyed, peace shattered, and moral codes established, often unsuccessfully. Hemingway thus presented man's moral and physical agony, as well as man's search for an answer of some kind, if only for a "separate peace." Violence is the theme most often associated with Hemingway's works—as a motif, violence in war, in sports, in bullfighting: "For Hemingway the great necessity [is] to be accurate in the statement of emotions. . . . The thing that stirs him most [is] violence, and the emotions of which he wrote were those stimulated by pain and killing—war and bullfighting . . . and love conceived as . . . something very akin to violence."[3] In short, violence as a theme, with a variety of motifs, is one which appears in nearly all of Hemingway's poetry and prose, whether set in Michigan, Spain, France, or Africa.

Probably the most violent of activities in Hemingway's world is war. At least five of Hemingway's novels and many of his short stories and poems closely associate violence and war, whether the violence is taking place in the time present of the novel, or the violence has occurred in time past, or the violence is yet to come and the foreshadowing is ominous. Such violence is not just that of soldiers killing and maiming one another, although there is certainly plenty of that. It is a broad spectrum of war violence: violence to civilians and their way of life (death, wounding, rape), and violence to the land (in an almost mythological sense), as well as violence to the warring nations themselves. The wounding of an individual soldier is a prominent and recurring motif in Hemingway. Frederic Henry, Jake Barnes, and many of the protagonists in the short stories, such as Nick Adams of "Now I Lay Me," are types of Hemingway's wounded soldier. The wounds are both physical and spiritual, and there is a sense of despair and agony. Hemingway's wounded soldier is not a *miles gloriosus*. The destruction of the land and of nations by war is evident in *For Whom the Bell Tolls* and *A Farewell to Arms*. These two novels, as well as many of the short stories, also portray the civilian suffering in the midst of the violence of war.

This interest in war and violence was, to a certain extent, natural for the artists of the 1920's. Many had served and suffered in World War I, and the memories were fresh. And yet those who had formed the original Dada group, for example, were draft-dodgers, many of them conscientious objectors who had fled to Switzerland to avoid active military service. Others, such as Hemingway's friend Strater, really did not want to think of the war:

3 W. M. Frohock, *The Novel of Violence in America* (Dallas, 1950), pp. 168–69.

"There was such a sense of relief that it was all over."[4] Certainly, if one examines the war novels of Hemingway's contemporaries, such as Cummings' *The Enormous Room* or Dos Passos' *1919*, there is little to compare to Hemingway's realistic, even naturalistic, approach to war and violence. And where is war depicted and described in terms comparable to Hemingway's in any Dada, cubist, futurist, or surrealist work of art? Only the novels of the Frenchman Henri Barbusse, especially *Le Feu Journal d'une escouade* (1916),[5] and certain paintings on the German expressionists, such as Otto Dix and George Grosz, can in any way compare with Hemingway's brutal and realistic portraits of violence. In fact, until the Spanish painters, such as Quintanilla and Picasso, later began to express their horror at the Spanish Civil War, only a few painters or writers contemporary with Hemingway expressed the universal quality and particular agony of war and violence.

Actually Hemingway had written quite realistically of the civilian sufferings in war in articles for the *Toronto Daily Star* before he attempted to develop such themes in fiction. In 1922, Hemingway was sent by the *Star* to the Middle East to cover the Turkish and Greek war. It was the sufferings of the civilians, himself included, that most impressed him. At Adrianople, he saw "the entire Christian population of Eastern Thrace . . . jamming the roads to Macedonia." His description, of which this passage is only a part, is a mass of physical detail, a few adjectives, a series of nouns and verbs:

> It is a silent procession. Nobody even grunts. It is all they can do to keep moving. Their brilliant peasant costumes are soaked and draggled. Chickens dangle by their feet from the carts. Calves nuzzle at the draught cattle wherever a jam halts the stream. An old man marches bent under a young pig, a scythe, and a gun, with a chicken tied to his scythe. A husband spreads a blanket over a woman in labor in one of the

4 Personal interview, Ogunquit, Maine, August 24, 1968.

5 Translated as *Under the Fire* (1917). In *A Farewell to Arms,* Frederic Henry says that *Le Feu* is not "any good" (270).

> carts to keep off the driving rain. She is the only person making a sound. Her little daughter looks at her in horror and begins to cry. And the procession keeps moving.[6]

The sheer physicality, the evocation of the senses, the depiction of civilian suffering in wartime indicates, to a great extent, just how Hemingway will treat similar but fictional scenes in his novels and short stories. Hemingway clearly had an excellent eye for physical detail which, in this scene, strongly suggests and underscores the suffering and violence.

This description of the evacuation at Adrianople, although a piece of journalism, is nevertheless quite closely related to Hemingway's early poems of war, such as "Captives," "Champs d'Honneur," and "Riparto d'Assalto"—all of which deal with the sufferings of the soldiers themselves. The surface of these poems is very physical, very sensual: "[Dying] soldiers pitch and cough and twitch—/All the world roars red and black;/Soldiers smother in a ditch" read lines 5–7 of "Champs d'Honneur." In short, the imagist techniques, such as the use of a physical image or the emphasis upon the correct word, appear in these poems and even in the account of the evacuation at Adrianople.

And then Hemingway began to create scenes of violence in prose fiction, the first of which were certain of the vignettes in *in our time.* These vignettes composed the entire 1923 Paris edition of the book and were slightly altered and rearranged between the short stories in the New York editions of *In Our Time*, published in 1925 and 1930. Many of these vignettes deal with war and violence, and many are based on Hemingway's own experiences. They remain physical on the surface, but they are expressed in a manner different from his journalistic prose and, to a certain extent, even from his poems. Compare, for example, this vignette, which is obviously based upon Hemingway's own experience and the resulting *Star* article concerning the evacuation at Adrianople:

6 "A Silent, Ghastly Procession Wends Way from Thrace," *The Toronto Daily Star,* October 20, 1922, reprinted in *By-Line: Ernest Hemingway,* pp. 51–52.

> Minarets stuck up in the rain out of Adrianople across the mud flats. The carts were jammed for thirty miles along the Karagatch road. Water buffalo and cattle were hauling carts through the mud. No end and no beginning. Just carts loaded with everything they owned. The old men and women, soaked through, walked along keeping the cattle moving. The Maritza was running yellow almost up the bridge. Carts were jammed solid on the bridge with camels bobbing along through them. Greek cavalry herded along the procession. Women and kids were in the carts couched with mattresses, mirrors, sewing machines, bundles. There was a woman having a kid with a young girl holding a blanket over her and crying. Scared sick looking at it. It rained all through the evacuation.[7]

The entire scene has been shortened, the physical detail piled up more tightly. The carefully constructed sentences of the earlier newspaper article have been reduced to phrases and fragments. The use of slang words, such as the impersonal "kid," as well as the use of such words as "herded," reduces these people to a mass, not individuals. Only one little girl who, instead of the husband as in the *Star* article, is holding the blanket over the woman in labor is clearly identifiable, and she is horrified at what should be a natural event but is, in fact, an unnatural act in the context of the evacuation. Finally, the rain, which is to become so symbolically important in the same way in *A Farewell to Arms*, is now clearly associated with the misery and suffering of humanity.

Such stark, naked realism has been compared by Edmund Wilson to Goya's lithographs,[8] but only in terms of the bullfight vignettes, not with reference to the vignettes of violence and war. By the comparison, Wilson was not necessarily implying that Goya had directly or profoundly or even technically influenced

7 *The Short Stories of Ernest Hemingway*, p. 195. For another discussion of these two passages, with a different emphasis, see Charles Fenton, *The Apprenticeship of Ernest Hemingway: The Early Years* (New York, 1954), pp. 229–38.

8 Edmund Wilson, "Mr. Hemingway's Dry-Points," originally published in *Dial* (October 1924), reprinted in *Hemingway and His Critics: An International Anthology*, ed. Carlos Baker (New York, 1961), p. 58.

Hemingway's vignettes; yet there are simply too many similarities between Hemingway's many expressions of war and Goya's paintings and etchings of war and violence not to examine further for evidence of influence. Certainly Wilson's comparison was a valid one, not only with reference to the bullfight scenes, but also with reference to the scenes of violence and war. Even more important, in *Death in the Afternoon*, Hemingway himself associated the violence depicted in the vignettes specifically with Goya: "... in the case of an execution by a firing squad, or a hanging.... Goya tried to make them [permanent] in *Los Desastros de la Guerra*" (3). This series of at least eighty etchings[9] was made between 1808 and 1813. Handled with extreme naturalism, "The Disasters of War" was inspired by Napoleon's invasion of Spain. Goya, who himself apparently witnessed some of the atrocities he depicted, was profoundly moved by the suffering of the nation and her people in this war.

Technically the early vignettes, as well as many later scenes of war set into the novels and stort stories, are similar to Goya's etchings. Each scene is a stark statement with just a few figures. The attention of the viewer is forced upon the image of horror and suffering because of the very simplicity of the conception and design, or because of the few figures, the minimized background, and the clarity of action or scene. Goya depended heavily upon outline and broad planes to emphasize further the figures themselves. There is no fussiness, no busyness, as, for example, in Picasso's etchings executed in the late 1920's and the 1930's. Goya is not afraid to leave open space. The few details are those necessary for the realistic depiction of the horrible event. There is very little explicit symbolism as such. The statements can stand by themselves on a realistic plane. On the other hand, it is possible to find symbols. For example, Goya depicts a number of women in acts of bravery, as well as in positions of suffering. Is this woman an allegorical figure of Spain? Or, as one critic suggests, are "The

9 Not lithographs, as Edmund Wilson would have them. Some have been retouched with dry point. See Jose Gudiol, *Goya*, trans. Priscella Muller (New York, 1964), p. 52.

Disasters of War" about "the terror of man's nature" rather than simply "the terror of war"?[10]

As is evident from comparing the *Toronto Daily Star* passage concerning the Adrianople evacuation with its later fictive expression in the vignette, Hemingway cut the diverse elements of the scene to a very few; details have been omitted. For example, the old man with "a young pig, a scythe, and a gun, with a chicken tied to his scythe" is not mentioned in the vignette. The only isolated individual is the little girl who holds the blanket over her mother who is in labor. The elements of the scene are described directly and specifically, with little detail, almost in outline. Note the broad planes of the blanket, the river, the jammed carts (not individual ones). Indeed, the mass of people is seen as a *mass*, and could well be interpreted, in a painting or etching, in broad planes, as Goya did the spectators in "The Bullfight" (1810–20; New York Metropolitan Museum). Furthermore, there is no overt symbolism in the vignettes. The statements of horror are depicted on a very realistic level. Yet, as in the Goya etchings, symbols *can* be discerned, such as the rain in the evacuation passage or the "perfect barricade" which must be abandoned in the vignette which begins, "It was a frightfully hot day."

Thus Wilson was quite right in suggesting the relationship between Hemingway's vignettes and Goya's etchings. When Hemingway completed the vignettes, however, he had not yet been to the Prado. Yet there were Goyas at the Louvre, and the etchings were available in reproductions.[11] Hemingway made his first extended visit to Spain in 1923; many other trips to Spain and the Prado and the bullfights followed. Since Hemingway certainly considered Goya one of his favorite artists, there is good reason to suppose that he studied Goya's etchings and paintings much as he did Cézanne's landscapes. Hemingway's own reference to the accuracy and reality with which Goya depicted dead mules (in the passages opening this chapter) is an indication of

10 Frederick S. Wright, *Goya* (New York, 1966), unnumbered.

11 In the late nineteenth century, for example, Toulouse-Lautrec had even designed a cover for a new edition of "The Disasters of War."

his personal judgment and evaluation of Goya's talents. Hemingway is undoubtedly referring to the dead mules (and perhaps to the horses, too) which Goya scattered throughout the "Tauromaquia" (etchings #17, 26, 27, 32, and B).

Among other interests, Goya and Hemingway certainly shared an obsession with violence, bullfighting, war, and death. Both were interested in and artistically expressed the violence of war as it extended from the actual fighting of the soldiers to the suffering of civilians and the destruction of the land and the nation. The landscapes in Goya's "The Disasters of War," for example, are desolate and bare, with an occasional shattered tree or a destroyed building. Hemingway also noted the destruction of the land in such scenes as the opening of *A Farewell to Arms* and the reminiscences of battle by Colonel Cantwell in *Across the River and into the Trees*. Each artist was able to center quite realistically and without flinching upon a horrible scene of suffering, whether it involved gaping wounds or brutal rape.

By the time Hemingway wrote *For Whom the Bell Tolls*, the Goya influence is quite clearly in evidence. It is easy to find similar violence in war motifs, as well as similar techniques of expression, in Goya's "The Disasters of War" and in *For Whom the Bell Tolls* and other Hemingway works of the 1930's: scenes of rape (in Hemingway, Maria in *For Whom the Bell Tolls*, and in Goya, "The Disasters of War," etchings 9, 11, 13); brave women (Pilar in *For Whom the Bell Tolls* and etchings 4, 5, and 7); scenes of the dead (the opening of "A Way You'll Never Be" and etchings 21–24); prayers of the condemned showing various physical positions (the Fascists in *For Whom the Bell Tolls* and etching 26); and others. Indeed, certain scenes show a very similar—almost too similar—depiction of the same act. Compare the descriptions of the praying Fascists with the praying Spanish patriots in etching 26. Is it too much to suppose that, just as Hemingway was able to incorporate elements of his actual experiences into his fictional prose, so he could incorporate certain of Goya's figures into his prose?

Both expressed a horror at the violence done to a nation, especially in Hemingway's writings of the 1930's and in Goya's "The Disasters of War." The brave and tortured women of "The Disasters of War" can easily be associated with the bravery and suffering of the Spanish nation. Goya, in fact, did see his nation's suffering as a kind of crucifixion—a view which is more clearly manifest in two major paintings which were also based upon events of the Napoleonic invasion: "The Third of May" and "The Second of May, 1808," which is also titled "The Charge of the Marmalukes" (both painted after 1814 and both at the Prado). Note especially the center prisoner in "The Third of May," in his white shirt, with arms stretched up and out. If one looks closely, there is even an indication that his palms are pierced. One art historian associates this central figure with Christ on the cross—the antagonist of the French anti-Christ.[12] The huddled figure of a Virgin Mary can be noted in the far left corner of this painting.

The Virgin Mary, more particularly the Senora del Pilar to whom the church of Saragossa is dedicated, is the national saint of Spain. According to what was proved to be a forged document of church history, it was at Saragossa in the year 37 that the Virgin appeared on a pillar to St. James.[13] Here St. James built his church, and the Feast of the Immaculate Conception was first celebrated. It is not coincidental that the wise and brave peasant heroine of Hemingway's *For Whom the Bell Tolls* is named Pilar (and that Hemingway named his boat "Pilar").

The only mysterious elements in this novel are associated with Pilar, "who is both a woman and a kind of witch."[14] And it is Pilar who organizes and leads, who knows that Maria (Mary) will find health or a natural life with Jordan. Pilar also knows that Jordan needs Maria for his own understanding of self. The rape of Maria, her close association with Pilar, Pilar's wisdom, bravery, and qualities of mystery—all these point to Hemingway's association of

12 Folke Nordstrom, *Goya, Saturn, and Melancholy* (Uppsala, 1962), p. 178.

13 Henry Charles Lea, *Chapters from the Religious History of Spain Connected with the Inquisition* (New York, 1967), p. 118.

14 Carlos Baker, *Hemingway: The Writer as Artist* (Princeton, N.J., 1963), p. 253.

"Never did I submit to any one. Always I fought. . . ."

—MARIA IN *For Whom the Bell Tolls*

Francisco Goya, "The Disasters of War" #9. 1863. Etching and aquatint. Courtesy of The Hispanic Society of America.

"You're shaking like a Goddamn woman. What the hell is the matter with you? . . . I'll bet that Goddamn woman up above isn't shaking. That Pilar."

—ROBERT JORDAN IN *For Whom the Bell Tolls*

Francisco Goya, "The Disasters of War" #7. 1863. Etching and aquatint. Courtesy of The Hispanic Society of America.

Pilar-Maria with the Virgin Mary and hence with the violence done to the Spanish nation during the Civil War.[15] This is not to say that Pilar-Maria is an allegorical representation of the Virgin, or that Jordan is a kind of God-Christ figure. The characters are far too complex, too real, for that; I do not think Hemingway was interested in allegory in this novel. Yet if *For Whom the Bell Tolls* is "a prose epic of the Spanish people,"[16] then Pilar-Maria must be associated not only with the people, but also with the national religion of a very religious country.[17]

Indeed, this theme alone suggests why Hemingway loved and might have been profoundly influenced even at an early stage of his writing by Goya. They both viewed the violence of war as reaching to all levels—with special emphasis upon the violence. They even chose similar scenes to describe the horror of this universal violence. The tragedy of the Spanish Civil War was quite closely related to that other Spanish tragedy of Goya's day. Finally, the techniques of expression, especially in Hemingway's early vignettes, can be viewed as parallel to Goya's use of outlines, broad planes, and simplicity of design in the etchings of "The Disasters of War."

Hemingway and Goya were not the only artists to see Spanish wars as tragedies, nor were they the only ones to emphasize the violence of Spanish wars. Carlos Baker has pointed out that Hemingway's *For Whom the Bell Tolls* "has in fact much of the nightmare quality of Picasso's allegorical painting," such as "Guernica."[18] Hemingway himself indirectly indicated a relationship between Goya and the Spanish Civil War; in his preface to *All the Brave*, a collection of etchings by Quintanilla concerning the Spanish Civil War, Hemingway noted that Quintanilla's etchings are obviously related to those of Goya (8). It is sig-

15 For other associations of Maria and religion, see F. I. Carpenter, "Hemingway Achieves the Fifth Dimension," in Baker, ed., *Hemingway and His Critics*, pp. 197–98.

16 Baker, *Hemingway: The Writer as Artist*, p. 247.

17 Robert Jordan says that Spaniards are not Christian, that they are "idol" worshippers (355); but the idol they worship, of course, is the Virgin.

18 Baker, *Hemingway: The Writer as Artist*, p. 258.

"He looked at the man twice; once in the daylight, once with a flashlight. That too would have made a good etching for Goya, the visit with the flashlight, I mean."

—"A Natural History of the Dead"

Francisco Goya, "The Third of May." 1814. Oil, 135 x 105 in. Prado.

nificant that Quintanilla was also obsessed with war and violence on all levels and in all modes. Finally, one art historian has noted that all Spanish artists of the 1930's viewed the war as a kind of crucifixion of the Spanish nation: "the events that took place on the Peninsula from 1936–1939 are the poetic equivalent of a Crucifixion."[19]

Closely related to the war motif of violence is death. Of course people, dogs, mules, and horses die in war, or later from wounds. But death in Hemingway is not always just immediate physical death, although there is a great deal of that; it is also spiritual or emotional death. Very few of Hemingway's protagonists physically die in the course of the fictional work. In the novels, Colonel Cantwell and Harry Morgan die, and Robert Jordan and Thomas Hudson will die very shortly; but generally the Hemingway protagonist, especially in the works of the 1920's and 1930's, suffers a different kind of death. Indeed, Santiago of *The Old Man and the Sea* is "the only hero who is not left alone, at the end of the story, with death and despair."[20] Thus there are two types of death for the Hemingway protagonist: actual physical death, for which Hemingway had "a fascination with highly stylized dying,"[21] and spiritual death, which some characters suffer and never really overcome and which others may suffer and at least temporarily or partially overcome.

In Paris in the 1920's, it was the Dadaists who were much concerned with death. For all its advocacy of LIFE, the Dada nihilism and destructive objectives had only one result—death. The Dadaists "were haunted by the uselessness of life itself. To revolt against life! But there was only one wonderful remedy: suicide."[22] Fur-

19 Juan Larrea, "Light Illumined: Introduction to an Exhibition of Spanish Paintings," *Picasso, Gris, and Miró* (San Francisco, San Francisco Museum of Art, 1948), p. 31.

20 Melvin Backman, "Hemingway: The Matador and the Crucified," in Baker, ed., *Hemingway and His Critics*, p. 255.

21 Philip Young, *Ernest Hemingway: A Reconsideration* (University Park, Pa., 1966), p. 95.

22 Georges Ribemont-Dessaignes, "History of Dada," trans. Ralph Manheim, *The Dada Painters and Poets: An Anthology*, ed. Robert Motherwell (New York, 1951), p. 105.

thermore, "the Dadaist loves life, because he can throw it away every day; for him death is a Dadaist affair."[23] Involved in such a concept of death is a view of both life *and* death as essentially "nothing." The teasing of death or the dangerous courting of death could and did lead to many "daring" feats among the Dadaists; thus "Death is a thoroughly Dadaist business, in that it signifies nothing at all."[24]

Curiously enough, in view of Hemingway's own suicide and that of his father, none of his major protagonists commits suicide. In fact, only once in Hemingway's major works is suicide discussed to any extent. In *Islands in the Stream*, Thomas Hudson tells his sons that his friend the painter Pascin had committed suicide. Hudson and his sons had been discussing Pascin in the three previous pages (72–74). Hemingway himself devoted a chapter in *A Moveable Feast* to a chance meeting with Pascin in a Parisian café with, however, no mention of his suicide. Pascin clearly appears to be one of Hemingway's favorite twentieth-century painters. He committed suicide in 1930, having spent the last half of the 1920's prostituting his art to the rich, much like Harry in "The Snows of Kilimanjaro."

One might say that both Colonel Cantwell and Robert Jordan bring about their own deaths directly: the Colonel by overexertion, considering his heart condition, and Jordan by his acceptance of what is clearly a suicide mission. Yet they both faced death as a meaningful conclusion to their lives. Neither faced death in the insane and melancholic condition with which Hemingway and his father and the Dadaists presumably faced their own deaths.

No, death is not "nothing" in Hemingway. As Nicholas Joost has pointed out,

> At bottom Hemingway was opposed to the sweeping destructiveness of Dada; he was far too traditional in attitude.

23 Richard Huelsenbeck, "En Avant Dada: A History of Dadaism," in Motherwell, ed., *Dada Painters and Poets*, p. 28.

24 Ibid., p. 44.

> In "Riparto d'Assalto," the vignettes published in *The Little Review*, and "Indian Camp," he asserted a sardonic pessimism, but his vision was no bleaker than Mark Twain's. He still sought to communicate, he somehow still saw art as a positive resource, he still wished to come to terms with the bourgeois world and to make his success according to its standard. Despite the wit of Dada, its vision was a darker one than Hemingway's.[25]

It is possible to counter Joost's statement with the Dadaists' own continuing attempts to create communicative art, as evident in this statement of Tzara: "Must we cease to believe in words? Since when have they expressed the opposite of what the organ emitting them thinks and wants?"[26] Yet although Hemingway and his father and a few Dadaists chose suicide, Hemingway's protagonists choose to confront death, to struggle against death, or at least to maintain an ideal in the face of death. In the fictional works of Hemingway, death is not "nothing," but "something."

To be sure, "regardless of the particular situation, the Hemingway hero is always concerned with the problem of death."[27] It takes many forms: war, bullfighting, murder, and childbirth, for example, on the literal level; but also from a lack of conviction or compassion, or from despair, for example, on the spiritual level. Among Hemingway's favorite painters, a number depict death in all its various forms. Goya bluntly depicted physical death in both war and bullfighting, but he also depicted a spiritual death and death-sickness in both paintings and etchings, such as "The Caprices" (1796–97) and "Proverbs" (1814–19). El Greco and Mantegna both depicted religious martyrs as well as ordinary citizens who are on their way to heaven. And it was Bosch and Brueghel who painted allegorical Deaths killing people in various ways.

25 Nicholas Joost, *Ernest Hemingway and the Little Magazines: The Paris Years* (Barre, Mass., 1968), p. 100.

26 Tristan Tzara, "manifesto on feeble love and bitter love," trans. Ralph Manheim, in Motherwell, ed., *Dada Painters and Poets,* p. 87.

27 Joseph De Falco, *The Hero in Hemingway's Short Stories* (Pittsburgh, 1963), p. 195.

"That was the first time I ever saw a German dog eating a roasted German Kraut."

—COLONEL CANTWELL IN *Across the River and into the Trees* (1950)

Pieter Brueghel the Elder, "The Triumph of Death." 1560–62. Tempera and oil on wood, 46⅛ x 63¼ in. Prado.

A Brueghel painting in the Prado, "The Triumph of Death," abounds in sickle-bearing skeletons, dead and dying men and women of all social classes, ruined architecture, crosses, and sterile nature. There is "every conceivable horror."[28] It is interesting to note that in the lower left center of this painting is an emaciated dog eating a body. In *Across the River and into the Trees*, Cantwell ponders a scene in a recently captured village where a German dog was "eating a roasted German Kraut" (257). Moreover, the sterility of the landscape is a prominent feature in "The Triumph of Death." It is, in fact, rather similar in its desolation to the landscape described in the first pages of *A Farewell to Arms*.

It is specifically Bosch's image of Death which Cantwell remembers; he tells "old brother death," "with its ugly face that old Hieronymous Bosch really painted," to sheath his scythe. Cantwell seems to be referring to another painting owned by the Prado, "The Deadly Sins," in which there is an allegorical representation of Death, complete with scythe. (I must wonder, however, if Cantwell has not confused Bosch's Death with Brueghel's Death, since the Brueghel image is more obvious and spectacular.) Still another Bosch painting at the Prado depicts all sorts of horrible deaths: the "Hell" panel of his famous and controversial "Garden of Earthly Delights." The horrors of death, both means and suffering, are thoroughly examined in this macabre and pre-surrealistic scene. Interestingly enough, Thomas Hudson and his friend Bobby create a watery, Bimini counterpart of Bosch's "Hell" in *Islands in the Stream*: " 'We can paint the End of the World. . . .' 'Hell,' Thomas Hudson said. 'No. Before Hell. Hell is just opening. . . . There's a big sort of hatch open and devils are carrying Negroes and church people and . . . everyone into it and they go out of sight. Water's rising all around the island. . . .' 'There was a man named Bosch could paint pretty well along those lines' " (19–20).

Yet it is in a way other than the actual depiction of physical death that Hemingway is more closely related to these painters.

28 R. H. Wilenski, *Dutch Painting* (New York, 1955), p. 42.

"We will lay it on the line once more and the hell with it, and with its ugly face that old Hieronymous Bosch really painted. But you can sheath your scythe, old brother death, if you have got a sheath for it."

—COLONEL CANTWELL IN *Across the River and into the Trees*

Hieronymous Bosch, "The Deadly Sins." ca. 1480. Painted tableboard, $58\frac{1}{2}$ x $58\frac{1}{2}$ in. Prado.

The spiritual death suffered by so many of Hemingway's protagonists is, in essence and on a symbolic level, what Bosch and Brueghel both emphasized. The tortured souls on their way to death or suffering in afterlife in Bosch's and Brueghel's paintings are really representative of a spiritually sick mankind. Whether such a death is the result of the loss of idealism or virtue or hope, the death is frightening and is perhaps best indicated by the celebrated Hemingway theme of *nada*. The sick and suffering souls of Brueghel and Bosch and Goya have found that the agonies of life result in *nothing*—that the agonies of life are, in fact, *nothing*.

In Hemingway's "A Clean, Well-Lighted Place," an old man with "plenty of money" is slowly getting drunk in a cafe, which is clean and well lighted. The old man is in despair about "nothing" (*nada*). Two waiters, an older man and a young one, discuss the old man: "The great skill displayed in the story is the development through the most carefully controlled understatement, of the young waiter's mere *nothing* into the old waiter's Something —a Something called Nothing which is so huge, terrible, overbearing, inevitable, and omnipresent, that, once experienced, it can never be forgotten."[29] The older waiter concludes the story with the anti-prayers, "Our nada who art in nada" and "Hail nothing full of nothing," and then goes home to face his own insomnia and *nada*. The *nada* theme is also evident in other Hemingway works, such as "A Way You'll Never Be," *The Sun Also Rises*, "The Gambler, the Nun, and the Radio," and the conclusion of *A Farewell to Arms*.

It is possible to trace this concept of nothingness to the wasteland theme of the 1920's—the sterility and hopelessness of western civilization so closely associated with T. S. Eliot's "The Waste Land." It is also possible to identify Hemingway's *nada* with the Dada "Nothing." Indeed, Tzara at times drew remarkably close to the basic image of "A Clean, Well-Lighted Place." As Tzara followed the Dada nihilism to its full implications, he suddenly

29 Baker, *Hemingway: The Writer as Artist*, p. 124.

"It was a nothing that he knew too well. It was all a nothing and a man was nothing too."

—"A Clean, Well-Lighted Place"

Francisco Goya, "The Disasters of War" #69. Etching. Courtesy of The Hispanic Society of America.

realized: "that is something to cry about the nothing that calls itself nothing."[30]

Goya also developed a theme of *nada*. In etching 69 of "The Disasters of War," Goya depicted a skeleton arisen from his grave in order to write the single word, "Nada." In two bunches or clouds around and above the horrible image appear howling faces of people and animals. The etching is composed of heavy planes of jet black, relieved only by the white used to designate the figures. It is possible to interpret the specter's message of *nada* as indicating a nothingness beyond the grave, or as *nada*, the nothing of life. Or, too, considered in the context of "The Disasters of War," etching 69 might also indicate the *nada* of war. In short, the message itself is ambiguous, but the sense of despair dominates the etching. The two clouds of howling demons emphasize the nightmare quality of the image.

This sense of despair in Goya's etching is thus unrelated to any specific cause, as it often was in Hemingway. The despair of *nada* is simply a general agony. In "A Clean, Well-Lighted Place," there is no obvious cause for the old man's sense of *nada*, just as there is no definite explanation of the *Nada* written by Goya's figure. The grotesque skeleton in the dark, shadowy atmosphere could very well be the dead spirit of the old man or the old waiter in Hemingway. What Hemingway has expressed with controlled understatement, Goya has stated with a more dramatic, visual image. Note, too, that Hemingway's old man has moved to a clean, well-lighted place. In fact, unlike the melancholy figures of many Goya etchings, the Hemingway protagonists who experience the sense of *nada* at least search for a relief; they search for some type of clean, well-lighted place. For example, in "Big Two-Hearted River," Nick has found the woods and stream a place for therapy.[31]

This is not to say that the feeling of frustration or nothingness is always unrelated to particular causes in the works of either

30 Tristan Tzara, "manifesto of mr. aa the anti-philosopher," tr. Ralph Manheim, in Motherwell, ed., *Dada Painters and Poets*, p. 83.
31 Suggested in Baker, *Hemingway: The Writer as Artist*, p. 127.

Goya or Hemingway. In *A Farewell to Arms*, Frederic Henry is at first disillusioned and disheartened by war and, later, by Catherine's death; Jake Barnes, another of Hemingway's wounded soldiers, like Henry, must leave the light on in his room at night (i.e., his room must be well lighted) because of recurring nightmares. Harry, the protagonist of "The Snows of Kilimanjaro," reviews the failures and frustrations of his life with a heavy sense of *nada*.

The horrors of the world are clearly evident in nearly every one of Goya's series of etchings, except perhaps "Tauromaquia." In "The Disasters of War," it is the terror of war itself; in "The Caprices," it is all manner of despair from an abstract lack of reason to the more concrete disillusionment of sexual faithlessness. One major difference between Goya and Hemingway is that, at least in the later etchings and paintings of Goya, the black is unrelieved. Goya's Saturn who eats his children is the black *nada* of man. On the other hand, most of Hemingway's protagonists, even in failure, find some sort of resolution or adjustment, whether in a final act of courage (such as Francis Macomber) or in nature (such as Jake Barnes), or in themselves (such as Harry Morgan in *To Have and Have Not*, and Santiago in *The Old Man and The Sea*):

> For what Hemingway does, essentially, is to catalogue the disillusionment of contemporary man in his struggle to come to terms with a world he cannot truly understand.
>
> The implications of this continuing challenge provide the central conflict in many of his stories. As the characters demonstrate, the possibility of understanding and overcoming the contingencies are small. Feats of heroic magnitude are demanded of the individual, but not everyone is capable of the effort. Although Hemingway's heroes fail, the successful few emerge as heroes of a different stature.[32]

One of the most evident and recurring manifestations of the *nada* motif, as well as of world terror, is the nightmare or dream.

32 De Falco, *The Hero in Hemingway's Short Stories*, pp. 1–2.

Jake Barnes, Robert Jordan, Colonel Cantwell, Thomas Hudson, the Nick Adams of "Now I Lay Me" and "A Way You'll Never Be," the old waiter in "A Clean, Well-Lighted Place," and the protagonist of "On the Quai at Smyrna"—all these must suffer and confront nightmares, the subconscious manifestations of terrors, fears, and *nada*. These dreamers of nightmares seek escape in a variety of ways. Jake Barnes's night light temporarily suspends the terror; for Nick Adams of "Now I Lay Me," there seems to be no relief; Thomas Hudson admits that "you will never have good dreams anymore" (384); but Robert Jordan has "won over his incapacitating nightmares; he has held off giants and grasped the code, worked his way out of his long bitterness and blown the bridge, which was his job to do."[33] Indeed, by the time Hemingway writes *The Old Man and The Sea*, the dreams, although still recurring, are not at all horrible. They are peaceful memories of Santiago's youth—of Africa, of yellow and white beaches, and of lions. He no longer "dreamed of storms, nor of women, nor of great occurrences, nor of great fish, nor fights, nor contests of strength, nor of his wife" (27). Santiago did not need to spend his evenings in a clean, well-lighted place in order to escape from the dark and tortured world of the subconscious.

Certainly the progressive triumph over nightmares by the Hemingway protagonists (from Jake Barnes to Santiago) is one of the most interesting developments in the thirty-odd years that Hemingway wrote. Not all of Hemingway's protagonists suffered nightmares, but his major ones did: "Hemingway—who wrote, among other things, his nightmares—made both simple and justifiable the identification of 'fiction' and 'nightmares.' "[34] Hemingway himself, as a result of war experiences, suffered from nightmares at various times in his life, and it is as easy to understand the tortured dream worlds of Hemingway's fictive protagonists in terms of Hemingway's own nightmares as it is to see the wounded soldier motif as an extension of Hemingway's own wound in World War I, as Philip Young has interpreted this

33 Young, *Hemingway: A Reconsideration*, p. 114.
34 Ibid., p. 166.

motif. Yet the dream-nightmare motif might also reflect the surrealist interest in the subconscious and dreams which was especially dominant in Paris in the 1920's: "The surrealist aesthetic can be reduced to one theme: the attempt to actualize *le merveilleux*, the wonderland of revelation and dream, and by so doing to permit chance to run rampant in a wasteland of bleak reality."[35]

For the surrealist, the relevance of meaning of the dream was that it might produce otherwise unknown truths or relevations. The surrealists were searching for the "marvelous" and felt that logical and rational inhibitions had been placed upon man's subconsciousness and imagination (two terms which André Breton tended to use almost interchangeably). Thus in "Manifesto of Surrealism" (1924), Breton stated, "Surrealism is based on the belief in the superior reality of certain forms of previously neglected associations, in the omnipotence of dreams, in the disinterested play of thought. It tends to ruin once and for all all other psychic mechanisms and to substitute itself for them in solving all the principal problems of life."[36] Often, indeed, the examination of dreams led to the "marvelous"–a marvelous horror. In painting, especially, surrealistic introspection led to the melancholy and mystery of de Chirico or to the often bloody and ghastly images of Dali and Tanguy. The surrealist novels often incorporated Gothic-like castles, ghosts, and other horrors in order to create the dream fantasy. Breton's "marvelous" was not always beautiful.

Yet the Hemingway protagonist generally ran away from his dreams and his nightmares. Bad dreams, in Hemingway's fiction, are evidence of a psychic disturbance or failure or fear or sense of *nada*. Many Hemingway protagonists simply mention that they have nightmares and then try to find an escape in the conscious world of physical reality. For Jake Barnes, the night light was a means of escape; for Robert Jordan, following a code in a

35 Herbert S. Gershman, *The Surrealist Revolution in France* (Ann Arbor, 1969), p. 1.
36 André Breton, *Manifestoes of Surrealism*, trans. Richard Seaver and Helen R. Lane (Ann Arbor, 1969), p. 26.

physical manner (i.e., deciding to act in a heroic and relevant way and then pursuing a goal even in the face of that greatest of *nadas*, death) was the means to conquer his nightmares; the protagonist of "On the Quai at Smyrna" simply left Smyrna. The protagonists generally do not say what is terrifying about their nightmares. Hemingway did not feel that it was necessary for these tortured souls to reveal their dreams: "I have the nightmares and know about the ones other people have. But you do not have to write them down. Anything you can omit that you know you still have in the writing and its quality will show."[37] Furthermore, the protagonists do not consciously study the images of their nightmares in an attempt to find the "marvelous." The true surrealist, of course, finds the means to record not only his nightmares, but also his daydreams. No, the Hemingway protagonists who suffer from nightmares are not surrealists in the sense that they find revelations in their dreams.

On the other hand, there are three protagonists whose dreamscapes Hemingway specifically reveals. Harry experiences a death dream in "The Snows of Kilimanjaro"; Thomas Hudson has good dreams as well as bad; Santiago's dream of peace reoccurs in *The Old Man and the Sea.* As Harry dies, he dreams that the airplane has finally arrived to take him to civilization and to doctors. In very realistic terms, he describes the take-off and first moments of flight, but "then there were other mountains dark ahead":

> And then instead of going on to Arusha they turned left, he [the pilot] evidently figured they had the gas, and looking down he [Harry] saw a pink sifting cloud, moving over the ground, and in the air, like the first snow in a blizzard, that comes from nowhere, and he knew the locusts were coming up from the South. Then they began to climb and they were

37 Quoted in George Plimpton, "An Interview With Ernest Hemingway," in Baker, ed., *Hemingway and His Critics*, p. 28. Of all the Hemingway protagonists, only Thomas Hudson is allowed to reveal—briefly—his nightmares: "He slept and he dreamed that the cabin was burned and someone had killed his fawn that had grown into a young buck. Someone had killed his dog and he found him by a tree and he woke sweating" (384).

> going East it seemed, and then it darkened and they were in a storm, the rain so thick it seemed like flying through a waterfall, and then they were out and Compie turned his head and grinned and pointed and there, ahead, all he could see, as wide as all the world, great, high, and unbelievably white in the sun, was the square top of Kilimanjaro. And then he knew that that was where he was going [174].

Thomas Hudson dreams of a past happiness which is now lost forever:

> While Thomas Hudson was asleep he dreamed that his son Tom was not dead and that the other boys were all right and that the war was over. He dreamed that Tom's mother was sleeping with him and she was sleeping on top of him as she liked to do sometimes. He felt all of this and the tangibility of her legs against his legs and her body against his and her breasts against his chest and her mouth playing against his mouth. Her hair hung down and lay heavy and silken on his eyes and on his cheeks and he turned his lips away from her and took the hair in his mouth and held it [343].

Santiago's recurring dream is of Africa:

> he dreamed of Africa when he was a boy and the long golden beaches and the white beaches, so white they hurt your eyes, and the high capes and the great brown mountains. He lived along the coast now every night and in his dreams he heard the surf roar and saw the native boats come riding through it. He smelled the tar and oakum of the deck as he slept and he smelled the smell of Africa that the land breeze brought in at morning. . . . He only dreamed of places now and of the lions on the beach. They played like young cats in the dusk and he loved them [26–27].

These are dreams of "peace," whether in Harry's case, peace at death; or in Thomas Hudson's case, peace of the past; or in Santiago's dream, peace of rest and sleep.[38] Yet, as dreams, they are

38 Baker, *Hemingway: The Writer as Artist,* p. 308.

remarkably sensual: not only are they described in visual color, they are also expressed with reference to sound, and in Santiago's dream, also with reference to smell. For Thomas Hudson, the dream experience is tangible. They are sensually complete dreams —an evocation of man's senses in the midst of a subconscious dream state. These dreams represent a new mental reality correlated with what should be responses of the conscious physical world. In fact, so carefully did Hemingway overlap the two worlds that most readers mistake Harry's dream as the real event, rather than a dream trip to death—at least until the final words of the story.

Such a physically accurate description or representation of what are actually non-physical experiences is one method often used by the surrealists, both writers and painters. For the surrealists wanted "to present the imagined as real";[39] "dreams are its reality."[40] For example, in the dream sequences of such writers as Breton and Soupault, the most realistically presented details are used to describe fantastic images. Or in the paintings of de Chirico and Dali, the trompe-l'oeil effect is used to juxtapose and contrast diverse and contradictory elements in order to create the unreality of the dream and the subconscious.

Indeed, the illusionism of painters like de Chirico and Dali can perhaps be seen in Santiago's dream of the beaches. The static beaches, capes, and mountains—especially the white beaches "so white they hurt your eyes"—are strongly outlined in their vivid colors. The lions playing and the native boats with their smell of tar and oakum are made small, but special, because of their juxtaposition to the expanses of beach, sea, and mountain. There are no people, only things; there are no natives in the native boats. This is not a landscape or seascape inspired by Cézanne.[41] There are no series of planes, no geometric figures, no molding by color. There is a sharp distinction made between objects, but only be-

39 J. H. Mathews, *Surrealism and the Novel* (Ann Arbor, 1966), p. 40.
40 Gershman, *The Surrealist Revolution in France*, p. xl.
41 Note, however, in Harry's dream, that Kilimanjaro retains the characteristics of Cézanne's Mont Sainte-Victoire. For Harry, Kilimanjaro is "wide . . . great, high, and unbelievably white . . . the square top of Kilimanjaro."

cause of the purity of the colors. Yet while the technical presentation of the dream image suggests the illusionism of the surrealists, the message and general motif of peace in a nature without people suggest Cézanne. Santiago did not look to his dream for revelations or for the "marvelous," but for peace and order.

Surely it is significant that Hemingway chose a type of illusionist technique in the expression of a dream or subconscious state. The implications are several. For Hemingway, the inner world could be as real as the outer world. The very reality of the nightmares of Jake Barnes is, in fact, the reason that he must use a night light. On the other hand, in Hemingway, the nightmares and reality of the dream world can only be counterbalanced by a positive action of the protagonist in the outer reality, as terrible as such an action can be. For both Hemingway and the surrealists, the outer world was cruel and agonizing. The Hemingway protagonist was thus forced to "come to terms with a world he cannot truly understand."[42] "Every surrealist" feels he has been placed in a "largely antagonistic universe."[43] The surrealist turned to his inner world, whether the subconscious or the dream, for new revelations or for the "marvelous." Hemingway's protagonists, however, attempted to find a code or relevance in real life activities such as bullfights or love-making or fishing—even in violence itself—in order to drive out the terrors of the subconscious. For the Hemingway protagonist, the dream world was not only real but horrible. Only the old man Santiago and the middle-aged Thomas Hudson and Harry could also find a peaceful and symbolic reality in dreams, much as the surrealists could find significance in their dreams.

It should further be noted that certain of Hemingway's favorite artists, such as Goya, Brueghel, and Bosch, were also painters who often expressed fantastic images in an illusionistic style. Examine Bosch's "Garden of Earthly Delights." Here the juxtaposition of diverse elements, the fantasy, and the dream-like evocations have often been cited as pre-surrealistic. In fact, when George Plimp-

42 De Falco. *The Hero in Hemingway's Short Stories*, pp. 1–2.
43 Mathews, *Surrealism and the Novel*, p. 88.

ton asked Hemingway why he had added Bosch to his list of literary forbears, Hemingway admitted, "I have the nightmares and know about the ones other people have." Certainly the later etchings of Goya, with their fantasy and monsters, tend in the same direction. Indeed, it is interesting that while Hemingway was influenced in other ways by Goya, he did not choose to follow Goya's example of the depiction of nightmares and the terrible images of subconscious fantasy. Perhaps Hemingway, like Jake Barnes, simply preferred to keep on a night light; the terrors of the subconscious world were too real. On the other hand, one must assume that, aesthetically, Hemingway purposefully chose to avoid any direct description of nightmares or other subconscious horrors, except on rare occasions, because he wished to limit experience to the reality of the physical world, the world of the physical senses. When he does delineate dreams, they are described in purely physical terms. Such an emphasis upon physical reality does not minimize the force and significance of the psychic reality, for it is the mental reality which drives Jake Barnes, Robert Jordan, and Nick Adams to action in the physical realm.

Hemingway thus seems to have shared an interest in the dream world with the surrealists. Furthermore, their illusionist techniques seem to be quite parallel, especially to the images and techniques used to represent Santiago's dream of youth, as well as of Harry's death dream. There were, however, three artists whose paintings Hemingway owned[44] who were associated with the surrealists, but who remained outside the main surrealist movement to a certain extent: Miró, Masson, and Klee. Miró's "The Farm" has already been discussed because of his vision of the land—a vision quite similar to those of Cézanne and Hemingway. Yet the coincidence of Hemingway's ownership of paintings by these three artists calls for a further examination of each of them.

Hemingway owned five paintings by Masson, who once called

44 Personal letter from Mary Hemingway, October 6, 1969.

himself a dissident surrealist. Masson was actually more closely associated with the surrealists than either Miró or Klee. He was mentioned in Breton's first "Manifesto of Surrealism" and continued his association with the surrealists until 1923. His paintings exhibited in 1924 were an attempt to mobilize the cubist still life: "They were rigorously abstract constructions with firmly embodied representational references. But within and over the flat planes the curved outlines formed a mobile, sinuous arabesque which imparted an ecstatic movement to the whole composition."[45] Such movement is clearly evident in "The Dice Game," a painting which Hemingway owned. The still, stylized faces of the men can be traced to a painting like Picasso's "Les Demoiselles d'Avignon," but the curves, wavy lines, and circles keep the Masson composition from becoming static, like the Picasso masterpiece. The arabesque had clearly sprung from subconscious images, and these images were sometimes morbid: tombs, knives, ropes. Masson's later images, still originating from the subconscious, were drawn from nature: fish, birds, hands. Many of these natural images were created by "wavy lineaments"[46] similar to the techniques of his friend Miró. Indeed, another of Hemingway's paintings by Masson, "Composition," is a reduction of such lineaments to the basic geometric forms of the circle and oval. There is constant motion in any Masson picture: for him "the universe consists solely of rhythm and metamorphosis."[47] Such organic rhythm is especially evident in the three landscapes by Masson which Hemingway owned. The curved branches and trunks of the trees give the landscape a life of its own.

Hemingway owned one painting by Klee, who remained largely outside the surrealist movement but who was often identified with it. Many of Klee's paintings and drawings also depend

45 Werner Haftmann, *Painting in the Twentieth Century* I, trans. Ralph Manheim (New York, 1965), p. 275.

46 Ibid.

47 Maurice Raynal, Jacques Lassaigne, Werner Schmalenbach, Arnold Rüdlinger, Hans Bolliger, *History of Modern Art from Picasso to Surrealism*, trans. Douglas Cooper (Geneva, 1950), p. 184.

"One had a large flat face, flat and brown . . . with a nose flattened and broken, and the long thin Russian cigarette, projecting at an angle, made the face look even flatter."

—*For Whom the Bell Tolls*

André Masson, "The Dice Game." Oil on canvas, 25¾ x 32 in. Hemingway Private Collection, courtesy of Mary Hemingway.

on those "wavy lineaments" which Miró and Masson found so expressive. He too wished to express "images from the psychic realm," although he "never regarded himself as a mere sounding board for the unconscious."[48] His images were drawn primarily from nature, and his drawings have been referred to as "scrawls" because they often appear to be infantile or childish.[49] According to Strater, Hemingway liked Klee because of his humor.[50] Certainly, of all the painters whom Hemingway liked, only Klee revealed a healthy humor, neither sadistic nor oblique. Klee also asserted a sense of totality and unity in nature throughout his painting: "By looking deeply into the formal development of nature and the higher processes of its imagination, the intuitive judgment discerns the typical, essential forms, the roots of endless formal possibilities in addition to the limited examples provided by nature."[51] In this final sense, then, Klee must be seen along with Miró and Cézanne as sharing an essentially orderly vision of the land, or at least of nature. Hemingway's own painting by Klee, "Monument" (1929), is dominated by an enigmatic face, whose staring eyes suggest both wisdom and apprehension. The two angular laborers, the ladders, and the triangular scaffolding provide a contrast to the circular head with its wavy features. There is no humor in this painting; rather, there is a sense of profundity and durability manifest in the monument itself.

What do Miró, Masson, and Klee have in common, and why were they such favorites of Hemingway's? Werner Haftmann has specifically associated these three artists as painters who "stand in the same line of thinking."[52] All three wished to humanize, mobilize, naturalize, and poetize the still-life immobility and formal intellectualization of cubism. In their attempts, they turned to various techniques of surrealism in order to depict "the poetry of the heart." At one time or another, each practiced automatism,

48 Haftmann, *Painting in the Twentieth Century* I, pp. 244–45.
49 Marcel Jean with Arpad Mazei, *The History of Surrealist Painting*, trans. Simon Watson Taylor (New York, 1960), p. 148.
50 Personal interview, Ogunquit, Maine, August 24, 1968.
51 Haftmann, *Painting in the Twentieth Century* I, p. 245.
52 Ibid., p. 277.

"Hem learned to like abstract art at Gertrude Stein's."

—HENRY STRATER (1968)

André Masson, "Composition." Gouache on canvas, 8¾ x 10¾ in. Hemingway Private Collection, courtesy of Mary Hemingway.

or the technique of simply drawing a line with no preconceived plan. Thus each believed in the "found" picture, as prescribed by the surrealists, and each drew strongly upon images from the subconscious for motifs and symbols and attempted to depict the reality of psychic experience in their paintings. I suppose that it is superfluous to observe that each was influenced by Cézanne, since Cézanne influenced nearly every one of the moderns. Miró, as has been noted, was attracted early to Cézanne's geometrical forms and series of planes. Masson specifically called himself a follower of Cézanne, and Klee formed his first concepts of color from viewing Cézanne.

Nearly any one of these qualities might have drawn Hemingway to the paintings of Miró, Klee, and Masson. Certainly the depiction of psychic experience and the assertion of its reality and profound importance are an obvious parallel between these three artists and Hemingway, as well as between Hemingway and all surrealists. Perhaps a clearer parallel between Hemingway and Klee, Miró, and Masson, however, is their mutual interest in poetizing, naturalizing, and mobilizing the solid geometrical forms of cubism. In a letter to Edmund Wilson, dated October 18, 1924, Hemingway stated: "I've worked like hell most of the time and think the stuff gets better. Finished the book of 14 stories with a chapter of *In Our Time* between each story—that is the way they were meant to go—to give the picture of the whole between examining it in detail. Like looking with your eyes at something, say a passing coastline, and then looking at it with 15X binoculars. Or rather, maybe, looking at it and living in it, and then coming out and looking at it again."[53] Hemingway's description of the arrangement of the vignettes and short stories for the New York edition of *In Our Time* is simply a statement of simultaneity, in the sense of Cézanne and the cubists. That is, he was looking at a similar image (e.g., a wounded or dead soldier) from several different points of view and from several different angles. By arranging the short stories and vignettes in such a way, he was creating a work comparable to the typical cubist guitar which

53 Reprinted in Baker, ed., *Hemingway and His Critics*, p. 60.

Three versions of André Masson's "Landscape, Trees." Hemingway Private Collection, courtesy of Mary Hemingway.

was examined from various perspectives—top, bottom, side, inside, and so on. Thus it is especially important to note that, in several instances (e.g., 69, 136), the painter Thomas Hudson becomes aware of the differences of appearance caused by an altered perspective or by a simultaneous view of the sea and swimmers or a fisherman. Like the fictional Hudson, Hemingway owned paintings by Juan Gris, who was a cubist.

It is possible to suggest that the short stories are much like the flat planes of Masson's early paintings, with the vignettes as the "mobile, sinuous arabesque" playing within and among the static and solid planes of the larger fictive pieces. The immobile and mobile are images often contrasted in Hemingway: the immobility of the solid, orderly mountains (drawn, much as the cubists ordered their universe, from the static planes and outlines of Cézanne) as opposed to the mobility of man and other natural elements (the humanizing, poetizing, and naturalizing qualities).

Moreover, the "arabesque" of Masson and the "wavy lineaments" of all three painters depend upon natural, pictorial elements which are generally in a state of constant motion. The simplification of the technical elements which Hemingway so admired in Goya and which seems to be reflected in the vignettes is further extended by the lines and primitive or child-like line drawings of Klee, Masson, and Miró.

The agony of man was also expressed by these artists, although their despair did not extend to the sense of *nada* shared especially by Hemingway and Goya. For Miró, man must seek to find order in the disorder; we have already seen that his resolution to this problem was, at least in one sense, similar to Hemingway's and Cézanne's. Yet, as Marcel Jean has pointed out, there is even in Miró's most ordered pictures, "a fixed, perfected streak of violence"[54]—a primitive, dynamic, and universal violence with which man must cope. Masson's images often bordered on the morbid: men stick knives into their eyes, children eat raw fish, and birds are killed in flight. The images he drew from his subconscious were violent, macabre, and agonizing. Hemingway's

54 Jean, *The History of Surrealist Painting*, p. 155.

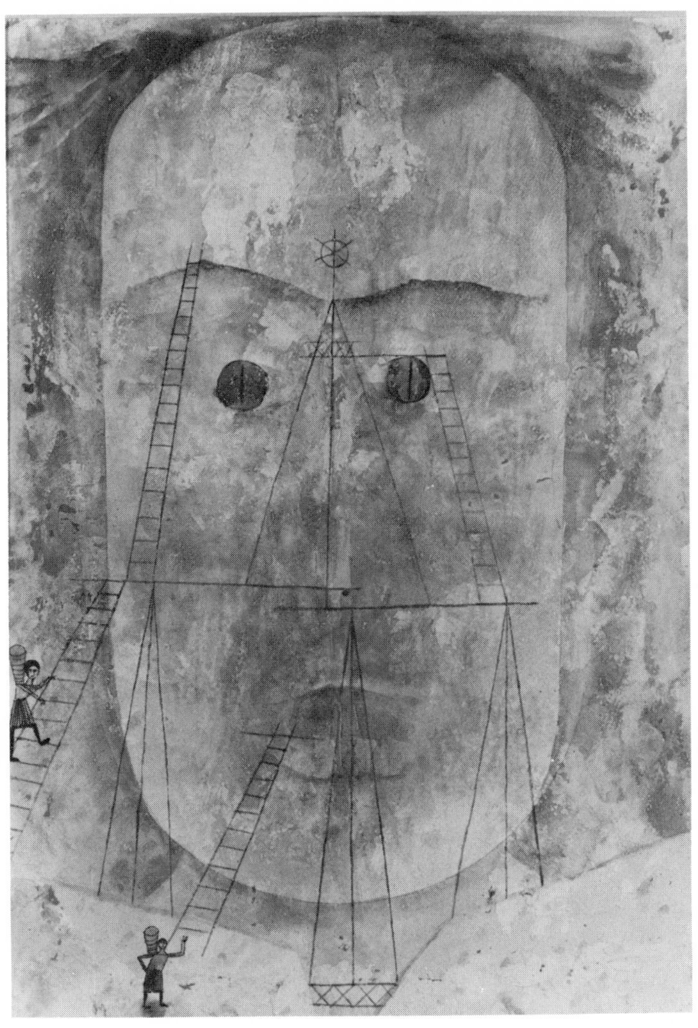

"... how frightened of it his wife had been until she had learned to accept its corruption and only see it as a painting. . . . It was a good picture and he liked to look at it."

—THOMAS HUDSON IN *Islands in the Stream*

Paul Klee, "Monument." 1929. Gouache and oil, 15 x 22 in. Hemingway Private Collection, courtesy of Mary Hemingway.

own paintings by Masson, however, reveal a different aspect of this painter. Hemingway had obviously chosen not to purchase the macabre canvases, but preferred for his own collection Masson's paintings of dice players, of vibrant trees, and of an abstract composition. Klee, with his gentle humor, offers relief; yet despite his ultimate assertion of transcendent order, he must seek that order. In his search, he finds dances of horror, unbalanced landscapes, or, in the early etchings and drawings which were sometimes inspired by Goya, grotesque human figures.

Robert Penn Warren has pointed out that Hemingway's emphasis upon the agony of man, especially the sleepless man, has religious overtones: "And the sleepless man—the man obsessed by death, by the meaninglessness of the world, by nothingness, by nada—is one of the recurring symbols in the work of Hemingway. In this phase Hemingway is a religious writer. The despair beyond plenty of money, the despair that makes a sleeplessness beyond insomnia, is the despair felt by a man who hungers for the sense of order and assurance that men seem to find in religious faith, but who cannot find grounds in his faith."[55] Thus the despair is total, rising from individual human agony to universal significance and suffering. Man has been placed in a world which is seemingly without order, either human or divine, and the result is the man who usually cannot sleep because of his nightmares. This agonized and agonizing man is obsessed with meaninglessness, with Goya's sense of *nada*.

Hemingway, it seems to me, thrusts beyond the nihilism and despair of his contemporaries, especially in the 1920's when he first expressed the *nada* theme. The nihilism of the Dadaists was directed at the established institutions and customs of their contemporaries; the surrealists, too, found fault primarily within their own contemporary setting. Both groups, the surrealists and especially the German Dadaists, saw hope in a revision of social institutions, usually in terms of Marxism. Even the wasteland vision of T. S. Eliot was centered upon the decay of western civilization. Hemingway's vision of *nada*, however, extends to all men, to all

55 Robert Penn Warren, Introduction, *A Farewell to Arms*, p. xvi.

Looking at the landscape from an airplane, "I began to understand Cubist painting."

—ERNEST HEMINGWAY, *The Toronto Daily Star* (1922)

Juan Gris, "Le Torero." 1913. Oil on canvas, 29 x 36½ in. Hemingway Private Collection, courtesy of Mary Hemingway.

times, and to all places. Although Hemingway's novels are set in a clearly recognizable historical time, usually a time contemporary with the author, the implication of despair is universal and transcendent for all men throughout history. It is for this reason that the existentialists of the 1960's claim him as their own. As John Killinger has pointed out, both for contemporary existentialists and for Hemingway, " 'nothingness' is a convenient designation for the inexplicable weirdness that lies beyond the rational boundaries of existence."[56]

That painters like Goya, Bosch, and Brueghel appealed to Hemingway is an indication of his profound understanding of their art in terms of this universal sense of despair which at one time or another affects individuals. After all, he could find the same motifs of violence, war, and death, which he himself wished to express, in their paintings—works executed many years earlier. Hemingway could even see that these painters too had long ago suffered from nightmares, from despair, and from *nada*. On one level, then, Hemingway's mention of these painters, as well as his borrowing of specific motifs, is evidence of an attempt to transcend any sort of limited temporal expression of the theme of the agony of man. Like Goya, Bosch, and Brueghel, Hemingway attempted to express universal despair. The wounded soldier in Goya is the ancestor of Nick Adams and Frederic Henry. The nightmares of Goya, Bosch, and Brueghel are reborn in Jake Barnes and the old man and old waiter in "A Clean, Well-Lighted Place." Hemingway's understanding of these painters is most clearly made manifest by his borrowing of actual images and specific techniques. Particularly from Goya, it appears, Hemingway learned to "draw" his vignettes and other scenes of battle, as Goya literally drew upon the plates for his etchings. On the other hand, it was the illusionist techniques of the surrealists, as well as of Goya, Bosch, and Brueghel, that might have helped Hemingway express dreamscapes in realistic, sensual images.

Hemingway's special interest in and affinity with Klee, Miró,

56 John Killinger, *Hemingway and the Dead Gods: A Study in Existentialism* (Louisville, 1960), p. 14.

and Masson emphasize just how important the mental world was to him. Although he examined in detail only a little of his protagonists' subconscious or dreams, Hemingway placed a profound importance upon the psychic experience. Like Klee, Miró, and Masson, who are attempting to express the mental reality through plastic images, Hemingway has attempted to suggest psychic experience through physical images. The sense of despair and *nada* suffered by Nick in "Big Two-Hearted River" is not simply told to the reader by the narrator, but is suggested by Nick's refusal to enter the swamp, as well as his need for order in the ritual of fishing. The orderliness of Nick's fishing is as clean and precise as Miró's order in "Catalan Landscape" ("The Hunter").

Thus Hemingway reached out to painters who shared his image of the agonized man in a chaotic and cruel universe. In his use of both motifs and techniques of these painters, he universalized the sense of despair he found in man. By involving Goya or Goya-like suggestions, for example, in the contemporary settings of stories, he transcended any sort of limited interpretation of man's agony. In short, these various painters suggested to Hemingway ways in which the flat pages of a literary work could be made more plastic and more evocative of all the senses, as well as indicating just how a particular image or motif could be made universally symbolic.

IV

Iconography and technical expression: the search for order

Greco liked to paint religious pictures because he was very evidently religious and because his incomparable art was not then limited to accurate reproducing of the faces of the noblemen who were his sitters for portraits and he could go as far into his other world as he wanted and, consciously or unconsciously, paint saints, apostles, Christs and Virgins with the androgynous faces and forms that filled his imagination.[1]

It was a feeling of consecration to a duty toward all the oppressed of the world which would be as difficult and embarrassing to speak about as religious experience and yet it was authentic as the feeling you had when you heard Bach, or stood in Chartres Cathedral or the Cathedral at Léon . . . or when you saw Mantegna and Greco and Brueghel in the Prado.[2]

Despite the sense of *nada* permeating and dominating so many of Hemingway's works, there is also manifest in his fiction an affirmation that there can be some relief for the agonized man's nightmares, insomnia, and despair. More often than not, this affirmation takes the form of a search for some means to confront the largely hostile world in which the Hemingway protagonist has been placed. Hemingway forces his protagonist to search for meaning or for honor in that very same world which has caused him such anguish and despair; Hemingway does not let his pro-

1 *Death in the Afternoon*, p. 204.
2 *For Whom the Bell Tolls*, p. 235.

tagonists wander through dreams searching for the "marvelous," as the surrealists did; he does not even allow his protagonists to counterbalance physical reality with the spiritual comfort of a god, except on rare occasions. No, the Hemingway protagonists must find meaning specifically and directly in the very reality which raped their innocence and which caused their nightmares and their sense of despair and *nada*.

Some protagonists never reconcile themselves to physical reality; in the major works, only Santiago is not left alone with death and despair at the end of the novel. Other protagonists make some partial adjustment to their universe, like Jake Barnes, whose stoic resignation represents one wounded soldier's solution, or like Nick Adams, another wounded soldier, who has made a separate peace in the vignette which begins, "Nick sat against the wall of the church."[3] Other protagonists, such as Frederic Henry or the young Nick Adams of "Indian Camp," are left with *nada* and with the necessity to continue the search whether or not they want to.

Those who do find a means of coping with their universe have generally found a code by which to govern their actions in the hostile, physical world. This code is not necessarily a set of rules like the Ten Commandments or a system of ethics expressed with philosophical implications. Rather, it is an establishment of some sort of order within the confusion and chaos. The search for order results in several partial answers but in no final, universal conclusions. We have already seen how Hemingway's vision of the mountains, for example, results in the home concept or idyll. Another means of confronting or counterbalancing the hostility of the world is sports or games, whether fishing and hunting or boxing and bullfights. Still a third manifestation of the code is the special significance of love and love-making, or the "love cult." A fourth means of confronting life is simply the confrontation of death—a theme which often becomes an examination of violence per se and which overlaps other themes, such as love and games. Finally, a fifth mode of order is religion, although not perhaps traditional, conventional religion. Like the themes and motifs

3 *The Short Stories of Ernest Hemingway*, p. 236.

of the agony of man, the themes of a search for order reoccur as different motifs and, in one or two instances, in ever-expanding symbolism.

Hemingway's code can thus be defined as an expression of order, whether order in the natural world or order essentially created by man within the civilized or non-natural world: "the code and the discipline are important because they can give meaning to life that otherwise seems to have no meaning or justification. In other words, in a world without supernatural sanctions, in the God-abandoned world of modernity, man can realize an ideal meaning only in so far as he can define and maintain the code."[4] Certainly if Hemingway's choice of painters for his personal collection is any standard, his taste in art reflects the assertion of the need for order in the world of his fictional protagonists. The cubists, with whom Gris is classified, used Cézanne's geometric forms, overlapping planes, and static atmosphere to assert a sense of order in their simultaneously viewed objects. The order, to be sure, is often an artificial order imposed by the painter, but the immobile solidity of the geometric forms is aimed at giving "a chronological structure to form" or at expressing " 'the quest for the eternal in the object.' "[5] Moreover, the cubist forms through which Masson allowed his arabesque to play represent another expression of order. Both Klee and Miró found some sort of transcendent order in nature.

For Hemingway, the presence and importance of order in nature, especially with reference to the mountains, has already been shown to be a motif expressed in modes quite similar to Cézanne's. There are, however, certain critics, such as Robert Penn Warren, who feel that Hemingway lost his vision of the orderliness and solidity of the land. Warren points to a passage from "A Natural History of the Dead" to show that, in Hemingway, "The order of nature [does not imply] meaning in the world."[6] Baker has pointed out that the mountain sanctuary "is

4 Robert Penn Warren, Introduction, *A Farewell to Arms,* p. xiii.

5 Marcel Jean with Arpad Mazei, *The History of Surrealist Painting,* trans. Simon Watson Taylor (New York, 1960), pp. 21 and 23.

6 Warren, Introduction, *A Farewell to Arms,* p. xv.

"On the wall over his bed was one of his favorite paintings, Juan Gris' 'Guitar Player.' "

—A. E. HOTCHNER (1949)

Juan Gris, "Guitarist." 1926. Oil on canvas, 29 x 36½ in. Hemingway Private Collection, courtesy of Mary Hemingway.

. . . open to invasion and destruction by fascist bombers" in *For Whom the Bell Tolls.*[7] Yet Hemingway's final statement of man's search into nature for a code is another affirmation of order. As Baker later admitted, Santiago has always had an alliance "with the natural laws and forces," an alliance which is "a sense of solidarity with the visible universe and the natural creation."[8] It is the same alliance which Jake Barnes formed with nature at Burguete and, later, with the sea at San Sebastian. It is the same sense of solidarity which Nick Adams comes to gain at "Big Two-Hearted River" or Harry finally achieves in "The Snows of Kilimanjaro."

In fact, the sea itself might be associated with the mountains as a manifestation of order and solidarity. As a motif, the sea does not reoccur as consistently as the mountains. Descriptions of the sea as a major image occur only in Hemingway's first and last major fictional works: *The Sun Also Rises*, *Islands in the Stream*, and *The Old Man and the Sea.* To be sure, the sea is the partial setting of *To Have and Have Not*, but there are no important descriptive passages of the sea and no symbolic suggestions associated with it. The sea in this novel provides only texture or background. In *The Sun Also Rises*, *Islands in the Stream*, and *The Old Man and the Sea*, however, something beyond texture is indicated by Hemingway.

Thus Jake Barnes swims in the ocean after he has denied himself as a true *aficionado* by introducing the innocent bullfighter Romero to the corrupt Brett. He is allowed to swim for only two days before Brett's cable for help arrives. The beach at San Sebastian, like the beach in Santiago's dream, is yellow, and in the first swim, Jake notices the breakers "out beyond the headlands of the Concha" where the open sea is (234–35). During his second swim, he rests on a raft and views the vista of the town as well as the headlands (237–38). His mood is not jubilant as it was at Burguete. Like Nick of "Big Two-Hearted River," he concen-

7 Carlos Baker, *Hemingway: The Writer as Artist* (Princeton, N.J., 1963), p. 258.
8 Baker, *Hemingway: The Writer as Artist*, p. 304.

trates on the details. Swimming in the waves and diving into deep water, he performs the ritual of swimming much as Nick would perform the ritual of fishing. And as Nick will not enter the swamp, so Jake will not swim across the harbor or even venture a swim in the open sea, although he views the headland and the sea often.

In *Islands in the Stream*, the reader is allowed to see Thomas Hudson view the sea and reproduce it on canvas. His conscious perceptions of the sea are generally simple descriptions, grounded in reality and used for texture, as, for example, this passage: "out across the flats the sand was bone white under the blue sky and the small high clouds that were traveling with the wind made dark moving patches on the green water" (49). Rain, storms, and sharks are carefully balanced against such calm seascapes. What Thomas Hudson paints, however, is more significant: "Pictures of Negroes in the water. Negroes on land. Negroes in boats. Turtle boats. Sponge boats. Squalls making up. Waterspouts. Schooners that got wrecked. Schooners building" (17). In the course of the novel, Hudson paints a picture of a waterspout and remembers in some detail a picture of a plover he had once painted. In short, both the peaceful and dangerous aspects of the sea are represented. Correspondingly, the dangers of the sea Hudson and his family overcome or at least happily or conveniently compromise.

Hudson's paintings most resemble the watercolors and canvases of Winslow Homer. Hemingway himself stated that, were he to write a book about the sea, he would like it to contain pictures by Homer.[9] It would, in fact, not be difficult to illustrate *Islands in the Stream* with certain of Homer's works, among them those which Hemingway admired at the Art Institute of Chicago. Homer first went to the Caribbean in 1885; from his visit in 1898–99, he painted Negroes, turtle boats, squalls, schooners, and waterspouts. See, for example, "The Gulf Stream" (1899; New York Metropolitan Museum of Art), in which a helpless Negro in a small, damaged sailboat which is surrounded by sharks is watching

9 Carlos Baker, *Ernest Hemingway: A Life Story* (New York, 1969), p. 466.

Thomas Hudson paints "pictures of Negroes in the water. . . . Negroes in boats. Turtle boats. . . . Waterspouts. Schooners that got wrecked."

—Islands in the Stream

Winslow Homer, "The Gulf Stream." Oil on canvas, 28⅛ x 49⅛ in. The Metropolitan Museum of Art, Wolfe Fund, 1906.

a waterspout. In the far back is a schooner. Or the Art Institute's "After the Tornado" (1899), in which a Negro and his damaged boat lie washed up on the beach. Homer also depicted the tropical sea in its calm moods, as in "Rum Cay" (1898 or 1899; Worcester Art Museum). Moreover, especially in the watercolors and oils done in the Caribbean, Homer's colors are bright and pure, much as Hemingway's fictional painter apparently depicted similar scenes in bright and pure blues and whites and greens.

Yet although the sea provides more than texture in this novel, the symbolic associations are vague and incomplete, much as in Homer's paintings. Thomas Hudson is clearly as allied to the sea as Nick Adams is to "Big Two-Hearted River." Hudson, however, is also aware of the dangers of the sea, as was Jake Barnes at Burguete, although, unlike Jake, Hudson ventures out. Indeed, in *Islands in the Stream*, there are only suggestions of the symbolic significance which the sea will have in *The Old Man and the Sea*.

In *The Old Man and the Sea*, the open sea itself is described more completely, and there are specific symbolic associations made with it. Most often, Santiago views the sea in terms of its vastness and the Gulf Stream in terms of its fecundity. He also shows awareness of the dangers of the open sea, as well as a recognition of "friends" who are present in the sea, such as the birds. In short, Santiago has that sense of solidarity and natural order with the sea which Jake Barnes discovered at Burguete or Frederic Henry found in the mountains of Switzerland. In this sense, then, Santiago's sea and the mountains of Hemingway's other works are related. If man has this sense of solidarity and alliance, he can find significance, home, or an idyll in the sea or in the mountains.

Yet Santiago admits to the great fish he has caught that he has, in a sense, failed them both because he "went out too far" (127). That is, even though the sea is a part of the natural order with which Santiago is in alliance, there is the danger of going "out too far." Such an admission is, in one sense, Santiago's admission of man's tenuousness and temporal limitation as opposed to the solid and eternal order of the sea—in the same sense that the mountains are opposed to evanescent man in other novels. In another sense, however, Santiago's admission that he ventured "out too far" is similar to Melville's dichotomy of land and sea "values,"[10] a dichotomy of certain men who, like Starbuck in *Moby Dick*, find safety and security in the land, as opposed to other men who, like Ahab, are willing to go "out too far" in the sea and who thus are willing "to take the greater risk where the greater prize is involved."[11] In this interpretation, a new significance is suggested for the sea. In the images of the mountains in other Hemingway novels, there is not really any suggestion of danger in going "out too far."

In fact, Santiago's few views of the land from the sea rather strongly support this contention. As Santiago is rowing out to sea, he looks back to the land: "The clouds over the land now rose like mountains and the coast was only a long green line with the gray blue hills behind it" (38); and later, "He could not see the green of the shore now but only the tops of the blue hills that showed white as though they were snow-capped and the clouds that looked like high snow mountains beside them" (44). The horizon line of the land is thus described in the colors and solidity so often associated with Hemingway's landscapes which are most similar to Cézanne's. It is significant that, because no real mountains were visible on Havana's shoreline, Hemingway substituted clouds for the peaks which generally appear in his mountain scenes. Santiago's hills and cloud "mountains" represent safety and home and are reminiscent of Cézanne's seashores, such as the cliffs and hills in "The Gulf of Marseilles, Seen from L'Estaque" (Art Institute of Chicago). Furthermore, it should be remembered that Santiago's dream of peace and youth is of land (beaches, "high capes," "great brown mountains") with the boats coming in to land, not leaving. In *The Old Man and the Sea*, therefore, the image of the land and the mountains is consistent with Hemingway's other works.

In a sense, then, the image of the sea as holding a danger of venturing "out too far" is special, perhaps even new, in Hemingway's works, although as a symbol it can be related to Nick's

10 Herman Melville, *Moby Dick*, Chs. 23 and 58, for example.
11 Baker, *Hemingway: The Writer as Artist*, p. 318.

"I was learning something from the painting of Cézanne that made writing simple true sentences far from enough to make the stories have the dimensions that I was trying to put in them."

—ERNEST HEMINGWAY IN *A Moveable Feast* (1964)

Paul Cézanne, "The Gulf of Marseilles, Seen from L'Estaque." 1886–90. Oil on canvas, 31¾ x 39¼ in. Courtesy of The Art Institute of Chicago.

refusal to enter the swamp in "Big Two-Hearted River" and Jake Barnes's fear of swimming across the harbor at San Sebastian. Then what is the sea, and how does Hemingway describe it? In *The Old Man and the Sea*, the sea is generally calm and flat: "the surface of the ocean was flat except for the occasional swirls of the current" (33), and "the flat sea sent [the glare of the sun] back so that it hurt sharply" (35). In these passages, the sea has solidarity and substantiality. The flatness and the tangibility are quite similar to the few images of the sea which Cézanne painted. In his shorescapes, the sea is solid blue, waveless, with only subtle color variations which suggest waves in a limited way.

Yet Santiago also notes "the phosphorescence of the Gulf weed" (31) and other weeds lying just under the flat surface of the sea. Moreover, the big fish, as well as the predator sharks, come from the deep. The deep as such is never really described, although Santiago tries to imagine it: "he could picture the fish swimming in the water with his purple pectoral fins set wide as wings and the great erect tail slicing through the dark. I wonder how much he sees at that depth" (74). Thus when Hemingway wants to describe the deep which is beyond the surface of the sea, he must reach into the imagination, beyond any realistic depiction. But Winslow Homer's rough and storm-tossed seascapes, which Hemingway so admired at the Chicago Art Institute and which Thomas Hudson painted, are not the calm sea of Santiago with its mysterious phosphorescence and its ambiguous depths.

No, Santiago's sea is not wholly like Cézanne's, nor does it resemble Homer's. It bears a much closer resemblance to the imaginative seas and fish of Klee, such as "Goldfish Wife" (1921; Philadelphia Museum of Art) or, more particularly, "Around the Fish" (1926; The Museum of Modern Art, New York). In the latter, the phosphorescent fish contrast vividly with the dark and mysterious background. Surrounding and imaginatively associated with the fish are symbolic figures, abstract geometrical designs, and vegetable forms. In the battle scene from "Sinbad the Sailor" (1923; Collection Madame T. Dürst-Haass, Muttenz), however, Sinbad must confront the terrible and fantastic creatures from

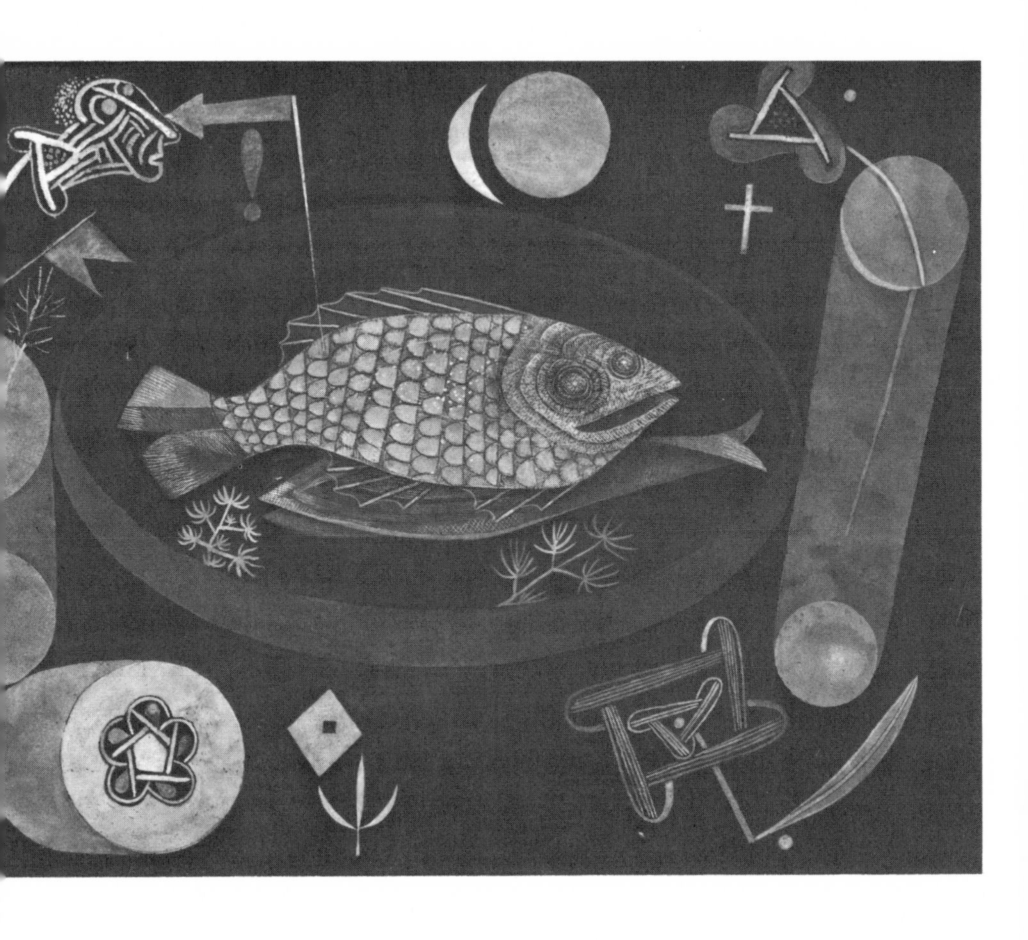

"He could picture the fish swimming in the water with his purple pectoral fins set wide apart and the great erect tail slicing through the dark."

—SANTIAGO IN *The Old Man and the Sea*

Paul Klee, "Around the Fish." 1926. Oil on canvas, 18⅜ x 25⅛ in. Collection, The Museum of Modern Art, New York. Abby Aldrich Rockefeller Fund.

the deep. Like Santiago, Sinbad is battling with a harpoon from a small boat. Like Santiago's sea, Sinbad's sea is calm, formed with a cubist pattern of parallel and right-angle planes of varying blues which become black at the edges of the picture. Purples and striped abstract patterns and designs describe Sinbad's fish, much as Santiago's fish was striped and had purple pectoral fins. In short, the imaginative fish and seas of Klee are remarkably similar to Santiago's fish and sea. It should be remembered that Hemingway himself owned one painting by Klee.

Santiago's imaginative attempt to picture the deep is a unique passage in Hemingway's works. Throughout all of Hemingway's poetry and prose, there is practically no description of an imaginative projection of the protagonist. When Jake Barnes describes the deep water at San Sebastian, he has made a dive into it. Even Santiago's dreams and Harry's death dream are psychic realities. But Santiago's description of the deep is almost totally imaginative. Other Hemingway protagonists are allowed to describe only what they have seen, felt, smelled, heard, or otherwise physically experienced. It goes without saying that Klee's undersea pictures or pictures of an event upon the sea, such as "Sinbad the Sailor," are also totally imaginative; yet, like so much else in Klee, they have sprung from his subconscious. For Klee, the essence of art was this: "Art does not render the visible; rather, it makes visible."[12] Such too was the aim of Hemingway in *The Old Man and the Sea.*

Finally, both Hemingway's and Klee's seas are made more mysterious by the choice of colors. In Klee's "Sinbad the Sailor," the blackness which the blue of the sea becomes is sharply contrasted by the bright reds and yellows of Sinbad's harpoon and of his clothes. The graduated purples and reds and light blues of the sea monsters provide a luminous, contrasting motion to the cubistically stable sea and primitively stylized and immobile Sinbad. Santiago's sea is blue, at times purple, at times black. Near its surface floats the phosphorescent seaweed, as well as other

12 Quoted in Herbert Read, *A Concise History of Modern Art* (New York, 1959), p. 182.

seaweed, both yellow and red. Once floating close to the skiff is the "purple, formalized, iridescent, gelatinous bladder of a Portuguese man of war, which has long deadly purple filaments" (39). The great fish Santiago catches is striped, with purple dorsal fins, while the sharks have "yellow cat-like eyes" (120). Hemingway's choice of colors for the depiction of the fish and the sea is almost exactly that of Klee, and its effect is similar to the magical, mysterious qualities of Klee's sea scenes.

In *Islands in the Stream*, Thomas Hudson makes special mention of Klee's colors. Discussing his own painting by Klee, "Monument in Arbeit," Hudson remarks that "the color was as indecent as the plates in his father's medical books that showed the different types of chancres and venereal ulcers, and how frightened of it his wife had been until she had learned to accept its corruption and only see it as a painting. . . . it was a good picture and he liked to look at it" (238). Only rarely does Hudson describe the sea in terms of Klee's corrupt colors, as, for example, when he describes a flock of flamingoes as a "roseate mass on a gray brown flat" (420), or when he sees phosphorescent strips of seaweed at night "like cold strips and patches of white, unhealthy fire in the water" (453). In contrast to these imaginative uses of color and also in contrast to Santiago's decorative fish, Davey Hudson's fish is described only as purple.

Thus the sea, in *The Old Man and the Sea*, is not really the same as the mountains which remain solid, substantial, and orderly. The sea is an area into which man can venture, but in which he must not go "out too far." The sea is a symbol of man's venture into the unknown or of man's heroic willingness to take the greater prize. As such, the sea is mysterious and ambiguous, even paradoxical. Such mystery, ambiguity, and paradox are evident in Klee's seascapes. Both the mountains and the sea, however, represent a kind of order, a type of the code for which so many of the Hemingway protagonists were searching.

At the same time, mountains and sea often provide the setting for the games and sports which Hemingway's people play. The favorite sports can be divided into two groups: those which are performed in nature and those which are performed in the city. Of the first group, the protagonist most often participates in fishing, hunting, swimming, or skiing. Any one of these sports may be performed alone. If other people are present, they are there only for companionship. Nick of "Big Two-Hearted River" chooses to fish alone, but Jake Barnes asks "good old Bill" to join him for the fishing idyll on the Irati River. In both cases, the presence of nature is as significant, if not more significant, than the game itself. Nick and Jake go fishing not only to fish, but also to find the peace and order of the hills. Like Thoreau at Walden, Nick and Jake "caught two fishes as it were with one hook."[13]

The city games, however, must be performed with at least one other person, and there is no sense of natural order or peace necessarily associated with them. The three most important city games are horse-racing, boxing, and bullfighting. They are social games, so to speak, but with this difference: boxing and horse-racing demand a highly competitive spirit. In this sense, but this sense only, they are individual sports like fishing or skiing. Bullfighting, on the other hand, demands a cooperation, a team effort, so to speak. In this sense, it is unlike any other sport in which the Hemingway people participate. The climax of the bullfight, however, is individual: the bullfighter alone, like the hunter, confronting death in the form of an animal. The bullfight is the only team sport, if it can in fact be called that, to interest the Hemingway protagonists. There is occasionally, in Hemingway's fiction, an almost incidental interest in the scores of football or baseball games in the United States, but there is no direct participation in these sports. Seldom, too, are the two categories of sports mixed. Only Santiago, while performing an individual sport in nature, thinks of a team sport which must be performed in the city (75 and 107). Yet his thoughts center not upon the New York Yankees as a team, but upon the bravery and heroism of Joe DiMaggio.

There was a great deal of interest in sports in the 1920's. Indeed, that Jake Barnes and Nick Adams are intrigued by games is evi-

13 Henry David Thoreau, *Walden*, Ch. 9.

dence of their milieu; it is part of Hemingway's realistic context for his fictional characters. One group in the 1920's, however, had a very special interest in games of all kinds:

> To the surrealists games were a method by means of which they might detach themselves from the world, a gesture meaningless in the context of ordinary life, but pointing toward a social distinction and suggesting a distinctive metaphysical outlook.... The beauty of the game lies in its being so clearly, so irrevocably ordered. No trespassing of the rules is permitted at the risk of denying the game, of breaking the magic circle, of opening the hothouse doors, to the cold wind of the world beyond. The game, in short, is a formal constructive which shuts out one reality while creating another, more nearly ideal one.[14]

The Freudian implications of this special surrealist interest in games are self-evident. Yet, although "almost from the very beginning the surrealists devoted what must have seemed to onlookers as an inordinate amount of time to games,"[15] there is very little depiction of sports in their artistic works. De Chirico and Dali may have painted a few bike-riders, charioteers, and hoop-rollers, but neither the surrealist painters nor novelists nor poets painted or wrote to any extent about the games and sports in which they participated.

Obviously Hemingway's interest in sports can be understood in terms quite similar to those used to describe the surrealist passion for sports. Certainly all of the sports to which Hemingway most frequently refers in his fiction are governed by specific rules or at least an implied order of fair play. The very ritual-like motions of preparing to fish and then the ordered steps of fishing itself are the most elaborately described actions of "Big Two-Hearted River." There is manifest, in fact, a ritual of fishing, an

14 Herbert S. Gershman, *The Surrealist Revolution in France* (Ann Arbor, 1969), p. 10.
15 Ibid., p. 9.

order with a set of rules in which there is safety from the symbolic dangers of the swamp: "The whole of the fishing is conducted according to the ritualistic codes of fair play. When Nick catches a trout too small to keep, he carefully wets his hands before touching the fish so as not to disturb the mucous coating on the scales and thus destroy the fish he is trying to save. Down under, in short, the close reader finds a carefully determined order of virtue and simplicity. . . ."[16] It is in the social sports of the city, however, that the rules are most closely observed and ritualized—and needed. Good boxers and good bullfighters must fight cleanly; that is, they must observe the ritual and the rules. The order of the game must be asserted and obeyed.

The ritual of the bullfight has received the most attention in studies of Hemingway. From the first brief sketches of *in our time* to the full development of the theme in *Death in the Afternoon*, Hemingway perceived the bullfight as a different sort of reality, both for the participants and, vicariously, for the *aficionado*—a reality which is a highly ritualized activity in which death must be confronted and conquered only in the context of rules and order. The Hemingway bullfighter who has *pundonor* has been defined as a type of the crucified Christ, as a priest, or as a psychic expression of the Spanish culture.[17] Clearly, for Hemingway, the bullfight is a reality which, by way of its own controlled rules, is able to shut out that other reality of the world; it is indeed a nearly ideal reality, when performed bravely and cleanly: "I believe that the tragedy of the bullfight is so well ordered and so strongly disciplined by ritual that a person feeling the whole tragedy cannot separate the minor comic-tragedy of the horse so as to feel it emotionally"; and, with regard to the matador: "But the matador, if he knows his profession, can increase the amount of the danger of death that he runs exactly as

16 Baker, *Hemingway: The Writer as Artist*, p. 126.

17 See Melvin Backman, "Hemingway: The Matador and the Crucified," *Hemingway and His Critics: An International Anthology*, ed. Carlos Baker (New York, 1961), pp. 247ff.; Baker, *Hemingway: The Writer as Artist*, pp. 146ff.; and Joseph De Falco, *The Hero in Hemingway's Short Stories* (Pittsburgh, 1963), pp. 198ff.

much as he wishes. He should, however, increase this danger, *within the rules provided for his protection.*"[18]

Whether or not Hemingway was conscious of the special surrealistic interest in games cannot be known. Perhaps it is significant that Miró used to accompany Hemingway to his boxing matches. Hemingway had been introduced to all these sports—except bullfighting—as a young man in Michigan, Illinois, and Canada. He wrote about trout fishing when he was in Canada, before his first trip to Europe, but in "The Best Trout Fishing in the World Is at the Canadian Soo,"[19] there is really no intimation of the ritualistic significance with which Hemingway was later to associate fishing. There is only the expression of pleasure in the sense of fun. None of the intensity of Nick Adams is evident in the article for the *Star Weekly*. Thus it is probable that the special surrealistic interest in games may have had some influence upon Hemingway in the 1920's. Yet, as I have said, the surrealists very seldom depicted sports or games in their paintings, novels, or poems.

Bullfighting, the most important sport in Hemingway's fiction, even more important than fishing and hunting, was introduced to him only after he arrived in Europe. From 1923 on, Hemingway spent many hours watching the bullfights; it is evident that most of *Death in the Afternoon*, for example, is based upon his own observations. Most of the vignettes were written after he had seen the bullfights in Spain, and although the descriptions and the texture are amazingly accurate, the vignettes are highly stylized. Could there have been any artistic models for these very realistic images in the vignettes and even in the later scenes of bullfighting?

Baker felt free to associate *Death in the Afternoon* with Goya's "Tauromaquia" in subject;[20] and, as has been pointed out, Wilson alluded to these same Goya etchings when he discussed the bullfight vignettes. Certainly the vignettes suggest the Goya etchings,

18 *Death in the Afternoon*, pp. 8 and 21.
19 *The Toronto Star Weekly*, August 28, 1920, reprinted in *By-Line: Ernest Hemingway*, pp. 9–12.
20 Baker, *Hemingway: The Writer as Artist*, p. 143.

"Maera lay still, his face in the sand. He felt warm and sticky from the bleeding. Each time he felt the horn coming. . . . Once the horn went all the way through him and he felt it go into the sand."

—VIGNETTE

Francisco Goya, "Tauromaquia" #33. Etching and aquatint. Courtesy of The Hispanic Society of America.

"Finally the bull charged, the horse leaders ran for the barrera, the picador hit too far back, and the bull got under the horse, lifted him, threw him onto his back."

—"The Undefeated"

Francisco Goya, "Tauromaquia" B. Etching and aquatint. Courtesy of The Hispanic Society of America.

both in spirit and in subject. Goya's series of at least forty plates (mostly etchings) depict not only bullfighting, but also bull-baiting by dogs, bull-baiting from a horse's back, and other bull-man contests. The "Tauromaquia" is "the most naturalistic Goya series, the one that adheres with closest narrative fidelity to the visual truth in most of its plates."[21] The series was completed by 1815, just at the time that bullfighting was becoming Spain's national sport. As Wilson pointed out, the bullfight vignettes have the elegance of Goya's etchings. The gracefulness of the bull-fighters as well as of the bulls, and yet the omnipresence of death, are indications that Goya, like Hemingway, was an *aficionado.*

In fact, it seems more than circumstance that several scenes of bullfighting in the vignettes and in "The Undefeated," first published in 1925, can be paralleled in Goya's etchings. For example, a gored white horse, losing its entrails, appears in Goya's etchings 26 and 32 and in the vignette which begins, "They whack-whacked the white horse on the legs." Further, both Goya and Hemingway show a bull goring a man who is lying flat on the ground; Hemingway, in the vignette beginning "Maera lay still, his head on his arms," as well as in "The Undefeated," and Goya, in etching 33. In "The Undefeated," Hemingway describes a bull throwing a horse over his back, much like Goya's etching B. It is important to note that, in both scenes, the picador is falling safely away from the action. In view of the nature of the bull's attack on the horse, it is more than likely that the picador would have been dangerously involved in the action.

These scenes might have occurred in any bullfight; it is possible to assume that Hemingway could have described these scenes with originality without any influence from Goya. And yet even the mode of expression or the techniques are quite similar. Like "The Disasters of War," most of the etchings of "Tauromaquia" are stark, outlined statements. The action centers upon only one or two figures, with background elements and figures tending to blend into the chiaroscuro. The major figures themselves, bull and

21 Jose Gudiol, *Goya,* trans. Priscella Muller (New York, 1964), p. 62.

man in most cases, tend to be isolated; and there is movement, constant movement. Indeed, it is amazing that Goya could employ broad planes of shadow and light to describe such movement within such a limited part of the page. The etchings are dominated by light and shade, but even in his few paintings of bullfights, Goya's colors are whites and blacks, with an occasional splash of red. The bright costumes of the matadors and the picadors, as well as the colors in the crowd, are generally dulled: bright gold satin becomes a rather dusty yellow, and brilliant blues are heavily shaded with blacks. The colors or contrasts do not agitate the movement. It is the angle of a man's leg or the arch of a bull's neck which creates motion within the entire scene. There is, in a sense, a kind of shorthand in Goya's etchings. As in "The Disasters of War," Goya does not shrink from depicting the most bloody and horrible details: horses lose entrails, men spurt blood, bulls suffer and die with their tongues hanging out.

The same sort of stark statement is present in any of the early Hemingway bullfight scenes: the very naturalistic depiction of the most bloody details, the isolation of bull and man, the description in broad planes with practically no details (such as of costume), and, in most cases, constant motion. Even more amazing is the almost complete lack of color in Hemingway's early descriptions. In the vignettes which concern bullfighting, specific colors are mentioned only twice, the white of a horse and the red of a sword hilt. In the bullfight scenes of "The Undefeated," again there are practically no colors except for blacks, whites, and occasional reds. The broad areas of light and shadow of the stands and the sand are rendered simply as light and shadow. The occasional mentions of red are splashed through this colorless scene much as Goya highlighted his bullfight paintings with reds, such as "The Bullfight." Except for one brief reference to orange, no bullfighter's suit is described in terms of color in these early pieces of Hemingway's. Yet the bullfight is an immensely colorful spectacle. To be sure, Hemingway uses color sparingly, except in special circumstances; but the absence of color, especially in these early works, is notable. It is especially relevant to note here that, in *Death in the Afternoon*, Hemingway had praised Goya for his blacks and whites.

Thus it seems to me that Hemingway might have used Goya's etchings of bullfights much as he did Goya's etchings of war. Like the other series of Goya's etchings, the "Tauromaquia" was available in reproductions in Paris in the early 1920's. That is, Goya might have helped Hemingway to describe visually scenes of bullfighting, especially in the early passages. It is possible too that Hemingway connected Goya's etchings with his own special interpretation of the bullfight as another reality of ritual or order. It is certainly no coincidence that the powerful young bullfighter of *The Sun Also Rises* is named Pedro Romero. A popular bullfighter in Madrid in the 1770's and 1780's was also named Pedro Romero and was depicted by Goya in etching 30 of the "Tauromaquia." Like Hemingway's other "good" bullfighters, the fictional Romero has a special significance: "Pedro was exempt from the *mal de siècle* that beset the others, for his fighting with the bulls brought him into a fundamental relationship with life, which involved the pitting of his maleness against that of the bull. It is a life and death struggle that reveals not only the steel of his young manhood but a certain passion with which he met life—an intensity, a seriousness, a dedicated quality. Pedro had a place in the scheme of existence—and a role to fulfill."[22] Hemingway's Romero offers a meaningful contrast to the other characters in *The Sun Also Rises*; he has a code and courageously lives by it—a quality which is evident even to Brett. Goya's Romero is depicted just at the moment his sword enters the neck of the charging bull. He is a handsome young man, and, in the etching, his face is intense as he experiences the very moment of confronting death. Goya chose to depict him in the most heroic and dramatic moment of the bullfight.

Hemingway's Romero had a brief love affair for which Jake Barnes had acted as the liaison. Such an affair between the noble and innocent bullfighter and the sophisticated, pagan Brett held

22 Backman, "Hemingway: The Matador and the Crucified," p. 248.

"Out in the centre of the ring Romero profiled in front of the bull, drew the sword out from the folds of the muleta, rose on his toes, and sighted along the blade."

—JAKE BARNES IN *The Sun Also Rises*

Francisco Goya, "Tauromaquia" #30 ("Pedro Romero matando á toro parado"). 1815 edition. Etching and aquatint. Courtesy of The Hispanic Society of America.

the potential ruination of Romero's primitive innocence. Goya's friend Romero, it was rumored, also had a love affair which could have affected Goya himself quite deeply. Apparently the eighteenth-century Romero won the Duchess of Alba in 1793.[23] The Duchess had, of course, been a special "friend" of Goya's. Like Jake Barnes, Goya was wounded at this time: after a severe illness, Goya had been left deaf and quite weak. Unlike Jake, however, Goya could not stoically accept a woman's infidelity. His bitterness and anger at the Duchess is evident in "The Caprices," which were executed between 1793 and 1796. By the time Goya completed "Tauromaquia," apparently he had forgiven Romero; or perhaps he felt obliged to include at least one etching of this popular matador who was so prominent in the early years of Spain's national sport. Hemingway associated his fictional bullfighter with Goya's Pedro Romero, and it is highly probable that he found the name in Goya's "Tauromaquia." Whether or not Hemingway knew of the Goya–Duches of Alba–Romero triangle will probably never be known, but the parallel is nevertheless suggestive.

Final mention should be made of the significance of the bull himself in both Goya and Hemingway. For Hemingway, the brave bull has a very special quality—a virility and a sense of honor which parallels those qualities in the noble bullfighter: "The bravery of a truly brave bull is something unearthly and unbelievable. . . . The best of all fighting bulls have a quality, called nobility by the Spanish, which is the most extraordinary part of the whole business."[24] In the ritual of the game, the confrontation of death must be in heroic proportions, and the bull provides an honorable and noble opponent. In fact, in *Death in the Afternoon*, Hemingway observed that "the bravery of the bull is the primal root of the whole Spanish bullfight" (113). By recounting peasant and gypsy rituals and superstitions related to the bull, such as that concerning the two gypsy children who roasted and ate the

23 Jacques Lassaigne, *Goya,* trans. Rosamund Frost (New York, 1948), p. 55.
24 *Death in the Afternoon*, p. 113.

testicles of a bull which had killed their brother,[25] Hemingway suggests a mythological dimension (in the case of the two gypsy children, an association with ancient fertility cults).

For Goya, too, the bull became a very special symbol. Certainly throughout "Tauromaquia" the bull is depicted with nobility, majesty, and bravery. He is a worthy opponent of the brave matadors and picadors. In an etching prepared for "Proverbs" (1820–24), "Make Way for Bulls and Wind," Goya represents four bulls in a lyric and dancing fantasy. Free from harassing and torturing humans, the bulls dance and leap and kick. The background is solid and flat; there are no fences, buildings, or spectators. There is nothing at all to associate these bulls with the actual world. Overlapping, whirling, with tails flying, the bull dance is Goya's tribute to these brave animals. The bulls seem to reach back to the dancing bulls of Crete, though Sir Arthur Evans was not to discover the bull-dancing frescoes at the Palace of Knossos until 1900.

Certainly the number of similarities, on nearly every level, between Goya and Hemingway is convincing. From the reproduction of specific images to the mythological and symbolic significance of the bulls themselves, the parallels are numerous. Much as with "The Disasters of War," it is also evident that Hemingway might have been able to transpose specific techniques from Goya's medium to his own.

There is only one other artist whom Hemingway mentions with specific reference to bullfighting. In *Death in the Afternoon*, Hemingway begins with an analogy to Brancusi and continues with a statement concerning the impermanence of certain arts: "I know of no modern sculpture, except Brancusi's, that is in any way the equal of the sculpture of modern bullfighting. But it is an impermanent art as singing and the dance are, one of those that Leonardo advised men to avoid, and when the performer is gone the art exists only in the memory of those who have seen it and dies with them" (99). The Romanian Brancusi was for a

25 Ibid., pp. 24–25.

time associated with the cubists, but, unlike the cubists, he never let the image itself deteriorate by means of a simultaneous viewing of the object and its consequent imaginative reconstruction. His forms remained representational, though highly abstract. He attempted to achieve the most simple and elemental statement of the object. His work often took the form of simple geometrical forms with appropriate variations. In this sense, his art is closely related to Cézanne's. In fact, according to Herbert Read, "it might be argued that Brancusi has shown a better understanding of Cézanne's intentions than any of the Cubist painters—certainly a more consistent attempt to 'realize' the organic structure of natural objects."[26] Brancusi was thus not the type of sculptor whom Frederic Henry so disliked. Like Cézanne, he described the world in terms of order: the geometrical shapes of the cone, the sphere, and the cylinder.

Hemingway's reference to Brancusi suggests that Brancusi's sculpture was able to capture some elemental and primordial qualities which a bullfight also made evident. The archetypal theme of man and the animal, the ritual of the encounter, the confrontation of death—all these are as elemental as "Bird" or "Sleeping Muse." Both the bullfight and Brancusi express a sense of life in its most reduced and thus real sense. Moreover, the clean lines of Brancusi's geometrical forms are an expression of order in the world, just as were Cézanne's. For Hemingway, too, the bullfight represented a kind of order. The geometrical shapes with which Brancusi had learned from Cézanne to express the reality of his world would surely have appealed to Hemingway, who also saw nature and the mountains manifesting the same forms.

In Hemingway, however, the bullfighters were not always as majestic and brave as in Goya's etchings, nor were their perform-

26 Read, *A Concise History of Modern Art*, p. 104. It is interesting to note that the "sculpture" which most interested Thomas Hudson is driftwood: "he watched the sculpture that the wind and sand had made of a piece of driftwood. It was gray and sanded and it was embedded in the white, floury sand, It looked as though it were in an exhibition. It should be in the Salon d'Automne" (337). Certainly, the driftwood suggests works by Brancusi because of its purity of line and its evident organic structure.

ances always a sculptured art like Brancusi's; more often than not, the *aficionado* left the plaza with disappointment. With the bravest of bulls and matadors, however, the bullfight offered a new reality which was the reward of the Hemingway protagonists' search. Love affairs in Hemingway also had a way of disappointing. Jake Barnes's capacity for love and his incapacity for sexual intercourse and Brett's incapacity for love and her nymphomania are indicative of the many kinds of problems from which the characters in Hemingway's works must suffer. As often as not, love is as frustrating and anguished as the reality of the world which the lovers are trying to counterbalance. Leslie Fiedler has observed that Hemingway is really only comfortable in dealing with men without women and that "perhaps he is best of all with men who stand alone. . . ."[27] Certainly very few of Hemingway's early protagonists find any kind of happiness in their love affairs; yet as Hemingway himself grew older, the love affairs in his fiction became more successful. Frederic Henry can be happy, at least for a while, with Catherine. Harry Morgan can find happiness in his marriage; the novel concludes with a lamentation and elegy by his wife. Robert Jordan and Colonel Cantwell, just before their deaths, are able to love their mistresses quite successfully. Thomas Hudson had once been very happy, especially with his first wife.

Robert W. Lewis, Jr., sees the progressive ability of the protagonists to form happy sexual unions as indicative of a growing feeling of agape in Hemingway's fiction. This sense of agape takes its final form in Santiago, who, although another man without a woman, "learns that mankind is one other thing that he cannot help but be involved in."[28] Yet despite the apparent happy progression of love affairs, there is no real permanence in them: Jake and Brett survive, but cannot make love; Catherine dies in childbirth; Harry Morgan, Robert Jordan, Colonel Cantwell, and Thomas Hudson all die; Santiago does not even dream of his wife

27 Leslie Fiedler, *Love and Death in the American Novel* (New York, 1960), p. 305.
28 Robert W. Lewis, Jr., *Hemingway on Love* (Austin, Tex., 1965), p. 213.

anymore. Yet love is an important theme, and it does represent an attempt on the part of the anguished protagonist to order his universe.

It is safe to say, I'm sure, that the happiest love affairs in Hemingway are sentimentalized, that they are idyllic, and that the woman is too subservient to the dominant male: in short, that they are unreal, especially in the realistic context of any Hemingway novel or short story. Certainly the most extreme example of this kind of love affair is Maria's and Robert Jordan's in *For Whom the Bell Tolls.* Indeed, the ecstasy of their sexual union, as described by Hemingway in Chapters 13 and 37, is generally considered a "minor blemish" in an otherwise successful novel.[29] Yet such ecstasy does not last, for apparently happy love between a man and a woman is only temporary in Hemingway's fictional world. In this sense, Hemingway's treatment of love places him solidly in the post–World War I context: "One of the most persistent themes of the twenties was the death of love in World War I. All the major writers recorded it, often in piecemeal fashion, as part of the larger postwar scene; but only Hemingway seems to have caught it whole and delivered it in lasting fictional form."[30]

There was one group in the 1920's, however, who refused to see love as dead. For the surrealists, love was alive and well and living in Paris. The surrealists elevated love or *amour fou* to mythic proportions, often raising the *femme-enfante* "to a position comparable to that held by Mary in the Church."[31] For them, love was another illogical and chance-governed means of finding *le merveilleux.* Their myth of love lifted man from everyday reality to mysteries which could be sought and found in flesh and blood. Love was an all-consuming passion and hence was regarded, in its most "mad" form, as a mystical experience. Although not a surrealist, Jules Pascin also elevated or sentimentalized woman much in the manner of Breton or Desnos. In his paintings of prostitutes

29 Joseph Warren Beach, "How Do You Like It Now, Gentlemen?," in Baker, ed., *Hemingway and His Critics,* p. 241.
30 Mark Spilka, "The Death of Love in *The Sun Also Rises,*" ibid., p. 80.
31 Gershman, *The Surrealist Revolution in France,* p. 5.

and models, for example, these women appear as soft-featured innocents in virginal surroundings. In *A Moveable Feast*, Hemingway states that Pascin was "a very good painter" (102); for Thomas Hudson, Pascin "could paint more beautifully than anybody then" (73).

At least three love affairs in Hemingway's novels could be discussed in terms very similar to those which describe *amour fou*: the brief affairs of Frederic Henry and Catherine, Robert Jordan and Maria, and Colonel Cantwell and Renata. The affairs both of Frederic and Catherine and of Jordan and Maria clearly represent an attempt to escape from a horrible reality—a counteraction, so to speak. For Frederic and Catherine, the flight to the mountains of Switzerland from the war-torn plains of Italy is an attempt to isolate themselves in a home image. That they have sought such protection in the order and beauty of the mountains is especially significant in terms of Hemingway's concept of nature. The idyll is only temporary, as the reality of the hostile world breaks the spell when Catherine dies in childbirth. Much like Prince Prospero in Edgar Allan Poe's "The Masque of the Red Death," Frederic has learned that death cannot be eliminated by isolation and beauty or *amour fou*.

The affair of Jordan and Maria also takes place in the mountains, and it is this affair that most resembles the *amour fou* of the surrealists.[32] The association of Pilar-Maria with the Virgin Mary was noted in the last chapter. Moreover, the passages describing the ecstasy of the sexual union of Jordan and Maria certainly approach the mystical experience which the surrealists sought in love affairs. Note, for example, this passage of Jordan's consciousness: "For him it was a dark passage which led to nowhere, then to nowhere, then again to nowhere, once again to nowhere, always and forever to nowhere, heavy elbows on the earth to nowhere, dark, never any end to nowhere, hung on all time always to

32 Breton's *L'Amour fou* was published in 1937; *For Whom the Bell Tolls* was begun in 1939. Breton had formed his theories earlier and had published them in "Here Come the Mediums" (1922) and "Introduction to a Lecture on Reality and Its Limits" (1924).

nowhere, this time and again for always to nowhere, now not to be borne once again always and to nowhere, now beyond all bearing, up, up, up and into nowhere, suddenly, scaldingly, holdingly all nowhere gone and time absolutely still and they were both there, time having stopped and he felt the earth move out and away from under them" (159). The images are certainly unlike any Hemingway has used in other works. Note the cosmic significance which is suggested: time stands still, and the earth moves "out and away." Hemingway has used language daringly in this passage. As innovative as he may have been in some techniques, he usually used words in their traditional grammatical forms. In this passage, however, he invents the words "scaldingly" and "holdingly." The "nowhere" in this passage is not a "nowhere" of *nada.* It is the "nowhere" of a dark tunnel which is a turning inward, a searching, or a manifestation of a psychic state. It is the same (undoubtedly Freudian) tunnel of the Gothic castles of surrealist novels or the paintings of Tanguy. It is the mystical ecstasy also evident in such surrealist poems as Éluard's "L'Amoureuse." For both Éluard and Jordan, "woman . . . was the means by which an erotically charged universe was rendered visible."[33]

Finally there is, for once in Hemingway, a good result of a love affair. Maria again becomes healthy, and Jordan loses many of his self-doubts and nightmares. He can face death in a brave and courageous manner. In the cosmic proportions of their sexual union, Jordan certainly approached *le merveilleux.* With Maria and Jordan, Frederic and Catherine, and the Colonel and Renata, Hemingway has asserted a type of love cult quite similar to that of the surrealists. As Robert Penn Warren has pointed out, "The initiates of the cult of love are those who are aware of nada, but their effort, as members of the cult, is to find a meaning to put in place of the nada. That is, there is an attempt to make the relationship of love take on a religious significance in so far as it can give meaning to life."[34] For the surrealists, *amour fou* was also a kind

33 Gershman, *The Surrealist Revolution in France*, p. 57.
34 Warren, Introduction, *A Farewell to Arms*, p. xix.

of substitute religion, a means of finding meaning in their hostile world.

Colonel Cantwell's love affair with Renata is not just a final fling before his death. One critic, at least, sees Renata as an agent of castigation and purgation.[35] She is the agent who encourages the life analysis, the loss of ego-centeredness, which leads to Cantwell's happy death. In short, she does represent Maria to a certain extent in that her effect is health or a happy death. In surrealist terms, *le merveilleux* is Cantwell's own coming to terms with his life and himself.

These three examples isolated from three of Hemingway's major works seem to indicate that love affairs can be happy, if short-termed, and that the mystical love motif of the surrealists might have had an influence on Hemingway. But there are simply too many other love unions in Hemingway's other novels and short stories which are not happy and which are perverted or loveless or stale or sick in some way or another. The surrealist cult of *amour fou* may have had some influence upon Hemingway's creation of Robert and Maria, Frederic and Catherine, and the Colonel and Renata; the death of love was not total. Perhaps the title of Hemingway's unpublished novel, *The Garden of Eden*, is a better indication of Hemingway's general treatment of love: there is a paradise which can lead to a hell.

The Garden of Eden is a motif used by many artists in many different ways; more specifically it is also the name given to the first panel of a triptych by one of Hemingway's favorite painters, Hieronymous Bosch. The left panel represents Adam and Eve in the Garden of Paradise; the center panel, "The Garden of Earthly Delights," depicts naked men and women in various positions of love-making, bathing, or marching; the right panel contains one of Bosch's most terrifying visions of the tortures of hell, perhaps the one which Thomas Hudson mentions to his friend Bobby. Bosch's art, especially the center panel of this painting, contains much symbolic imagery of a very personal nature. Most critics

35 Horst Oppel, "Hemingway's *Across the River and into the Trees*," trans. Joseph M. Bernstein, in Baker, ed., *Hemingway and His Critics*, p. 221.

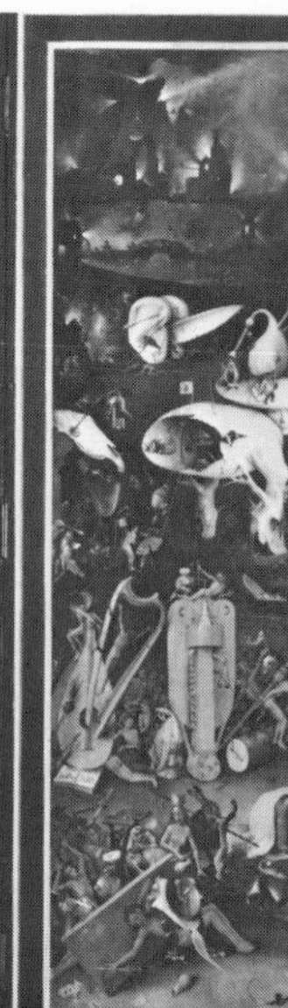

"We can paint the End of the World." . . .
"There was a man named Bosch could paint pretty well along those lines."

—Islands in the Stream

Hieronymous Bosch, "The Garden of Earthly Delights." ca. 1500. Triptych; oil on wood, 86⅝ x 153 in. Prado.

see the center panel as representing "the seductive world of desire and dreams which is avidly yielded to and only leads to perdition";[36] the triptych is a morality piece. Another critic understands the major imagery of the center panel as "a pictorial dithyramb in which the extreme of reckless voluptuousness seems to be used as a vehicle for an ecstatic state of communion with the Divine"; the center panel represents "an ecstatic Nature-cult, with its Dionysiac raptures."[37]

Yet in understanding Bosch's triptych, one must stress the importance of the total image of the work, for the three panels are hinged together, physically and symbolically. There is paradise; there are nudes and their delights; there is a hell populated by grotesque figures and suffering humans in a dreamscape. The temptation of Adam and Eve has already begun; whether the painting is a morality piece or not, there is manifest a statement of man's dangerous situation. Bosch "seeks and finds a new means of expressing in visual terms his immense unhappiness at the state of the world."[38] Viewed strictly in terms of human love, the successive panels of Bosch's painting state that there is indeed a danger in paradise, that there is fleshly pleasure, but that there may also be horrible suffering.

It is not difficult to find parallels between Hemingway's general treatment of love and Bosch's triptych. The failure or death of love is evident in many of Hemingway's works and in Bosch's dreamscape of hell. Note too how many of Hemingway's failed or "dead" lovers must push bad dreams from their consciousness. Jake Barnes avoids his nightmares with a night light, but the affair with Maria helps Jordan to overcome his nightmares. In *The Sun Also Rises*, the loose sexual allegiances and Brett's nymphomania suggest the fleshly delights of Bosch's center panel. In fact, Baker's suggestion that Brett is a kind of pagan fertility goddess[39] cor-

36 Robert Genaille, *Flemish Painting from Van Eyck to Brueghel*, trans. Leslie Schenk (London, 1954), p. 98.

37 Wilhelm Fränger, *The Millennium of Hieronymous Bosch*, trans. Eithne Wilkins and Ernst Kaiser (London, 1952), p. 113.

38 Margaret Whinney, *Early Flemish Painting* (London, 1968), p. 107.

39 Baker, *Hemingway: The Writer as Artist*, p. 91.

responds, to a certain extent, with the interpretation of the center panel as a "Dionysiac rapture." Finally, the dangers of paradise, the loss of innocence, and the intrusion of suffering into paradise is the theme of many Hemingway short stories, such as "The End of Something," but is also manifested in Catherine's death at the end of *A Farewell to Arms*, as well as in the deaths of Robert Jordan and Colonel Cantwell.

There are more specific parallels between the Bosch triptych and Hemingway's abortive novel, *The Garden of Eden*. In speaking of this novel, Hemingway said that paradise could, in fact, only be lost: "the happiness of the Garden that a man must lose."[40] In the center panel of the Bosch painting, the figures are nude; one of the pairs of lovers in the Hemingway novel enjoys sunbathing in the nude. Both sets of lovers in Hemingway's *The Garden of Eden* attempt to mingle identities, not only by transference of sexual identities but also by their efforts to look alike. In Bosch's "Garden of Earthly Delights," the individual sexual identity of those bathing and loving figures is difficult to discern. Each figure in the myriad of nudes must be examined if one wishes to be certain of sexual identities; but then, it is not really necessary to distinguish the difference. Both Bosch and Hemingway seem to be suggesting that there are, indeed, many delights in the garden, but both also point to the "happiness" that "a man must lose."

Perhaps one of the most interesting qualities of Hemingway's *The Garden of Eden* is that it concerns two sets of lovers: Catherine and David Bourne and Barbara and Nick Sheldon, one couple honeymooning at a seaport village and the other couple struggling in Paris. Hemingway was apparently intending to treat love on two levels or in two ways or from two perspectives. He had paralleled sets of lovers in other novels, such as *To Have and Have Not*, but one couple was clearly the major concern, while the other provided a counterbalance. In his unpublished novel, however, the two couples are both major, offering balance to each other. Both sets are paralleled in their attempts to mingle identities, yet neither is a mirror of the other. The pairs form, as it were, a

40 Baker, *Hemingway: A Life Story*, p. 460.

diptych, a two-paneled composition of the progress of love. Further speculation, I suppose, must cease here because the novel was never really finished and has not been published.

Thus love is not totally dead for Hemingway's characters. For the moment, without any reference to the past or the future, there can be a meaningful, mystical union, much as the surrealists believed. On the other hand, this moment of love must eventually lead to a loss of innocence and beauty; it is "the happiness of the Garden that a man must lose," as Bosch certainly would have agreed.

This cult of love, the search into nature for order, and the ritual reality of sports and games all generally involve violence of one kind or another. In the preceding chapter, violence was examined as an antagonistic part of the hostile universe in which Hemingway's agonized protagonists had been placed. Yet violence also offered an alternative course, a counteraction to the hostile world, and a path to order. Violence is clearly a part of the sports in which the characters participate, either directly or vicariously; it is part, too, of the natural world which the Francis Macombers must face, and it is often related to love affairs, as in *For Whom the Bell Tolls*. In short, violence can be another means of counteracting violence. The violence in Hemingway which is related to man's search for order is a violence of sensual involvement; it is a physical violence—killing, injuring, destroying, maiming. Primarily it is a confrontation with death, whether in the form of a bull or a bridge. In this confrontation, the protagonist must be brave and must follow the rules. It is this type of physical violence which can counteract the nightmares and the *nada*.

What Hemingway wrote of Goya indicates the profound sensual reaction with which Hemingway associated Goya's etchings and paintings. Hemingway himself wrote what he saw, felt, smelled, and drunk, long after Goya had painted "what he had seen, felt, touched, handled, smelled, enjoyed, drunk, mounted. . . ." Moreover, in the bullfight etchings or in those etchings depicting bravery in "The Disasters of War," the violence can be beautiful, orderly, and clean. Other painters who evoke a sensual response, such as Klee, certainly suggest that violence is one means of confronting the hostile universe. One could review the works of nearly all painters who seem to have exerted some influence upon Hemingway to show that violence, if ordered and appropriate, is one means of following the code or of asserting order. In short, the violence of Pedro Romero, of Santiago, of Goya's bullfighters and brave women, and of Miró's hunter is another means of confronting a chaotic universe.

Of the various searches for order which the Hemingway protagonist must undergo, there remains the most traditional means —religion. There is little positive use of formal religion in any of Hemingway's works. These few instances of a positive expression are not difficult to remember: the peasants and the Fascist lieutenant in *For Whom the Bell Tolls* manifest a faith in the Roman Catholic Church; Jake Barnes at least tries to find consolation in the cathedral at Pamplona; Frederic Henry prays for Catherine while she is in childbirth; certain of Hemingway's short stories, such as "Today Is Friday," deal with Christ's martyrdom, but in an unconventional way; and there seem to be direct Christian analogies of a more traditional nature in the characters of Pedro Romero, Robert Jordan, Colonel Cantwell, and Santiago (St. James).[41]

On the other hand, the older waiter in "A Clean, Well-Lighted Place" prays "Our nada who art in nada" and "Hail nothing full of nothing"; Brett is unable to pray; Count Greffi in *A Farewell to Arms* has rejected religion. Thus the treatment of religion in Hemingway's works is paradoxical. Indeed, much of the ambivalence of Hemingway's expression of religion was established early; in the vignette beginning, "While the bombardment was knocking the trench to pieces at Fossalta," the desperate young soldier prays to Jesus but afterwards never tells anyone of his prayer. There seems to be a desire on the part of Hemingway's characters to find meaning in traditional religion, but at the same time an inability to relate in any successful way to the church and God.

41 Backman, "Hemingway: The Matador and the Crucified," pp. 245–58.

It has often been noted that certain activities take the place of religion for the Hemingway characters. F. I. Carpenter suggests that Hemingway is able to create a "fifth dimension" or "an intensity of experience beyond time" which comes "from a profound sense of participation in . . . traditional patterns of life experience" and which may result in mystical experience.[42] These traditional patterns appear in experiences as diverse as love-making, war, and bullfighting. The "fifth dimension" is most clearly perceived in Santiago, who performs "realistically the ritual techniques of his trade" and who "identifies the intensity of his own suffering with that of the great fish he is slaying." Hemingway was able to achieve this "fifth dimension" by a "synthesis of immediate experience and mysticism." In Santiago's fishing, as well as in love-making and bullfighting, Hemingway centered upon the realistic and ritualistic nature of the experience.

Correspondingly, as these rituals are emphasized, traditional religious ritual is almost totally negated. Apparently it is the religious experience itself which most interested Hemingway. Backman describes such experience in Hemingway's works as pain and martyrdom.[43] In Carpenter's study, the transcendence of time is closely related to religious mysticism. Perhaps an understanding of the role of traditional religion in Hemingway can be extended by an examination of the religious paintings which especially attracted him. In fact, most of the artists Hemingway admired painted works expressing traditional religious motifs.

El Greco, for example—for Hemingway, El Greco's art was "incomparable." He considered "View of Toledo" "the best picture in the [New York Metropolitan] Museum for me, and Christ knows there are some lovely ones."[44] He also seemed to like the painter's androgynous forms. More especially, El Greco was capable of stimulating a deep emotional response in Robert Jordan: "It is in Greco and in San Juan de la Cruz, of course, and in the

42 F. I. Carpenter, "Hemingway Achieves the Fifth Dimension," in Baker, ed., *Hemingway and His Critics*, pp. 200–201.

43 Backman, "Hemingway: The Matador and the Crucified," p. 245.

44 Quoted in Lillian Ross, *Portrait of Hemingway* (New York, 1961), p. 58.

others. I am no mystic, but to deny it is as ignorant as though you denied the telephone" (380). El Greco was a favorite of the artists in Paris in the 1920's and has been called the father of cubism and surrealism, as well as of expressionism.[45] Perhaps the best summation of El Greco's appeal to Hemingway and his contemporaries was written by Harold E. Whethey: "The Expressionist movements of the early part of this century, the general reaction in the world of art against realism, and a widespread concern for inner psychological values have created a critical climate in which a master of El Greco's unworldly nature and daring originality would best be understood and evaluated."[46] It is perhaps those "inner psychological values," especially the emotional and spiritual intensity of El Greco's religious paintings, which attracted Hemingway. El Greco painted many Christian martyrs who were mystics, and even his "View of Toledo" is charged with the movement and mystery of a spiritual and cosmically related storm. Indeed, El Greco went "as far into his other world as he wanted."

Yet it is this "other world" which Hemingway very seldom reveals in explicit terms. For Robert Jordan, any discussion or admission of a deep personal religious experience would be "embarrassing"—and Jordan is no mystic. The protagonist most nearly approaching any clear statement of Christian mysticism is Santiago of *The Old Man and the Sea*, a novel which some critics read as a moral parable.[47] Yet Santiago is hardly a mystic in the traditional sense. Perhaps, then, it was just the emotional and spiritual intensity of El Greco to which Hemingway responded. Such intensity, like Bosch's nightmares, might be an element which can be omitted: "Anything you can omit that you know you still have in the writing and its quality will show."

Other painters of religious works whom Hemingway specifically mentioned were Bosch, Brueghel, Giotto, Masaccio, della Francesca, and Mantegna. After El Greco, the most references to

45 R. Scott Stevenson, *In Search of Spanish Painting* (New York, 1956), p. 69.
46 Harold E. Whethey, *El Greco and His School* (Princeton, N.J., 1962), p. 65.
47 Mark Schorer, *New Republic*, October 6, 1952, p. 20.

any painter of religious works are to Mantegna. The advocate of world revolution in "The Revolutionist" did not like Mantegna. Colonel Cantwell, however, admired Mantegna (14), and, like El Greco, Mantegna could evoke a deep emotional response from Robert Jordan (220). Catherine Barkley remembers Mantegna as "very bitter," and Frederic Henry adds, "with lots of nail holes" (289–90). The "very bitter" picture with "lots of nail holes" is perhaps "The Dead Christ" (Milan, Pinateca di Brera).

Like Robert Jordan, but unlike El Greco, Mantegna is not a mystic. His paintings have been described as expressions of "archeological humanism."[48] He tends to give his figures "a noble stature."[49] Concerning Mantegna's paintings, however, Hemingway's characters remember not nobility or humanistic values, but bitterness and nail holes–and an emotional response. Certainly the bitterness and nail holes indicate that Hemingway viewed Mantegna in terms both of realism and of suffering and anguish. For example, in "The Death of the Virgin" (1462)–the one Mantegna owned by the Prado in the 1930's and hence the one which aroused emotion in Robert Jordan–Mary is a pudgy, unattractive old woman with a lined face, and she is quite obviously dead. Yet there is no indication of satire as in the surrealist Max Ernst's "The Virgin Spanking the Infant Jesus before Three Witnesses: A.B., P.E., and the Artist" (1928). Mantegna's Virgin is framed by rows of saints, her position set in the middle plane. The verisimilitude of the nail holes in "The Dead Christ" corresponds to Hemingway's realistic description of, for example, Passini's wounds in *A Farewell to Arms*: "One leg was gone and the other held by tendons and part of the trouser and the stump twitched and jerked as though it were not connected" (57).

That the starry-eyed young communist of "The Revolutionist" did not like Mantegna's paintings is further evidence of Hemingway's interest in the realism, rather than the "archeological

48 Andre Chastel, *The Flowering of the Italian Renaissance*, trans. Jonathan Griffin, in *The Arts of Mankind*, ed. André Malraux and George Salles (New York, 1965), p. 42.

49 Maud Cruttwell, *Andrea Mantegna* (London, 1901), p. 60.

"It was as authentic as the feeling you had when you heard Bach, or stood in Chartres Cathedral . . . or when you saw Mantegna . . . at the Prado."

—ROBERT JORDAN IN *For Whom the Bell Tolls*

Andrea Mantegna, "The Death of the Virgin." ca. 1462. Panel, 21¼ x 16½ in. Prado.

humanism," of Mantegna's works. In "The Revolutionist," Hemingway is demonstrating the foolishness of idealistic causes such as the revolutionist advocated. The young man's dislike of Mantegna reflects his inability to see the reality of the world in which his schemes of revolution will not work. As the story ends, the young idealist is eventually forced to face the immediate reality of jail.

The emotional intensity which Mantegna, like El Greco, is able to inspire is thus not so much a mystical experience as an affirmation of order and value, even with respect to man's painful condition. In fact, it is perhaps more to the paintings of Mantegna than to those of El Greco that Santiago is related. The wounded hands, the dried blood on his face, the taste in his mouth, the weight of the mast as he ascends the hill—these are all very real to Santiago and are described by Hemingway in specific sensual images. Santiago has suffered "plenty." But the emotional and spiritual experience itself transcends and is enhanced by the physical suffering and anguish.

Of all the painters of religious works whom Hemingway specifically mentions, only Mantegna combines the realistic and spiritual in such a way. The juxtaposition of the real and spiritual, physical and mystical, Brett and Maria, "bad" bullfighters and "good" bullfighters—this, it seems to me, is Hemingway's means of expressing man's transcendence or at least affirmation of value in the midst of the anguish and despair of the world. Thus religion could never be totally spiritual in Hemingway, nor could it be restricted to traditional forms. The order of nature, the ritual of games, the evanescent love affair, the expression of bravery in violent acts, and a spirituality which is never allowed to move too far from the physical—all of these took the place of traditional religion for Hemingway's searching man.

The search, therefore, was for order or for a means of ordering one's life. Generally, the search ends with some physical expression or action which manifests order. So physical and so sensual are both the agonies of man and his expressions of order in Hemingway's work that one critic has categorized them generally as the "cult of sensation."[50] Other critics, however, such as Young and Baker, see implications beyond the purely physical in Hemingway. For example, Baker asserts, "The consciousness of God is in his books. The tragic view of life comes out in his perennial contrast of the permanence of nature and the evanescence of man."[51] The point is that Hemingway's concentration on the physical and sensual activities of man is meant to suggest and symbolize not only man's empirical situation, but also his metaphysical and mythical relationships. In Hemingway's works, man must live and act empirically; he must work out his mental and metaphysical problems in physical, empirical activities. The non-physical world (on one hand, that of the subconscious; on the other hand, that of conceptualization, as of order) is asserted necessarily by means of physical images.

In short, Hemingway's concentration upon physical images is expressive of man's empirical and metaphysical situations. Thus his poetry and prose are dominated by physical images or by the presentation of empirical experience. For this reason, he was physically involved as an artist in both the experience and the creation of art. Accordingly, he attempted to evoke physical sensations by means of prose and poetry. His writings continually call forth sensual response in all its modes. It is a synaesthesia which begins in the artist's own consciousness, continues in the creative act, becomes the essence of the verbal image, and is thus transmitted and re-created for the reader. It is through such a complex synaesthetic mosaic that Hemingway has attempted to break down the purely visual quality of prose.

The images thus become of primary importance. It is significant that the artists whom Hemingway most admired were those who emphasized an expansion of the sensuous aspect of painting in one way or another or who sought to express metaphysical problems or spiritual and psychic reality in sensuous and dynamic images. Those motifs and symbols which Hemingway seems to have found meaningful in Goya and Klee, for example, are those of

50 Warren, Introduction, *A Farewell to Arms,* p. xix.
51 Baker, *Hemingway: The Writers as Artist,* p. 328.

actual physical expression or of psychic experience made visible through physical images. Hemingway seems to have studied the works of certain painters in order to learn just what iconographic images might be relevant in terms of his own vision of reality.

In his re-creation of these images, Hemingway also learned just how techniques of painting might be carried over into the expression of verbal images. In short, Hemingway proved that words could be made to act like paint, at least in the presentation of certain images. Just by his choice of artists and by his use of their techniques, he was able to expand the sensuous quality of his own art further toward a single art.

V

Color and chiaroscuro

> Goya did . . . believe in blacks and in grays, in dust and in light . . . El Greco believed . . . in blues, grays, greens, and yellows, in reds. . . .[1]

> He looked at the man twice; once in the daylight, once with a flashlight. That too would have made a good etching for Goya, the visit with the flashlight, I mean.[2]

A simple tabulation of the specific colors and frequency of their occurrences in the works of Hemingway indicates these conclusions: Hemingway used a disproportionate amount of blacks, whites, and grays. Of the primary colors, he used reds and many yellows–almost always pure. Of the secondary colors, he used much green and some orange and purple. His blues were seldom pure, often qualified with adjectives such as "metallic" or "muddy" or combined with other colors such as green. The color he used most often, however, is brown: people's faces are brown, mountains are brown, shadows are brown, and cathedrals are brown. The Hemingway palette was rather limited.

Actually, Hemingway did not use specific colors or tones very often. Some short stories, such as "Ten Indians," do not contain a single reference to any color; others, such as "Che Ti Dice la Patria?" or "Big Two-Hearted River," are comparatively colorful. In much the same way, *For Whom the Bell Tolls* is a relatively colorless novel, while *The Sun Also Rises* abounds in color. Some

1 *Death in the Afternoon*, p. 205.
2 "A Natural History of the Dead," *The Short Stories of Ernest Hemingway*, p. 544.

fiction is predominantly one color: "A Natural History of the Dead" is yellow; *A Farewell to Arms* is dominantly gray. Thus when Hemingway does mention a specific color, even the colorless all-color white, it is worth noting.

I have already noted two special instances of color usage. In "The Snows of Kilimanjaro," Hemingway seemingly attempted to imitate the complex color modulations of Cézanne. And in *The Old Man and the Sea*, the purples and phosphorescent reds, so unlike the usual colors used by Hemingway, seem to be intended for the same effects achieved by Klee in his marine paintings. These two examples are unique in Hemingway's fiction.

Hemingway consistently used certain colors for definition of specific qualities or elements. Dead people are nearly always yellow, unless they have been dead long enough to be yellow-green or black. The faces of peasants or of healthy men who work outdoors, such as Pedro Romero, are nearly always brown, sometimes tan or ruddy. Conversely, when Hemingway specifically mentions a white face, such as Lady Brett Ashley's in *The Sun Also Rises* (25), the reader is alerted to the indoor, unhealthy qualities of the character. Such a pattern of colors is not the result of intellectual or artistic laziness on Hemingway's part. Yellow bodies and brown faces are images grounded in reality. Dead people do, in fact, appear to be yellow, and the complexion of a woman like Brett would be white. On the other hand, the specific use of yellow intensifies the grotesque qualities of the dead, just as the designation of brown and white faces provides a symbolic shorthand for Hemingway.

The use of color as a symbol is not uncommon in Hemingway's fiction. In "The Short Happy Life of Francis Macomber," for example, the ruddy color of the face of the white hunter Wilson and the rose blouse of the dominant Margot Macomber are counterpointed by the red blood of the virile lion.[3] When Macomber succeeds in bravely facing and killing the buffalo, it is no surprise that he is now "natural" and that Wilson describes him as "a

3 See Joseph De Falco, *The Hero in Hemingway's Short Stories* (Pittsburgh, 1963), pp. 205ff.

ruddy fire eater" (133 and 130). Obviously, the red, ruddy, and rose tones are symbolic of dominance and of a virile strength.

Yet Hemingway was far more sensitive to color than my comments thus far might have indicated. In "Big Two-Hearted River," which is one of Hemingway's "colorful" short stories, color is more than visual; it becomes tactile: "He sat on the logs, smoking, drying in the sun, the sun warm on his back, the river shallow ahead entering the woods, curving into the woods, shallows, light glittering, big water-smooth rocks, cedars along the banks and white birches, the logs warm in the sun, smooth to sit on, without bark, gray to the touch; slowly the feeling of disappointment left him" (325). "Gray to the touch!" The integration of color and form! The creation of form by color was obviously one of Cézanne's major contributions to the modern school. Perhaps Nick Adams's tactile response to a visual quality can be associated with Hemingway's own observations concerning Cézanne's "Rocks of the Forest:" "This is what we try to do in writing, this and this, and the woods, and the rocks we have to climb over."[4] Hemingway's specific reference to "the rocks we have to climb over" indicates his own tactile response to the volumes of those large gray rocks in the shadowy forest of Fontainebleau. Cézanne had formed these volumes primarily by color which, at least for Hemingway, had become something tactile, something which it was necessary "to climb over."

The entire passage is quite consciously a study of volume and color, with the tones predominantly gray and white. The repetition of "shallow" as an adjective and then "shallows" as a noun gives volume to the river, as Hemingway's rather poetic[5] "water-smooth" gives a sculptured quality to the rocks. The sun's white glitter contrasts with the gray and is counterpointed by the white birches. Hemingway's refusal to designate the cedars as brown further emphasizes the dominant white-gray scheme. Indeed, it is clear that, in this passage, the omission of certain colors is a con-

4 Quoted in Lillian Ross, *Portrait of Hemingway* (New York, 1961), p. 60.

5 E. E. Cummings had already used this phrase, without the hyphen, in his poem "Buffalo Bill's," which was published in 1923.

scious attempt to emphasize those which are specifically mentioned. Thus although Hemingway attempted Cézanne's intricate color modulations only in "The Snows of Kilimanjaro," he obviously sought to mold volume in terms of color tones, as Cézanne had.

Indeed, all the landscapes in which gray, green, brown, and occasionally orange and red predominate seem to be those in which volume is most clearly emphasized and which must be based upon Hemingway's understanding of Cézanne. Examine, for example, this passage from *The Sun Also Rises*:

> The country was barren and rocks stuck up through the clay.... Far back the fields were squares of green and brown on the hillsides. Making the horizon were the brown mountains. They were strangely shaped.... Then the road came over the crest, flattened out, and went into a forest. It was a forest of cork oaks, and the sun came through the trees in patches, and there were cattle grazing back in the trees. We went through the forest and the road came out, and turned along a rise of land, and out ahead of us was a rolling green plain, with dark mountains beyond it. These were not like the brown, heat-baked mountains we had left behind. These were wooded and there were clouds coming down from them. The green plain stretched off. It was cut by fences and the white of the road showed through the trunks of a double line of trees that crossed the plain toward the north. As we came to the end of the rise we saw the red roofs and white houses of Burguete strung out along the plain, and away off on the shoulder of the first dark mountain was the gray metal-sheathed roof of the monastery of Roncesvalles [108].

Here the contrast of the two mountain ranges—the brown, heat-baked mountains at the beginning of the trip and the tree-covered range near Burguete—indicates the movement from the corrupt plain to the mountain idyll. In much the same way, the movement from the barren land of clay to the "rolling green plain" is further evidence of the more traditional, literary use of color symbolism. In this sense, Hemingway has allowed his colors to complement and even to foreshadow the psychological situation of the observer Jake. Note too that Hemingway has structured the vista in a traditional manner with his establishment of a foreground, middleground, and background.

On the other hand, there is a very careful arrangement of color in this passage. Hemingway has consciously highlighted this passage with specific colors. The plain itself is green and rolling, with the white road leading through it to the village and then to the dark, wooded mountains beyond. In the pictorial plane represented by a single mountain between the village and the mountain range is the gray monastery. Thus the dominant color is the green of the plain which is concluded by the dark mountains. Note especially that Hemingway has refused to designate the mountains as any particular color. They are simply "dark"; the color is neither the brown of the sterile mountains which Jake viewed at the beginning of the trip nor a blue or purple which might have diminished the dominating and closing effect which Hemingway desired.[6] Black would not be realistic, since the hills are wooded. Had Hemingway been painting this scene, he probably would have used a mixed color of some kind, perhaps green mixed with black or gray or blue.

The road which crosses the plain is emphasized by the double row of trees and is the usual type of diagonal used by both Cézanne and Hemingway in their landscapes. This road, however, is white and "showed through the trunks" of the trees—a seemingly unnecessary and superfluous touch. However, the white of the road is picked up by the cloud patches from the mountains and the white houses of Burguete. The gray of the monastery is also contrasted to the dark of the mountains; it moves the monastery out from its mountain background. The only bright or cool color in the vista is the red of the roofs of Burguete, which stand out aggressively.

In short, the entire vista is given life and movement by Hem-

6 Cézanne occasionally used dominant blue for his mountains, but the blue is carefully modulated in such a way as to maintain the position of the mountain solidly in space.

ingway's choice and placement of color. The scene is defined by color—an amazing achievement. A writer is working under a severe handicap if and when he might attempt to imitate the type of complex color modulation or color orchestration used by painters from Cézanne to the present. When Hemingway did try such a modulation, even to a limited degree, as in "The Snows of Kilimanjaro," he was forced continually to qualify his colors as "gray-yellow" and "purple-brown." Obviously, in any extended passage, such a constant qualification of color would be both boring and confusing to the reader. We can presume, I believe, that Hemingway was well aware of the limitations of labeling something as simply "green" or "dark": What is the tone or quality of "green"? What kind of "dark"?

Despite these limitations, in this passage from *The Sun Also Rises*, he has been able to create a really vibrant and dynamic vista without complex color modulation. It is a scene in which the reds and the whites jump out from the page and in which the gray clearly stands out from the solid and substantial darkness of the mountains. Cézanne could very well have created this scene on canvas; the planes are clearly marked, with the fences suggesting further geometrical divisions. Hemingway's specific mention of the trunks of the trees gives them solidity, and even the green plain is "rolling." Obviously the colors are Cézanne's—without modulation. The particular arrangement of the colors, however, is Hemingway's.

Hemingway has created a color orchestration based upon the most modern of color theories, for the plastic use of color or the use of color as an integral component of the formal structure of a painting has been one of the major discoveries in twentieth-century art. Today we can open even the most elementary handbook for Sunday painters to read of the theory of advancing and recessive colors. For us it is common knowledge that colors have dynamic properties: that blue, green, and blue-green recede, but that red, orange, and certain yellows advance. All paintings are created today with the consciousness of this principle, but in Paris in the 1920's, the principle was newly discovered, or perhaps newly realized. The excitement at this new understanding of color continued even into the 1930's and can be easily understood in this passage written by Sheldon Cheney in 1934: "But exceptional cases and non-color arts aside, the revolutionary truth is that color and texture have been discovered recently as harboring properties of 'movement' totally unrecognized in the preceding era. Important as may be the principles codified by the adherents of tonality and scaled values, this other matter of the dynamic properties of color is incomparably more important to the student of Expressionism."[7]

Apparently the artists following Cézanne simply discovered this principle from a close study of his color modulations. The moderns did not deny that artists preceding Cézanne had some understanding of this concept, but they insisted that pre-Cézanne painters simply worked out these properties in an intuitive manner, without any conscious understanding of this principle. Further, the moderns believed that it was the impressionists who had freed color from traditional schemes, but that it was Cézanne who fully understood and pictorially stated this principle. If used correctly in conjunction with form and design, color orchestration was an integral part of the new plastic art or of Cheney's "Expressionism," which included painters of nearly all the schools of the 1920's. Clearly this principle of color ultimately became the basis of such movements as Jackson Pollack's abstract expressionism and the recently current op art.

It is possible to assume that Hemingway simply imitated intuitively Cézanne's own color arrangements to create the vibrating passage describing the plain of Burguete. Hemingway could very well have been sensitive enough to Cézanne's color arrangements to reproduce them in a conscious or unconscious way. On the other hand, it is entirely possible that Hemingway fully understood the principles of the "dynamic properties of color." This "new" discovery was obviously still exciting knowledge in Paris in the 1920's and was used in one way or another by every artist whom Hemingway seems to have known at the time.

7 Sheldon Cheney, *Expressionism in Art* (New York, 1939), p. 246.

The passage from *The Sun Also Rises* is certainly constructed with some understanding–intuitive or otherwise–of this principle. The dominant green of the plain is recessive, moving the eye back over the rolling contours and the geometrical fields defined by the fences. The white of the road cutting through the plain advances and emphasizes the diagonal movement. Ending with the advancing reds and whites of the village, the road has carried the eye into the vista but at the same time has set up a tension with the recessive green. The perspective is concluded with the dark mountains which, in this color context, I would assume to be somewhat advancing. The "dark" situates the mountains clearly in space, keeping the eye from wandering into deeper space. Even more advancing are the presumably white clouds "coming down from them," which contribute to the plastic qualities of the vista in two ways: by their association with the whites of the road and the houses, and by carrying the movement across the mountains. The mountains are tied to the city and plain by the gray roof of the monastery–which is undoubtedly an advancing, rather than a neutral, gray, given the color context. And although the pictorial planes of the vista are clearly delineated, Hemingway was able to flatten and foreshorten the landscape much as Cézanne did. The receding, rolling green is counterbalanced by the dark mountains, the gray monastery, the red roofs, and the whites of the road, the houses, and the clouds. In short, Hemingway seems to have created this passage with full knowledge of the most sophisticated techniques of color orchestration known in his day.

It is no mean achievement. Hemingway has created on a white page with black type a vibrantly colorful vista–a vista which is, in fact, formed and defined primarily by color. It is a passage which commands the reader to use his total visual responses, as well as a tactile sensitivity. Amazingly enough, the novelist was able to create this color orchestration by techniques just opposite those used by Cézanne or by Matisse, who was a contemporary and friend of Hemingway's. Both of these painters employed a full palette to create their dynamic color effects. As a part of his orchestration, Cézanne's modulations for individual objects are well known. Matisse blended colors in a daring fashion within the total context; in order to push empty space forward, or, in a sense, to give empty space volume, Matisse might use reds or rose-grays. Hemingway, on the other hand, never let his colors wander far from reality (no red space for him!), nor did he try to modulate colors, except on rare occasions.

Using colors which would be familiar to any reader,[8] Hemingway consciously withheld too many mentions of even these colors in order to awaken the reader to their significance. Had Hemingway splashed various tones across his page, the reader would have become insensitive through the effort of trying to assimilate all these colors. Even in a passage such as Jake's view of the plain of Burguette, the colors have been slowly and carefully introduced. There is a conscious spacing between mentions of specific colors, and Hemingway has been careful to differentiate between the dark mountains near Burguete and the brown mountains which were seen at the beginning of the trip. Although Hemingway might have been employing the color orchestration of the moderns, he has been forced to find his own means for communicating it. By minimizing the number of colors in any one description, by simplifying the intricacies of color modulation, and by carefully arranging specific colors, Hemingway was able to create a dynamic vista in which color, volume, form, and arrangement are totally integrated.

This is not a unique passage, but it is the most successful in terms of color integration. Other passages in which Hemingway seems to be consciously creating a similar effect are scattered throughout his fiction.[9] The fact that most of these are landscapes suggests the general influence of Cézanne, but it is reasonable also to assume that Hemingway understood the principle

8 The only possible example of a color which might not be immediately recognizable to everyone is magenta, which Hemingway used to describe lobsters in *Across the River and into the Trees*, p. 192.

9 See, e.g., "Che Ti Dice la Patria?," *The Short Stories of Ernest Hemingway*, p. 388; "A Canary for One," ibid., p. 435; "Big Two-Hearted River," ibid., p. 325; *The Sun Also Rises*, pp. 93, 117, and 238; *For Whom the Bell Tolls*, p. 96; and *A Farewell to Arms*, pp. 215–16.

of plastic color since it was not common knowledge in the 1920's, but a very exciting discovery.

In passages other than landscapes, Hemingway used few such intricate arrangements of color. One passage, however, is noteworthy. In *For Whom the Bell Tolls*, the omniscient narrator juxtaposes, in color, the responses of Maria and Jordan as they make love: ". . . and for her everything was red, orange, gold-red from the sun on the closed eyes, and it all was that color, all of it, the filling, the possessing, the having, all of that color, all in a blindness of that color. For him it was a dark passage which led to nowhere . . ." (159). The bright and advancing colors of Maria's response are given a realistic basis because of the glare of the sun, but the startling burst of color emphasizes the dramatic nature of Maria's experience. Curiously, Hemingway's own modulation of these colors is from red to orange to gold-red. To be sure, each one is a strongly advancing tone. Were one to chart the color relationship, there would be a circular pattern: red (primary color) to orange (secondary) to gold (a form of yellow which is the next primary color) and back to red. In this description itself, there is obviously no contrast of advancing and recessive colors. Maria's response is simply a burst of brilliant color–comparable, for example, even in tone and modulation, to certain of Van Gogh's "Sunflowers" (National Gallery, London).

The red, orange, and gold-red are carefully juxtaposed to the dark, psychic tunnel of Jordan's sexual response. In this passage, the emphasis is clearly upon Jordan's experience, since he is, after all, the protagonist of the novel, as well as its central fictive consciousness. Clearly, Maria's colorful response is a preparation for the dark passage of Jordan's mind to nowhere. Although Hemingway has not really used color in this passage in the same sense that Matisse integrated it or that Hemingway himself had used it in certain landscape descriptions, the color is employed in a manner sophisticated enough to suggest further something of Hemingway's understanding of the moderns' principles of dynamic color.

The two colors Hemingway used most, however, do not have

consistently advancing or receding qualities—yellow and brown. To a great extent, each is a tone whose property depends ultimately upon the color surrounding it. Generally speaking, brown and yellow are advancing in Hemingway's fiction. If any color could be called a favorite of Hemingway's, it must be brown. Brown itself is composed of the primary colors red, yellow, and blue, although painters usually mix it by combining orange and blue or purple and yellow. It is an earthy, generally warm color. On the other hand, it is also a dry color, as of a dry, scorched, sterile earth. And therein, in this paradoxical nature of its connotations, I suppose, lies its special significance for Hemingway. For example, water can be dirty brown, muddy brown, or clear brown. In *Across the River and into the Trees*, the dirty canals of Venice are brown and contrast to the clean brass of the boat in which Colonel Cantwell is riding (145). Muddy brown water is generally the result of rain or is simply the color of a river itself, such as the Mississippi.[10] In "Che Ti Dice la Patria?" however, the muddy brown of a rain-swollen Italian river becomes symbolic of Fascist Italy: "A riverbed that, when we had passed, going into Italy, had been wide, strong, and dry, was running brown and up to the banks. The brown water discolored the sea . . ." (395). Yet clear, brown water can also be evidence of health, as in "Big Two-Hearted River": "Nick looked down into the clear, brown water, colored from the pebbly bottom, and watched the trout keeping themselves steady in the current with wavering fins" (307).

Paradoxical also are brown mountains. In *The Sun Also Rises*, they are evidence of a kind of wasteland which Jake and Bill are leaving as they go to Burguete: "The country was barren and rocks stuck up through the clay. . . . Making the horizon were the brown mountains. They were strangely shaped" (108). Yet Santiago's brown mountains are associated in his dream with peace and youth: "He was asleep in a short time and he dreamed of Africa when he was a boy and the long golden beaches and the white beaches, so white they hurt your eyes, and the high

10 *Across the River and into the Trees*, p. 26.

capes and the great brown mountains" (26–27). Other browns are not used with such ambiguity: brown fields almost always suggest a dry and sterile land, as in *The Sun Also Rises*, in which the sterile brown land corresponds with the brown mountains. Generally, brown land is contrasted with white, as in, for example, "Hills Like White Elephants": "The girl was looking off at the line of hills. They were white in the sun and the country was brown and dry. 'They look like white elephants,' she said" (371). The imaginative response of the girl to the hills indicates her sense of helplessness and pathos as she faces an abortion. The brown land, obviously, corresponds to the sterility of her love affair, ending as it does with an abortion and an insensitive lover. "Medium brown" locusts, however, are good for fishing—better even than those other locusts with "varied wing colors."[11]

In short, brown is a color which served many functions for Hemingway. It can simply provide the realistic texture, as of brown rivers and brown locusts. As Hemingway used brown, it can also be symbolic, but in a paradoxical fashion. By associating brown with other descriptive words or with certain characters, Hemingway was able to use brown for different symbolic purposes. Finally, brown is a color which can be either advancing or receding, depending upon its color context; hence it can be a versatile element within any color orchestration. If any artist used brown to a great extent, it was Cézanne. His tones were seldom pure, but, blended with oranges and yellows, Cézanne's browns created mountains, land, tree trunks, rocks, and even clouds. The warm, earthy color of brown would undoubtedly have attracted both Cézanne and Hemingway, who shared a love of the earth. Their own complex visions of the land could be expressed both symbolically and visually by this versatile color.

Although numerically there are more mentions of brown in Hemingway's fiction, his use of yellow is more interesting. Yellow is also a versatile color, another tone that recedes or advances as its color context dictates. Much as he used brown, Hemingway entrusted yellow with a number of responsibilities. Yellow is not

11 "A Way You'll Never Be," *The Short Stories of Ernest Hemingway*, p. 509.

only the color of the dead; it is also the color of the near dead as in *The Sun Also Rises*: "Belmonte's jaw came further out in contempt, and his face turned yellower . . . and always the pain that any movement produced grew stronger and stronger, until finally his yellow face was parchment color" (214). Yellow is also the color of explosions or of the earth following explosions: "he threw four grenades into the . . . torn yellow-stained explosive-stinking earth before he climbed out of the bomb crater."[12] And there are other unpleasant associations: the eyes of the sharks in *The Old Man and the Sea*; the yellow of the flooding Maritza River in the vignette which begins "Minarets stuck up in the rain out of Adrianople"; and the yellow mucus of Spanish influenza.[13]

Fields of crops and flowers are also yellow, however, and they provide a life-associated contrast to the death or war yellow: "The hills ahead were not wooded, and there were great fields of yellow gorse" or "in the valley the grain-fields were yellow."[14] Moreover, the beaches at San Sebastian where Jake swims to recuperate from the festival at Pamplona are yellow (234), and "yellow gray" (an unusual color modulation for Hemingway) is the color of the sun as the Colonel and Renata watch it displace the gray stormy light over the Venetian canals (205). In short, the symbolic significance of yellow depends upon the context, but Hemingway's associations with this color are generally unpleasant.

Mention should be made of one special and unique yellow with which Hemingway suggests a sense of dynamic movement in *The Sun Also Rises*: "Ahead of the formal procession and behind it danced the *riau-riau* dancers. There was one mass of yellow shirts dancing up and down in the crowd" (155). Shortly before this passage, he has described another *riau-riau* group: "When the

12 *For Whom the Bell Tolls*, p. 322. This is a very common use of yellow. See, e.g., *The Fifth Column and Four Stories of the Spanish Civil War*, pp. 110–11; "A Natural History of the Dead," *The Short Stories of Ernest Hemingway*, p. 542; and *For Whom the Bell Tolls*, p. 310. Sometimes explosions are red, as in *A Farewell to Arms*, p. 41, and *For Whom the Bell Tolls*, p. 321.

13 "A Natural History of the Dead," p. 543.

14 *The Sun Also Rises*, p. 117, and "Wine of Wyoming," *The Short Stories of Ernest Hemingway*, p. 548.

fifers stopped they all crouched down in the street, and when the reedpipes and the fifes shrilled, and the flat, dry, hollow drums tapped it out again, they all went up in the air dancing. In the crowd you saw only the heads and shoulders of the dancers going up and down" (153). The yellow is here quite advancing, blended with the action of the dancers.

Even more interesting in this passage is Hemingway's attempt to describe the motion of the dancers, first in terms of only a part of their bodies and next in terms of color. This is not the way Goya created movement in his etchings, such as those of "Tauromaquia," nor is it the way Hemingway has created movement elsewhere, as in fistfights or bullfights. The technique of creating movement in these two short passages is related more closely to the methods originally formulated before World War I by the Italian futurists and the orphists, but continued into the 1920's by painters such as Picabia, Delauney, and Duchamp.

While the cubists were examining objects simultaneously and representing them in static planes, the futurists and orphists were using simultaneous techniques to express the speed and movement of modern life, with emphasis upon machines and steel. The Italian group stated that, for example, a running horse had twenty feet, not four: "They therefore painted horses, or dogs, or human beings, with multiple limbs in a serial or radial arrangement. Sound, too, could be represented as a succession of waves, color as a prismatic rhythm."[15] The bold colors of the Italian group influenced others, especially the orphists.[16] Eventually the dynamism of modern life which the futurists and orphists attempted to express became the domain of cinematography, but futurism and orphism left lasting effects.

The best-known expression of this dynamic simultaneity and a painting with which Hemingway was certainly familiar is Duchamp's "Nude Descending the Stars" (1912). Here Duchamp depicted the action of the nude by giving her a number of geo-

15 Herbert Read, *A Concise History of Modern Art* (New York, 1959), p. 110.
16 Werner Haftmann, *Painting in the Twentieth Century* I, trans. Ralph Manheim (New York, 1965), pp. 110–11.

metrically designed legs, arms, torsos, and heads. In order to create an action of a group, Picabia, for example, used overlapping and interweaving triangles to represent the upper torsos and heads of the participants, and he only suggested the swifter movement of legs by highlighted grays and a few long black rectangles. Indeed, Picabia's "Procession in Seville" (1912) might very well have been the pictorial model for Hemingway's *riau-riau* dancers, so close in the expression of action are they. Where Picabia used an advancing and bright orange to suggest shirts, Hemingway used yellows. Whether or not Hemingway had ever seen Picabia's "Procession in Seville" will probably never be known, but he was familiar with Picabia's work: "Ezra [Pound] also liked Picabia's painting but I thought then that it was worthless."[17] Presumably, sometime later, Hemingway discovered a value in Picabia's works.

All of these uses of yellow are obviously related in a realistic manner with their natural context. Recently dead faces are yellow, and grain fields are yellow. This is not to say that their symbolic significance is not important; it is. There are other uses of yellow, however, in which the symbolic quality of the color is not necessarily related to any natural yellow or to any special use of plastic color. In dream scenes or passages of psychic confusion or introspection, yellow is almost always a central or dominant color.

Consider Santiago's dream: "He was asleep a short time and he dreamed of Africa when he was a boy and the long golden beaches and the white beaches . . ." (26–27). Or, in "A Way You'll Never Be," the shell-shocked and half-mad Nick associates a yellow house and river with the terror of the war: "but those were the nights the river ran so much wider and stiller than it should and outside Fossalta there was a low house painted yellow with willows all around it and a low stable and there was a canal, and he had been there a thousand times and never seen it, but there it was every night as plain as the hill, only it frightened him" (506). Later, when his friend Captain Paravicini tells Nick to lie down, the delusion returns: "He [Nick] shut his eyes, and in place of the man with the beard who looked at him over the sights of the

17 *A Moveable Feast,* p. 107.

rifle, quite calmly before squeezing off, the white flash and club-like impact, on his knees, hot-sweet choking, coughing it on to the rock while they went past him, he saw a long, yellow house with a low stable and the river much wider than it was and stiller" (512). Of course, the Captain does not shoot Nick; Nick has lost touch with reality after the words "the man with the beard." Gray-yellow is the color of a plain in Harry's death dream in "The Snows of Kilimanjaro" (174). Other colors appear in these passages, but yellow is the only tone which Hemingway used consistently in passages of illusion. In each of these instances, yellow represents a certain sense of peace or safety. The yellow of Santiago's African beaches, the yellow of the house beside the still river to which Nick escapes in his delusions, the yellow shading of the plain as Harry flies to Kilimanjaro—all indicate another world of reality in which the protagonists have found peace.

Such a use of yellow is odd since it is a color not usually associated with peace and safety. In the colloquialism which Hemingway himself had used in "Today Is Friday," yellow connotes cowardice (456). And I have already shown that yellow, for Hemingway at least, more typically suggests war and death or, occasionally, the beauty of a field of flowers. Yellow as symbolic of a kind of spiritual rest is simply not a usual connotation. In the epigraph to this chapter, however, Hemingway states that yellow is one color that El Greco "believed in."

If we examine El Greco's use of yellow, it is clear that his yellows often describe the faces of saints experiencing a spiritual vision or ecstasy, as in "The Martyrdom of St. Maurice" (ca. 1580–82; Escorial), or unworldliness, such as the Gloria of "The Burial of Conde de Orgaz" (1586–88; Sante Tomé, Toledo). El Greco, of course, blended his yellows (that is, he muted or heightened them) as he felt necessary, but it is his particular uses of yellow which art critics and historians nearly always note first when they examine El Greco's color integrations. Harold E. Wethey has observed, "His use of pale tones of yellow, green, blue, and rose in the Gloria of the 'Burial of Conde de Orgaz' and in later works . . . cannot be considered apart from the all-pervading delicacy of color in the Italian Mannerist schools of painting. . . . Nevertheless, he sought unique effects in dazzling contrasts of yellow against blue and against rose. . . ."[18]

Indeed, it seems to me that it is El Greco's yellows which contribute so much to the disembodied reality of his androgynous forms. It should be remembered that El Greco's use of color is one characteristic which Hemingway's friend Henry Strater claims attracted the moderns to El Greco. In fact, in a book like Cheney's *Expressionism in Art*, El Greco's paintings are reproduced almost as often as Cézanne's or Matisse's and are cited as precursors of the modern developments in color orchestration as well as color-volume relationship. In short, both symbolically and technically, El Greco's yellows could have suggested to Hemingway this very special use of yellow.

Santiago, Nick Adams, and Harry were not experiencing any sort of spiritual vision or ecstasy as they dreamed or mentally projected their yellow beaches, yellow houses, and yellow plains. Nor was Santiago or Nick or Harry ascending to a yellowish Gloria like the Conde de Orgaz. They were, however, experiencing a beauty and peacefulness which, in Hemingway's fictional world anyway, corresponds to the heavenly and spiritual bliss of El Greco's saints and spirits. Nor has Hemingway been especially conscious of color integration in these passages of dreams and delusions (except in the passage from "The Snows of Kilimanjaro"). Yet the recurrence of yellow in such passages, written as they were over a span of nearly twenty years,[19] suggests that yellow has a very special significance for Hemingway.

It should be clear by now that Hemingway's refusal to splash his pages with pigment is the result of his respect for color and his rather sophisticated understanding of its uses. Thus when a color is mentioned in Hemingway's fiction, it is nearly always an alert. When he specifically mentions a color, Hemingway is asking the reader to take special note, whether of the symbolic qualities of

18 Harold E. Wethey, *El Greco and His School* (Princeton, N.J., 1962), p. 57.

19 "A Way You'll Never Be" was completed in 1932, "The Snows of Kilimanjaro" in 1936, and *The Old Man and the Sea* in 1951.

the passage or of the artistic merit of the color orchestration or integration within the passage. Color was thus a very carefully considered and consciously applied element in Hemingway's fiction.

It is easy to understand that Hemingway, as an artist, was sensitive to color and that his sensitivity found expression in the concepts underlying the most sophisticated color orchestrations of Cézanne and the moderns. It does not seem too great a conjecture to speculate that Hemingway physically associated colors with sense impressions. His fictional figures actually associated color with physical sensations. I have already noted that in "Big Two-Hearted River," Nick responded in a tactile manner to the gray of the tree trunks: "the logs . . . gray to the touch." Throughout *For Whom the Bell Tolls*, there is a veritable synaesthesia of sense and color: Maria's sexual climax is "red, orange, gold-red." Robert Jordan smells yellow: "His face was down against the pebbles as the bridge settled where it had risen and the familiar yellow smell of it rolled over him in acrid smoke" (445). The noise and force of a bomb explosion is comprehended by El Sordo as a color: "Then, through the hammering of the gun, there was the whistle of the air splitting apart and then in the red black roar the earth rolled under his knees" (321). Finally, the motion of the *riau-riau* dancers in *The Sun Also Rises* is yellow: "There was one mass of yellow shirts dancing up and down in the crowd."

In all these passages, there is a conscious attempt to associate physical sensations with colors. In a sense, Hemingway combined techniques of both the verbal and pictorial arts in creating this color-sense coordination. A painter can only make an object smell as it does or feel as it does by a limited number of devices, one of which is color. It is the artist of words who can tell what something smells like or feels like. For a writer of fiction to achieve a real sensual suggestion (not just an abstract "this is what it smells like") is quite difficult; he might be forced to a metaphor or to an extended explanation, which could be awkward. Hemingway, it seems to me, used color as a painter might: to suggest the actual sensual quality. As an artist of words, however, he could also add a word or two to explain further the specific sensual quality.

Cézanne must depend upon colors—greens, blues, and browns—to suggest the clean, fertile smell of Aix-en-Provence; Goya can only suggest the sound of the clash of battle between the Spanish and the Marmalukes by the tumult of the action and by the brilliant splashes of reds and whites. Hemingway, however, was able to combine the two methods in a most effective manner. When El Sordo experiences the bombing of the hill, Hemingway can use both the colors ("red black") and the word ("roar"). He has thus created an even more specific suggestion of sensation. In a passage such as this, he has succeeded in making words act like paint. He has been able to transpose into words a technique originally created for the canvas. In so doing, he has further extended the sensual aspects of his own fiction. El Sordo's "red black roar" is a sensual statement with both visual and audile qualities. In short, Hemingway has borrowed from another art form to create a synaesthetically sensual fiction.

Thus far in this chapter, I have emphasized only color, not blacks, whites, or grays. Hemingway used a great many of these tones—all generally pure, but occasionally modulated with colors such as green or yellow. Sometimes blacks, whites, and grays are used to describe an object realistically, often simply to provide texture. For example, in *Across the River and into the Trees*, a sausage which the Colonel eats is "black pepper-corned" (190). Occasionally a black and white contrast suggests a simple symbolic significance. Thus in *The Sun Also Rises*, before Pedro Romero is introduced to Brett, he wears a matador's suit of white linen (163), but after he has spent the night with Brett, he chooses a black suit for the bullfight (212). It is significant that the only dress described in this novel is Brett's black evening gown (146).

On the other hand, Hemingway often used blacks, whites, and grays for a very special effect which can best be described in the language of the pictorial arts as chiaroscuro, or the balance of light and shadow, generally for a dramatic effect. In the paintings of artists such as Rembrandt and Caravaggio, in whom the effect is quite pronounced, the light is generally white or yellow and emanates from, for example, a lantern, the sun, or a religious figure. The shadows are heavy and dark and are often quite sharply juxtaposed to the brightness of the light. It is not to Caravaggio and Rembrandt that Hemingway's use of chiaroscuro is related; in the epigraph to this chapter, Hemingway has especially noted the use of chiaroscuro in the works of Goya: "a good etching for Goya, the visit with the flashlight."

Goya's works, especially the etchings, are today models for the use of light and shadow. With a great economy of means, Goya employs only a few shades (jet black, one or two grays, and white) to create the heightened dramatic effects of "The Disasters of War" or "The Caprices": "Goya's chiaroscuro, which regulated the entire lay-out and becomes his unmistakable signature, brings *The Caprices* directly into line with the tradition of Rembrandt. As Beethoven extended the range of emotional expression in music, so did Goya extend it in the plastic arts, at much the same time."[20] Paradoxically, the boldness and simplicity of Goya's etchings are thus the cause of their symbolic and dramatic richness. In a large sense, this same economy is present in Goya's paintings. Light seems to emanate from the white shirt of the Christ-like central figure in "The Third of May." The light is actually being reflected from a lantern in front of the firing squad. Thrown into the shadow on the right are the stiff and impersonal soldiers, on the left the huddled figure of the Virgin Mary. The brilliant white of the prisoner's shirt dominates and controls the scene, which is expressed with a minimum of color variation and modulation.

In many scenes, Hemingway was able to achieve a similar dramatic effect with an economy of means. Thus, for example, in many of the outdoor scenes in *For Whom the Bell Tolls*, Hemingway constantly juxtaposed the whiteness of the snow and the black or darkness of rocks or of a silhouetted horseback rider: "Now in the night he lay and waited for the girl to come to him. . . . The trunks of the pines projected from the snow that

20 Pierre Gassier, *Goya* (New York, 1955), p. 54.

covered all the ground. . . . He . . . settled deeper into the robe as he watched, across the snow, the dark break in the rocks that was the entrance to the cave. The sky was clear and there was enough light reflected from the snow to see the trunks of the trees and the bulk of the rocks where the cave was" (258). Lying in his sleeping robe in the snow, Jordan is waiting for Maria to come to him from the dark entrance of the cave; he becomes fearful that she might not come to him or that she might not come into the whiteness, where he was waiting, from the black depths of the cave.

Even without the natural chiaroscuro effect of night, moon, snow, and rocks, Hemingway could create a scene with dazzling and dramatic light effects. In a passage with symbolic overtones, Robert Jordan is described just before dawn of the morning he is to blow the bridge—the last morning of his life: "Robert Jordan lay behind the trunk of a pine tree on the slope of the hill above the road and the bridge and watched it become daylight. He loved this hour of the day always and now he watched it; feeling it gray within him, as though he were a part of the slow lightening that comes before the rising of the sun, when solid things darken and space lightens and the lights that have shone in the night go yellow and then fade as the day comes" (431). As the passage continues, those darkened "solid things" become colorful, as, for example, the pine trees become brown. Hemingway carefully and consciously constructed this passage, which introduces and foreshadows the final scene in the novel when Jordan once again is lying beneath the pine trees, but this time waiting for death. In both passages, Jordan's newly found happiness and peace with Maria are reflected in his sensitivity to nature or, as in this passage, in the grayness of the dawn which he feels "within him."

In other passages of chiaroscuro, Hemingway does not mention black or gray or white. He is able to achieve the dramatic effect simply by the use of the words "light" and "shadow," as in the opening passages from "A Clean, Well-Lighted Place": "It was late and everyone had left the café except an old man who sat in the shadow the leaves of the tree made against the electric light.

In the day time the street was dusty, but at night the dew settled the dust. . . . [The two waiters] sat together at a table that was close against the wall near the door of the café and looked at the terrace where the tables were all empty except where the old man sat in the shadow of the leaves that moved slightly in the wind. A girl and soldier went by in the street. The street light shone on the brass number on his collar" (477). Only three shades are indicated here: the brightness of the electric light and the street light, the shadow made by the tree, and the darkness of the night. The light and shadow placement itself is similar to many of Goya's etchings, such as etching 35 of "The Disasters of War," in which the prisoners are placed in the shadow of a building or tower. Goya has used at most four different tones in this etching: black, white, and two shades of gray. In etching 69, "Nada. Ella dira.," which is so closely related to the *nada* of "A Clean, Well-Lighted Place," Goya has used only three tones, with the whites most often contrasted with and directly juxtaposed to the jet black which melts into grays at the edges of the etching. In "A Clean, Well-Lighted Place," the analogy of light to safety and darkness to *nada* creates the tension within the short story. Hemingway has chosen to introduce and dramatize the psychological status of both the old man and the old waiter with a pictorial, chiaroscuro effect.

Much like Hemingway's sensual associations with colors, light too can have a tactile quality, as in this passage from *The Sun Also Rises*:

> At the end of the street I saw the cathedral and walked up toward it. . . . I went inside. It was dim and dark and the pillars went high up, and there were people praying, and it smelt of incense, and there were some wonderful big windows. I knelt and . . . prayed for everybody I thought of. . . . I was a little ashamed, and regretted that I was such a rotten Catholic. . . . And I only wished I felt religious . . . and then I was out in the hot sun on the steps of the cathedral, and the forefingers and thumb of my right hand were still damp, and I felt them dry in the sun. The sunlight was hot and hard . . . [97].

The dark of the cathedral has been carefully juxtaposed to the light of the sun. At first the darkness of the cathedral is a solace and comfort to Jake, but as he realizes that he is not religious, at least this time, he welcomes the brightness of the "hard" sunlight. The sensual description of the sunlight emphasizes the physical reality of the world to which Jake is returning from his unsuccessful attempt at communicating with the spiritual. Further emphasizing the chiaroscuro effect of this passage is the fact that the cathedral is dim and dark, even though it has "some wonderful big windows." That is, *some* light streams through those "wonderful big windows" of the cathedral—and Hemingway purposefully chose to ignore it. Had he wished to create a mystical, otherworldly scene inside the cathedral, he could have done so quite easily with the blending of colors from the windows, the smell of incense, and the deep shadows of the recesses of the cathedral interior. No, the scene has been quite consciously written in order to contrast the dim, dark interior of the cathedral with the tactile brightness of the sunlight.

Hemingway was also capable of creating a scene which is dramatically dominated by a single source of light. Against a generally dark background, he could flash a light which both illuminates and dominates the scene, as in this passage from *A Farewell to Arms*: "I ate the end of my piece of cheese. . . . Through the other noise I heard a cough, then came the chuh-chuh-chuh-chuh—then there was a flash as when a blast-furnace door is swung open, and a roar that started white and went red and on and on in a rushing wind" (56–57). Much as Goya chose to emphasize the white, light-reflecting shirt of the central peasant with his yellow trousers in "The Third of May," so has Hemingway complemented the white flash of the explosion with the advancing red. In both scenes, the whites advance strongly, with the help of yellow in Goya's canvas and red in Hemingway's passage.

Hemingway has been able to use the pictorial effects of chiaroscuro to create a number of dramatic effects. He was no doubt well aware of what he was doing. He himself obviously liked paintings which involved such dramatic contrasts of light and dark. Moreover, he could realize the pictorial effect of flashing a light in a dark room, as in the epigraph to this chapter. Goya's paintings and etchings, however, were not his only source for an understanding of chiaroscuro. The Italian artists, such as Titian and Tintoretto, whom Hemingway cited specifically, employed this particular pictorial technique.

At times Hemingway used black, white, and gray as colors. Gray, especially, is used quite often in scenes which are not created by means of chiaroscuro. I have already shown that gray was used, either as a pure color or in combination with other colors, in landscapes. It is also the color of the eyes of many characters, as well as the color of the horse upon which Robert Jordan is attempting to escape after the blowing of the bridge. For Colonel Cantwell, the Grand Canal is gray in the late afternoon of winter. There are a great many mentions of gray which could be termed an element of context or the realistic background.

Curiously enough, it is not with Goya that Hemingway seems to associate gray, but with Degas. In *Across the River and into the Trees*, Colonel Cantwell remarks that the Grand Canal "was now becoming as grey as though Degas had painted it on one of his greyest days" (71). Hemingway himself stated that "Degas is another wonder painter. I've never seen a bad Degas."[21] Goya, of course, was a master of gray modulation, especially in portraits such as "Woman in Grey" (ca. 1805; Louvre). Degas is not really noted for his use of gray, yet gray is a major color of his palette. Unlike the other impressionists who refused to use grays and blacks in shadows, Degas composed his shadows of grays and often created the diaphanous skirts of ballet dancers with grays, as, for example, in "Dancing Class at the Opera" (1872; Louvre). Actually his use of gray is much like Goya's, especially when one compares the skirts of Degas's ballet dancers and the gown of Goya's "Maja Clothed."

Perhaps it was the tactile qualities of Degas's gray skirts and Goya's gray gowns that suggested the "gray to the touch" logs which Nick senses in "Big Two-Hearted River." Gray was also

21 Quoted in Ross, *Portrait of Hemingway*, p. 50.

audile for Hemingway, as in *For Whom the Bell Tolls*: " 'Pull it farther back and let it snap lightly forward,' the *civil* said, and I have never heard such a tone of voice. It was grayer than a morning without sunrise" (101). Like the colors, gray is capable of sensual association and thus expands the synaesthetic qualities of Hemingway's fiction.

On the other hand, gray can also evoke symbolic and expressionistic associations. Hemingway noted that one of his favorite paintings in the New York Metropolitan Museum of Art was El Greco's "View of Toledo," which is a predominantly gray painting.[22] The eerie light emanating from a gray, stormy sky highlights the buildings of Toledo. Such unrealistic blue-white outlines of the buildings, as well as the foreboding gray clouds, create a dream-like atmosphere for some viewers, a symbol of mental turmoil and anguish for others. El Greco was not attempting to describe Toledo realistically; he has, for example, altered the lines of some buildings and rearranged others. His object here was effect, and his technique was a highly sophisticated use and contrast of gray, blue-white, and green.

It is curious that, as sensitive to color as Thomas Hudson is, only once does he describe a work or planned work in terms of color. Hudson continually notes the colors of the world around him, as in his descriptions of the sea, sky, and land, which are realistically perceived in pure, bright blues, greens, whites, and yellows (e.g., 3, 4, and 49). Only occasionally does Hudson perceive colors imaginatively or artistically, as, for example, when he sees a flock of flamingoes as a "roseate mass on a gray brown flat" (420). Of his paintings or planned paintings, only the images or subjects are described—except in one instance: "Then he thought that he should be painting it [a scene of nude men bathing in a rainstorm] himself with the ship against the roaring white of the surf that came through the driving gray outside with the

22 El Greco's "View of Toledo" probably appealed to Hemingway also for another reason: "With little cubic volumes of bluish-white paint the walls and buildings of Toledo are constructed bit by bit in a fashion which anticipates in a surprising way Cézanne's still more abbreviated methods." Harold E. Wethey, *El Greco and His School* (Princeton, N.J., 1962), p. 51.

black of the new squall coming out and the sun breaking through momentarily to make the rain silver and to shine on the bathers in the stern" (382–83). Clearly, Hudson is here interested not so much in the specific subject (the men bathing) as in the grays, silvers, blacks, and whites.

The sun in this painting would not really be a source of light so much as a giver of form and contrasting texture. The surf, the rain, and the squall would create their own illumination simply by their contrasting colors and forms. The spot of sun would be used to alter the texture of the rain and to define the forms of the bathing men. The painting itself would be a study in white, silver, gray, and black—with each tone an active, not neutral, color.

Interestingly enough, these same tones reoccur in Hudson's memories of "the happiest times" in Paris in the 1920's: as he rides his bicycle down the Champs Élysées, he sees the "high gray of the great arch" and the "blooming horsechestnuts," whose trunks are black and whose blossoms are "white and waxen" (448). These are the only colors in the entire passage! The simplicity and economy of tones suggest Goya's etchings. Yet it is Manet whom Hudson mentions at the end of the passage. Manet and the other impressionists often examined such scenes in terms of broad blocks of color, often using blacks and whites with no half-tones. Of course, the alternate title of James Abbott McNeill Whistler's portrait of his mother is "Arrangement in Black and Gray" (1872; Louvre). Yet as a group, the impressionists were far more colorful than Hudson's remembrance of the Champs Élysées or his projected painting of the bathing men.

Such gray scenes in *Islands in the Stream* are counterbalanced by the bright, sunny beaches and waters of Bimini. Two novels, *A Farewell to Arm* and *Across the River and into the Trees*, are generally "gray" novels. In *A Farewell to Arms*, gray is synonymous with hostility, the war, death—the agony of man. In the opening pages especially, the gray of the army is accentuated again and again. Later the gray of the storm clouds, the rain, and the plain indicates an alliance between violent man and violent nature. Frederic Henry can only take Catherine and escape to the clean, white mountains of Switzerland to achieve his separate peace. Significantly, the only gray mentioned during their sojourn in the Swiss mountains is the gray of a lake which lies below them in the valley where Catherine will die. To emphasize the contrast, Hemingway writes that the lake "down below" is "gray as steel" (302).

In *Across the River and into the Trees*, gray is also associated with death. Symbolically the Grand Canal is generally gray; morning is "gray-yellow"; the dead at Hurtgen were gray and yellow, Colonel Cantwell recalls (257); and a wolf is gray (24). In fact, in the most colorful passage in the novel, the dominant color is gray. The Colonel visits the fish market and describes with color the shrimp, the eels, and the sea itself, but it is the lobster which he examines most totally in terms of color: "In the market, spread on the slippery stone floor, or in their baskets, or their rope-handled boxes, were the heavy gray-green lobsters with their magenta overtones that presaged their death in boiling water" (192). In symbolic terms, the lobsters are just one other gray association with death which Cantwell makes as he contemplates his own death. Artistically, the Colonel's sensitivity to color and form is much like a painter's; his references to the textures of the "slippery stone floor," "their baskets," and "their rope-handled boxes" provide a visual, as well as tactile, contrast with the lobsters.

It is no coincidence that, as the Colonel enters the market, he looks "at the amount of fat on each carcass in the butcher section, as though he were enjoying the Dutch painters; whose names no one remembers, who painted, in perfection of detail, all things you shot, or that were eatable. A market is the closest thing to a good museum like the Prado or the Accademia" (191–92). Other than that this passage shows the Colonel as a connoisseur of both good paintings and good food (psychologists tell us that the two often go together), its most remarkable suggestion is the paralleling of the sensual stimulation of a market and a museum.[23] Food

23 Hemingway himself visited museums when he was hungry: "You got very hungry when you did not eat in Paris. . . . You could always go into the Luxembourg museum and all the paintings were sharpened and clearer and

is obviously a commodity which satisfies physical senses; on one level, the Colonel suggests that a museum stimulates him in much the same way! In fact, a market is the closest thing to a good museum. Certainly such an analogy suggests the type of response which paintings stimulated in the Colonel—and presumably in Hemingway.

Those Dutch painters whose names the Colonel has forgotten are easily identified. There were many of them: for example, at the Prado, Peter Boel, Frans Snyder, Gabriel Matsu, and others. The Accademia, which the Colonel also mentions, is devoted to the works of Italian painters; thus the Colonel's mention of this gallery is for association with Venice, the setting of the novel. Hemingway himself liked paintings of food. According to Henry Strater, "One day in a museum, we came upon a Rembrandt of a side of bloody beef. Hem said, 'Isn't that beautiful?' "[24]

That the thoughts of Dutch painters, the Prado, and the Accademia should lead the Colonel to a consciousness of the floor and baskets and lobsters—a consciousness which is dominated by pictorial elements—is a further indication of the artistry with which Hemingway constructed this and other passages. Hemingway's use of color is a continual attempt at re-creating pictorial effects with pictorial techniques. That Hemingway uses color so sparingly but so emphatically is evidence of his respect for its properties and its effects.

Beginning painters are taught that a single stroke of a brush can function in four ways: it can draw or describe edges, add a note of color, indicate volume, and define spatial position. A per-

more beautiful if you were belly-empty, hollow-hungry. I learned to understand Cézanne much better and to see truly how he made landscapes when I was hungry. I used to wonder if he were hungry too when he painted; but I thought possibly it was only that he had forgotten to eat. . . . Later I thought Cézanne was probably hungry in a different way." *A Moveable Feast*, p. 69.

24 Personal interview, Ogunquit, Maine, August 24, 1968. Although Strater could not remember which museum he and Hemingway were visiting, the painting is undoubtedly "The Slaughtered Ox" (1655; Louvre). This particular canvas has always excited interest; especially notable are copies made of it by, among others, Eugène Delacroix in the nineteenth century and Chaim Soutine in the twentieth century.

fect stroke can accomplish all of these functions at once. Artists like Goya or Cézanne emphasized economy and demanded that each brush stroke function as completely as possible. For them, a brush stroke was intensive and essential, as, for example, Cézanne's "color patches."

In much the same way, especially with reference to color and chiaroscuro, Hemingway was able to make words function. The exact and perfect word for which Hemingway continually searched corresponds to the exact and perfect brush stroke which artists like Cézanne and Goya always hoped to attain. Thus a bit of color in a scene, such as Jake's view of the plain of Burguete, can indeed describe edges, add a note of color, indicate volume, and define spatial position. In this sense, Hemingway has perhaps most successfully approximated with words the techniques of a painter.

However, to say "green" is not to paint green. Hemingway must still depend heavily upon the reader's willingness to transpose the word to the color or to read, as it were, in technicolor. As I have pointed out before, the limitations of the words themselves do not allow for the creation of exact colors or of extensive color modulation. On the other hand, an epithet of color in conjunction with a word or two of further explanation can sometimes be more effective and more exact than a painting. It seems to me that Hemingway was able to work out these problems with an artistry and sophistication based upon his own thorough understanding of both words and paint. At the same time, he was able to use techniques of painters to extend the synaesthetic quality of his own fiction.

VI

Character development and the psychological portrait

"We are devotees of the pictorial arts."

"I was looking at him as at a drawing by Goya. Faces are pictures too."[1]

These two passages indicate two different aspects of character development. In the first statement, Colonel Cantwell invites a waiter to show him a portrait of Renata in the middle of a hotel dining room during dinner. The statement itself may have been made in gentle jest, but it is an affirmation of the Colonel's interest in art—an affirmation which is confirmed and reconfirmed throughout the course of the novel. It is a statement concerning the personality of a character: what he values, what he enjoys, and what he thinks about.

The second statement, also the Colonel's, is his justification for staring at an American writer who happens to be drinking at Harry's Bar when the Colonel and Renata arrive. With this reference to Goya, Hemingway is suggesting that the description of the physical aspects of a character's face assumes a pictorial quality: that a true description of a face may demand the technical capability and devices of a painter. This is a statement concerning technique. Yet, as I have shown, technique in Hemingway's fiction is almost always inextricably associated with concept, symbol, or theme. Thus, with reference to the Colonel's specific mention of Goya, the careful depiction of a face in Hemingway's fiction might quite justifiably be considered a psychological por-

1 *Across the River and into the Trees*, pp. 144 and 90.

trait such as Goya himself painted. Both aspects of character development (as I have illustrated them in these two statements) eventually join together in the total development of a character.

One of the most interesting progressions throughout Hemingway's fiction is the increasing reference to art, until, in *Across the River and into the Trees*, Colonel Cantwell is allowed to assert, "We are devotees of the pictorial arts." Hemingway's next protagonist, Thomas Hudson, is himself a painter. By "reference to art," I mean the specific mention of an artist, a painting, a collection of etchings, a museum, or any other associated object. For example, in *The Sun Also Rises*, there is no specific mention of any kind of art. Yet this book abounds in Cézanne-inspired landscapes as well as other implied references to art. Thus the description of the bullfighting techniques of Pedro Romero (168) looks forward to Hemingway's comparison of a matador's "purity of line" to the sculpture of Brancusi in *Death in the Afternoon* (99). Throughout Hemingway's fiction of the 1920's, there is practically no mention of art, except in "The Revolutionist," which is a short story enlarged from one of the early vignettes of *in our time*, and in *Torrents of Spring*.

At the same time, however, Hemingway himself was studying art at the Prado, at the Luxembourg, at the Louvre, at Gertrude Stein's, at Ezra Pound's, and elsewhere. He was learning technique, apparently, from Miró and Strater; he was drinking in the cafes with artists like Pascin; he was buying paintings. His articles for *The Transatlantic Review* appeared with ones by artists and art spokesmen like Tzara. Yet even in these nonfictional pieces, there is very little direct comment concerning all the art that Hemingway must have been studying and thinking about at the time. In 1922, he does compare fields of crops, as seen from an airplane, to cubist paintings,[2] and he does criticize Tzara in an article, "And Out of America," in the August, 1924, number of *The Transatlantic Review*. In *Torrents of Spring*, the ref-

2 "A Paris to-Strasbourg Flight," *The Toronto Daily Star*, September 9, 1922, reprinted in *By-Line: Ernest Hemingway*, p. 43.

erences to artists have nothing to do with art.[3] In short, in the 1920's, although Hemingway was incorporating into his fictional works technical elements from the pictorial arts, his non-fictional pieces and even his fiction contain very few direct, specific references to artists, their paintings or sculptures, museums, or buildings of architectural merit.

Two possible reasons for Hemingway's avoidance of direct mentions of art in his work of the 1920's immediately come to mind. First, as a young artist who was consciously laboring to create his own style and type of art, he might have felt that what he had learned from, for example, Cézanne and how he had been able to transpose such techniques into words was a discovery too precious, too hard-earned, to share at this point in his career. Had Jake Barnes looked at the plain of Burguete and said "This looks just like Cézanne's 'Mont Sainte-Victoire' paintings" and then continued with the description as it now stands, the technique would have been there for all to see. Hemingway was selfish with his art.

After all, it was not until 1932, with the publication of *Death in the Afternoon*, that Hemingway was very willing to talk in any extensive way not only about the pictorial arts, but even about the methods of a writer of fiction. In 1934, he wrote the account of his purchase of Miró's "The Farm" for *Cahiers d'Art*, which was the first of several non-fiction pieces written in the 1930's, such as the *Esquire* articles on Quintanilla, devoted to the pictorial arts. And it was not until the 1950's that Hemingway seemed openly willing to associate directly the methods of painters and his own work, as in the Plimpton interview. Thus it was not until the 1930's, when Hemingway was well established, that he was willing to make known his own interest in the arts. And it was not until the 1950's that he was willing to indicate publicly that he might have learned something from painters, although intima-

3 Mandy mentions only that Rodin, Cézanne, Renoir, Picasso, and Stuart had had to support themselves by working "with hands"; i.e., at menial labor. *Torrents of Spring* in *The Hemingway Reader,* p. 40.

tions of this admission are clearly evident as early as 1932 in *Death in the Afternoon.* It is no coincidence that the first protagonist in a Hemingway novel who admitted to any true interest in the arts is Frederic Henry in *A Farewell to Arms* (1929).

Another reason that Hemingway might have hesitated to indicate his special interest in the arts in his fiction of the 1920's is perhaps his own fear of pretentiousness. Surrounded as he was in Paris by the most important artists of the time, as well as by such connoisseurs as Gertrude Stein, he may simply have been hesitant to proclaim any special, personal knowledge of the arts. The references to artists in "The Revolutionist" are to traditionally accepted masters: Mantegna, Giotto, Masaccio, and Piero della Francesca. The analogy of farm fields to cubist paintings, which appeared in the *Toronto Daily Star* article was by no means innovative. Even the references to art in *A Farewell to Arms* are to "safe" painters, such as Mantegna, Titian, and Rubens. Only Frederic Henry's derogatory remarks concerning sculpture show any daring and originality. Again, it is not until *Death in the Afternoon* that Hemingway was willing to risk comparing the silhouette of a bullfighter to the forms of Brancusi or to commit to paper his personal opinions of Goya, El Greco, and Velázquez. In *A Moveable Feast*, Hemingway indicated that both of these reasons—his fear of pretentiousness and his unwillingness to share his techniques—accounted for the scant number of direct references to art in his fiction of the 1920's: "I was learning very much from [Cézanne] but I was not articulate enough to explain it to anyone. Besides it was a secret" (13).

For whatever the reason or group of reasons, it is clear that Hemingway's fiction and non-fiction do not indicate, by specific references, his own depth of interest in the arts until the 1930's. In his fictional works, an interesting pattern is formed if such a yardstick is applied. If we consider five major novels of Hemingway in order, *The Sun Also Rises* (1926), *A Farewell to Arms* (1929), *For Whom the Bell Tolls* (1940), *Across the River and Into the Trees* (1950), and *Islands in the Stream* (written in the early 1950's), we note that art and architecture play a progressively more important role. Three novels are obviously omitted from this sequence: *Torrents of Spring* (1926), *To Have and Have Not* (1937), and *The Old Man and the Sea* (1952). *To Have and Have Not* and *The Old Man and the Sea* concern men of the sea who have little education and who would not in reality necessarily have any knowledge of art. Significant also is that all three of these novels are set in America: *Torrents of Spring*, in Michigan; *To Have and Have Not*, in Key West, Cuba, and the water between; and *The Old Man and the Sea*, in Cuba and the Gulf Stream. On the other hand, four novels are set in Europe: *The Sun Also Rises*, in Paris and Spain; *A Farewell to Arms*, in Italy and Switzerland; *For Whom the Bell Tolls*, in Spain; and *Across the River and Into the Trees*, in and around Venice. The fifth novel, *Islands in the Stream*, is set in America (Bimini, Cuba, and surrounding waters) but concerns an artist whose formative years were spent in Paris. Clearly, the American who has been placed in a European setting is more interested in art, à la Henry James, than is the American who stays at home. Perhaps Jackson's description of his hometown museum (in *Across the River and Into the Trees*) is indicative of Hemingway's general opinion of American culture: "All they got in the local museum is arrowheads, war bonnets, scalping knives, different scalps, petrified fish, pipes of peace, photographs of Liver Eating Johnson, and the skin of some bad man that they hanged him and some doctor skinned him out" (16).

Whatever Hemingway's assumptions concerning Americans abroad and Americans at home, Frederic Henry, Robert Jordan, Colonel Cantwell and Thomas Hudson, are all "devotees of the pictorial arts" in one degree or another. In *The Sun Also Rises*, as I have said, there is really no direct reference to art, except perhaps during Jake's visit to the cathedral of Pamplona in which he notes those "wonderful big windows." Frederic Henry and Catherine Barkley remark only rather superficially concerning Rubens, Mantegna, and Titian. Their dialogue is involved only with identification of specific painters so that Catherine might pass as an artist at the customs inspection in Switzerland. Robert

Jordan, however, indicates an emotional response to art—a response which is, in fact, not just to the pictorial arts, but to all of art: "it was as authentic as the feeling you had when you heard Bach, or stood in Chartres Cathedral or the Cathedral at Léon and saw the light coming through the great windows; or when you saw Mantegna and Greco and Brueghel at the Prado" (235). He further indicates familiarity with the Prado by noting that Pablo's horse "looked as though he had come out of a painting by Velasquez" (13).

Obviously, Jordan is far more sophisticated in his knowledge and understanding of art than is Jake Barnes or Frederic Henry. First, his response is specifically to music and to the pictorial arts and to architecture. He has expressed a unitary sense of art. That is, the reality and intensity of his response is the same whether it has been stimulated by music, paintings, or cathedrals. Moreover, his response to these arts is interpreted as an integrity of feeling which Jordan associates with religion and "a feeling of consecration to a duty toward all of the oppressed of the world" (235). These are all healthy and noble sentiments. In fact, in the context of Jordan's revolutionary political action in this novel, the coupling of art, religion, and social conscience ("a duty toward all of the oppressed of the world") is amazingly parallel with the aims of surrealistic art: "The arts are conceived to exist not in and of themselves but as a function of desire, of pleasure, of the need for a change—which change must be social as well as aesthetic."[4]

Jordan is not a surrealist—although, as I have mentioned, his love affair with Maria certainly approaches a type of *amour fou*, and his unitary response to art is in line with surrealist concepts. Jordan's association with the communists in the Spanish Civil War is consonant with surrealist political preaching in the 1930's.[5] But

4 Herbert S. Gershman, *The Surrealist Revolution in France* (Ann Arbor, 1969), p. 18.

5 "From 1928–1938 the history of the surrealist involvement in politics resembles that of a mad tea party: the Communist Party's directions were also those of the surrealists, as long, that is, as they in no way interferred with surrealist practices. . . . They were consummate fellow travelers, but

Jordan is not a communist, either, even though he fights for the republicans: "You're not a real Marxist and you know it. You believe in Liberty, Equality, and Fraternity. You believe in Life, Liberty, and the Pursuit of Happiness" (305). In short, Jordan's unitary response to art, his *amour fou*, and his association with the communists all suggest a certain surrealistic influence. Yet his refusal to classify himself as a Communist, his desire to rid himself of dreams, and his generally pragmatic approach to life indicate a different side of Jordan. As Carlos Baker has observed, "Jordan will remain as an essential nonconformist."[6]

That Jordan is able to identify Pablo's horse as the type painted by Velázquez suggests that he does not respond simply with emotion to a painting. He has looked hard and long enough at one of Velázquez's equestrian paintings to notice the actual details of the horse.[7] Since Jordan mentions the Prado in the later passage, perhaps the Velázquez horse is that ridden by Isabel de Bourbon or the one ridden by the Duke of Olivares in equestrian portraits or simply one of those ridden by noblemen in "The Surrender of Breda." Actually, only noblemen ride horses in Velázquez's paintings. Is it possible that Jordan associates Pablo's horse with Velázquez's in order to suggest a kind of inherent nobility, but incipient sickness, in Pablo, who is to betray Jordan by stealing the detonator? No matter what symbolic association might be made, however, Jordan's mention of Velázquez's horse must be read in conjunction with the later passage concerning Bach, Chartres, and the painters. In this sense, both passages suggest that Jordan is a cultured and sensitive man who is not totally committed to violence and sex.

The introduction of Jordan's knowledge and appreciation of art—slight as these references are in this long novel—adds a dif-

only of a parallel star, and were constantly surprised when they stumbled." Ibid., p. 93.

6 Carlos Baker, *Hemingway: The Writer as Artist* (Princeton, N.J., 1963), p. 245.

7 One reason that Hemingway himself might have been quite aware of Velázquez's horses is that Velázquez is generally quite unconvincing with animals. See, for example, the grotesque pony which Prince Balthasar Carlos rides (Prado).

ferent dimension to the general context of the action. That is, the general narrative force is a violent act of death and destruction—the blowing of the bridge. This theme is complemented and supplemented by Pilar's account of the massacre of the Fascists and by the death of El Sordo's band. Juxtaposed to this dominant force, however, is the health and affirmation of life suggested by Jordan's and Maria's love affair. In short, the major themes are violence and sex—as beautiful as sex may be in this novel. Jordan's consciousness of art provides a different frame of reference. In this sense, the introduction of art contributes to the epic qualities of the novel, for an epic must encompass as many different aspects of life as possible. Jordan's longer reference to art—to Bach, Chartres, and the painters—is much like a Homeric simile. That is, it is a simile; it is extended (extended further, at least, than Hemingway's similes usually are); and it does introduce a different aspect of life. Carlos Baker has already pointed out Hemingway's oblique references to Homer's *Odyssey* in *The Sun Also Rises*,[8] and it was Baker who first termed *For Whom the Bell Tolls* "a prose epic of the Spanish people."[9]

More important is the fact that Robert Jordan is a man who is not interested just in sex and violence. He has a knowledge and appreciation of art which can help to give him self-understanding and identity in a time of crisis. Had Robert Jordan not died in the 1930's among the pine trees in Spain, he could very well have been riding with Renata in a Venetian gondola in the 1950's with the pseudonym of Colonel Cantwell. Colonel Cantwell has blown many bridges, so to speak, and wants to do battle no more. He has not yet finished with women, however, and Renata and Maria are quite similar, despite the fact that one is a Spanish peasant (although the daughter of a mayor) and the other is of the oldest Venetian nobility. Cantwell is not a university professor as Jordan is, but Cantwell's interest in and knowledge of the arts classify him as an intellectual.

Besides the references to the pictorial arts, architecture, and

8 Baker, *Hemingway: The Writer as Artist*, pp. 87–90.
9 Ibid., p. 247.

sculpture, *Across the River and into the Trees* contains more reference to literature than any other of Hemingway's fictional work since the early *Torrents of Spring*. Hemingway's first novel, however, is a harsh parody of the styles of certain of Hemingway's friends, such as Sherwood Anderson; moreover, the references to the literary and popular journals of the day (such as *The American Mercury* and *The Saturday Review of Literature*) can easily be read as parody of popular American culture. In *Across the River and into the Trees*, there is no parody of writers; authors are generally treated with respect. There are references to Lord Byron and the Brownings (48), Gabriele d'Annunzio (49–52), Walt Whitman (211), Shakespeare (171 and 230), Dante (124, 129, 246, and 269), and Rimbaud and Verlaine (259). Renata states that "I have read mostly the classics" (136). The Colonel and Renata also refer twice to musicians: both like Bach (88), and Renata associates Cantwell's voice with "Pablo Casals playing the cello" (113). Contemporary drama is part of the Colonel's consciousness when he observes a lady who reminds him of "the Lady Diana Manners playing the nun in Max Reinhardt's, 'The Miracle' " (86).

The references to the pictorial arts dominate. Six Italian painters are specifically mentioned, as are two Spanish painters, two Flemish, and a French impressionist. At one point, the Colonel states to his driver: "Painters? . . . I know quite a little about them" (14). Six museums are specifically noted: the Uffizi and Pitti in Florence, the Prado in Madrid, and the Accademia and the Scuola di San Rocco in Venice. Colonel Cantwell and his driver also discuss campaniles, St. Mark's Cathedral, and the Cathedral of Torcello; other points of architectural interest in Venice and Burano are noted throughout the course of the novel. To complete the total aesthetic atmosphere, the Colonel purchases a piece of jewelry for Renata. It is not the usual diamond necklace or ring, but a small piece of sculpture: "that small Negro with the ebony face and the turban made of chip diamonds with the small ruby on the crown of the turban. I should wear it as a pin" (105).

Across the River and into the Trees is a moveable feast of art history and art appreciation. The characters wander easily from consideration of one art form to another. There is obviously manifest a response to all of art—a response which assumes in the characters, especially the Colonel, a unitary approach to art. All art is one and can be appreciated and responded to in the same way. The response is primarily sensual, as the Colonel's analogy between the Accademia and the butcher market implies. However, the response is also intellectual and technical, as the Colonel's mention of Goya's technique of portraiture indicates. Of all Hemingway's fiction, this is the work which most fully explores and illustrates his own interest in the arts—all of them. It is Hemingway's most intellectual novel, just as the Colonel is Hemingway's most intellectual protagonist.

The painter Thomas Hudson does not really display Colonel Cantwell's unitary understanding of art. There is no mention of music and little of literature or writers, although Hudson's friend Roger is a writer. The artistic references are most often to painters, especially to ones Hudson (and Hemingway) knew in Paris in the 1920's: Picasso (71), Braque (71), Miró (71), Masson (71 and 238), Peirce (71), Pascin (71–74 and 108), Gris (237), and Klee (238). Yet Hudson also mentions old masters: Brueghel (21 and 96–97), Bosch (21), Leonardo (96–97), Michelangelo (168), Dutch masters (238), El Greco (245–46), and Hogarth (246). The impressionists and post-impressionists form the smallest group: Renoir (7), Gauguin (7 and 318), Toulouse-Lautrec (317), Cézanne (382), and Manet (448). Hudson also is reminded of one pre-twentieth-century American painter, Thomas Eakins (382).

Of all the Hemingway protagonists, Hudson is most interested in sculpture. Frederic Henry had said that sculpture always reminded him of cemeteries, and Hudson also displays such an association: "Tom was still asleep. He lay on his back with his arms crossed and he looked like the sculpture of a young knight lying on his tomb. Thomas Hudson had sketched him that way using a tomb that he remembered from Salisbury Cathedral"

(446). Several young knights are so entombed at Salisbury. Here, however, Hudson might have been thinking of the famed statue of the "Boy Bishop," the recumbent figure of a boy who died during the children's festival of St. Nicholas. Yet Hudson also reflects upon the sculptured quality of driftwood and feels sorry about burning such pieces in his fireplace. Moreover, Hudson notes that Johnny Goodner's nose "looked as though it had been done by a modern sculptor who worked directly in the stone and had taken off just the shadow of a chip too many" (23). Thus Hudson shows a more healthy and intelligent interest in sculpture than do the other Hemingway protagonists.

Although Hudson does not really display a unitary sense of art, he does represent a unique consciousness in Hemingway's fiction. For with Hudson, Hemingway has tried to show just how an artist sees, feels, hears, smells, touches, and responds to the world. Hemingway has let Hudson demonstrate the particular angle of vision of a working, creative artist. Colonel Cantwell is not himself an artist; thus when he looks at the world, he can only associate what he sees or touches with art he already knows, as during his walk through the butcher market. But Hudson, sees and feels the world in his own creative fashion–take, for example, his response to driftwood, or, again, his interest in the colors of a particular scene, such as the flock of flamingoes which he sees as a "roseate mass on the gray brown flat" (420).

Perhaps the best example of Hudson's artistic perceptions at work is this passage:

> On the stern they were all bathing naked. They soaped themselves and stood on one foot and another, bending against the lashing of the rain as they soaped and then leaning back into it. They were really all brown but they looked white in this strange light. Thomas Hudson thought of the canvas of the bathers by Cézanne and then he thought he would like to have Eakins paint it. Then he thought that he should be painting it himself with the ship against the roaring of the surf that came through the driving gray outside with the black of the

> new squall coming out and the sun breaking through momentarily to make the driving rain silver and to shine on the bathers in the stern [382–83].

Hudson's immediate associations with Cézanne and then Eakins are indicative of Hemingway's own interest in art. Cézanne actually painted not one, but a series of "Bathers" or "Baigneuses," both men and women, in oil and in watercolor. His most famous is "The Great Bathers" (1895–1905; Philadelphia Museum of Art, W. P. Wilstach Collection), in which distorted female figures are integrated with a distorted landscape. With blue prevailing, both figures and trees form a triangular block. The distortion and integration of this painting later greatly influenced Picasso's "Les Demoiselles d'Avignon."

Cézanne's figures must have been too distorted for Hudson, who is himself a representational painter. His next choice is the more realistic Eakins—undoubtedly "The Swimming Hole" (1883; Ft. Worth Museum of Art). The figures in this painting also form a pyramid, but the bodies are handled more realistically (and monumentally). Their Apollo-like physiques remind one critic of Renaissance paintings[10] (Hudson mentions Michelangelo on page 168); the poetic, idyllic qualities of this painting remind another critic of Whitman's "Song of Myself," in which "twenty-eight young men bathe by the shore."[11] Eakins's colors are natural.

At this point, Colonel Cantwell would have had to stop his meditations, but Hudson begins his own creative reconstruction of the scene, as he would like to paint it. His interest has shifted from the original image of the bathing men to the stormy sea, the rain, the sun, the colors, and the textures. His painting would not have been anything like Cézanne's "Baigneuses" and Eakins's "The Swimming Hole." Thus Hudson begins with a scene of bathers in a storm and associates them with bathers in paintings with which he is familiar. Eventually his own artistic eye and imagination transform the scene into a study of color, light, and

10 Lloyd Goodrich, *Thomas Eakins: His Life and Work* (New York, 1933), p. 62.

11 Sylvan Schendler, *Eakins* (Boston, 1967), p. 86.

form. Thomas Hudson indicates to us just how an artist responds and then re-creates—or at least how Hemingway believes the creative process works.

Hemingway's own creation of Thomas Hudson is, in a sense, the culmination of the increasing intellectualization of his protagonists. Hudson does not simply respond to his world; he re-creates it in his mind and then in his paintings. With Hudson, Hemingway tried carefully to show how the outer reality is transformed in the artist's mind to a new inner reality. Then the inner reality becomes a painting—a new outer reality or thing.

Thus from Jake Barnes to Thomas Hudson, excluding the totally American-educated protagonists, there is a growing tendency for Hemingway to intellectualize his protagonists. References to art seem to be one of the major means which Hemingway has used to develop this more sophisticated protagonist.[12] Carlos Baker has associated Goya "the hero as artist" with "the fictional heroes from Lieutenant Henry to Colonel Cantwell."[13] For Baker, both Goya, at least as he was interpreted by Hemingway in *Death in the Afternoon*, and the Hemingway protagonists represent "the hero as pragmatist."[14] Certainly, to such a formula could be added "the hero as art buff"—with "art" used here in the general sense. An understanding of art becomes an integral quality of these Hemingway protagonists, culminating with Colonel Cantwell and Thomas Hudson.

It is too simple to assume that the gradual intellectualization of Hemingway's protagonists is a parallel with Hemingway's own life, much as Hemingway's wound in World War I is understood as the source of Hemingway's wounded soldiers. Hemingway himself, on the contrary, knew a great deal about art in the 1920's. Even more important, he was able to transpose into words the techniques of painters—a feat which demands more than just an

12 Another means of indicating an appreciation of art in his protagonists is the manner in which they speak of art. Compare the diction: Jake speaks of "some wonderful big windows" in the cathedral of Pamplona, but Robert Jordan talks of "the light coming through the great windows" at Chartres and Léon.

13 Baker, *Hemingway: The Writer as Artist*, pp. 154–55.

14 Ibid.

ability to identify paintings in a museum. I wonder if Hemingway's progressive interest in a more intellectual protagonist is not the result of his sensitivity to certain critics of the 1930's, especially Aldous Huxley and Wyndham Lewis. Both were critics who saw Jake Barnes and Frederic Henry as unthinking "animals." Lewis's article is correspondingly titled "The Dumb Ox, a Study of Ernest Hemingway";[15] the Huxley essay also clearly manifests his topic, "Foreheads Villainous Low."[16]

Hemingway was so incensed by the Huxley criticism that he lashed out at Huxley in public and in print. In *Death in the Afternoon*, Hemingway devoted nearly a page to quotations from Huxley's essay and another page and a half to refuting it. Hemingway seemed especially upset both with Huxley's comments concerning Frederic Henry's references to Mantegna and with this passage which Hemingway quoted: "There was a time, not so long ago, when the stupid and uneducated aspired to be thought intelligent and cultured. The current of aspiration has changed its direction. It is not at all uncommon now to find intelligent and cultured people doing their best to feign stupidity and to conceal the fact that they have received an education" (190). Immediately after quoting this passage, Hemingway refutes Huxley by asserting that "a writer should create living people. . . . A *character* is a caricature. If a writer can make people live there may be no great characters in his book, but it is possible that his book will remain as a whole; as an entity; as a novel. If the people the writer is making talk of old masters; of music; of modern painting; of letters; or of science then they should talk of those subjects in the novel. If they do not talk of those subjects and the writer makes them talk of them he is a faker . . ." (191). Apparently Hemingway's response to Lewis's article was more violent. Reportedly, after he read the article at Sylvia Beach's bookshop in Paris, "he punched a vase of tulips on Sylvia's table."[17]

15 Wyndham Lewis, "The Dumb Ox, a Study of Ernest Hemingway," *American Review* (June 1934), pp. 389–412.

16 Aldous Huxley, *Music at Night and Other Essays* (New York, 1931), pp. 111–15.

17 Carlos Baker, *Ernest Hemingway: A Life Story* (New York, 1969), p. 258.

Punching a vase of tulips was less effective, at least in terms of literary theory, than was Hemingway's response to Huxley in *Death in the Afternoon*. But Hemingway's justification there of his anti-intellectualism is begging the question. To plead that he is creating real people who do not happen to talk about art or who treat art casually is not really to answer Huxley's and Lewis's contentions that the Hemingway protagonist is like a "dumb ox." Huxley and Lewis saw Hemingway's protagonists as not only unintellectual, but even anti-intellectual. It is the *type* of people Hemingway creates—not that he creates people—that Huxley and Lewis criticized.

In support of Hemingway's "dumb ox," however, there was obviously a rather forceful anti-intellectual element throughout the 1920's. Discarding all traditional institutions, values, and rules, the Dadaists and even the surrealists discounted knowledge and understanding of, for example, old masters (except for a special few) or of any intellectual discipline before Cézanne. Based upon the Dada and surrealist emphasis upon sense and experience (both physical and mental), non-intellectualism often developed into anti-intellectualism. Contrast with the Dada and surrealist movements the esoteric "high intellectualism" of T. S. Eliot and his followers. Hemingway disliked Eliot about as much as he disliked Tzara.[18] His reasons for disliking both of them are more complex than simply the question of "high intellectualism" and anti-intellectualism, yet such a conflict cannot be discounted.

Whatever the reasons, for the progressive intellectualization of the Hemingway protagonists, references to art certainly increase until Colonel Cantwell's knowledge of art becomes a central consideration of his personality and Thomas Hudson is himself an artist. The Colonel's consciousness of art is more than simply a superficial knowledge of names. As Hemingway stated in *Death in the Afternoon*, "For a writer to put his own intellectual musings, which might sell for a low price as essays, into the mouths of artificially constructed characters which are more remunerative when issued as people in a novel is good economics perhaps,

18 Ibid., p. 135.

but does not make literature" (191). Art—all of the arts, as well as a consciousness of them—is functional not only with reference to the character development of Cantwell and Hudson, but also within the texture of the novels themselves.

As far as Cantwell himself is concerned, his references to art suggest a way of life and a particular response to the world. On one level, most references are to Italian artists—a simple fact which indicates the Colonel's devotion to Italy. After all, he has chosen to die in Italy; there is no thought of returning to America. He is truly an expatriate. On another level, all his references to painters are to old masters: there is not one reference to a contemporary or modern painter. Only Degas approaches the modern age. Hence the Colonel is a traditionalist in his taste in art—a tag which can indicate various conclusions. Is he searching for man's historical being, for some connection with the past, as he himself faces death and history? Is he simply affirming the values of the past? On still another level, the particular artists with whom he identifies are those who express themselves almost totally in highly emotional and sometimes violent paintings. These are, therefore, the artists who most appealed to him. On the other hand, Giotto, whom he mentions twice (13–14 and 54), is quite gentle. In still another sense, the specific references to art affirm the Colonel's particular response to the world: he can enter a butcher market or a fish market and discover art. He is by nature an artist: beauty, for him, exists in all of life. Such a listing of the importance of art in Cantwell's character development could be extended.

What of the function of such references to art within the novel itself? A common interest in and consciousness of art is one quality which Renata and the Colonel share. Readers have often wondered just what attracted Renata to the Colonel—and justifiably so. After all, Hemingway's own rather platonic relationship with nineteen-year-old Adriana Ivancich is far more logically motivated than the Colonel's and Renata's affair. Few intelligent nineteen-year-old girls would not want to become a confidante of a world-famous writer. Why, on the other hand, would Renata fall in love with Cantwell? Hemingway is too good a writer not

"She had that pure Renaissance beauty, black hair straight, eyes round at the bottoms, Botticelli skin, breasts of Venus Rising."
—ERNEST HEMINGWAY TO A. E. HOTCHNER (1949)

Sandro Botticelli, "Birth of Venus.' ca. 1482. Tempera on canvas, 66 x 108¼ in. Uffizi Galleries.

to offer some motivation. I believe that their common interest in art is one motivating factor. Renata is able to share the Colonel's musings on art. And, interestingly enough, it is she who makes reference to Pablo Casals, who is the only living artist mentioned in the novel. Thus, although she shares Cantwell's interest in the old masters, she is more a part of the contemporary world of art than Cantwell. It is she who survives.[19]

Also functional in the novel is the painting of Renata. For a man as concerned with art as Cantwell is, the portrait was an appropriate gift. Renata is not pictured realistically, but almost allegorically: "It is very romantic. My hair is twice as long as it has ever been and I look as though I were rising from the sea without the head wet. Actually, you rise from the sea with the hair very flat and coming to points at the end" (97). Obviously, a comparison can be made by the reader with Botticelli's "Birth of Venus" (ca. 1486; Uffizi[20]). Hemingway himself described Adriana to A. E. Hotchner with reference to this painting: "She had that pure Renaissance beauty, black hair straight, eyes round at the bottoms, Botticelli skin, breasts of Venus Rising."[21] Botticelli's Venus has risen from the sea and is making her way toward land; her hair is dry—a bit windblown, perhaps, but dry. Individual strands of hair are blown from the lock across her breast. Her hair is also extremely long, as in other Botticelli portraits of Venus, the goddess of love. The portrait's association of Renata with Venus is also a reference to Venice, a city which was named after the goddess. Moreover, the Colonel remembers the first day he saw Venice in this way: " 'Christ, I love it,' he said, 'and I'm so happy I helped defend it when I was a punk kid, and with an insufficient command of the language and I never saw her until

19 I am reminded here of Robert Jordan's musings concerning youth and old age in *For Whom the Bell Tolls*: "Look at her [Pilar] walking along with those two kids. She is like a mountain and the boy and the girl are like young trees. The old trees are all cut down and the young trees are growing clean like that" (136).

20 The Uffizi Gallery is mentioned by the Colonel (p. 14).

21 Quoted in A. E. Hotchner, *Papa Hemingway* (New York, 1966), p. 33.

that clear day in winter when I went back to have that small wound dressed, and saw her rising from the sea' " (45).[22]

The allegorical representation of Renata should be understood and correlated with the Colonel's own association of Renata with the Virgin Mary, as well as with Renata's association of the Colonel with Jesus. The Colonel asks Renata, "Would you ever like to run for Queen of Heaven?" (83). A few paragraphs later, she asks to hold his hand, crippled from war wounds, and comments, "I want to feel it because all last week, every night, or I think every night, I dreamed about it, and it was a strange mixed-up dream and I dreamed it was the hand of Our Lord" (84). Such allegorical and religious suggestions parallel those in *For Whom the Bell Tolls*, especially with reference to Renata and Maria and Pilar. There is no clear and precise allegorical pattern here, but simply the suggestion, such as the reference to Brett as a kind of Circe in *The Sun Also Rises*.

Yet the Colonel himself does not compare Renata's portrait to Botticelli's Venus, but to portraits by Tintoretto and Velázquez: "It was a beautiful portrait; neither cold, nor snobbish, nor stylised, nor modern. It was the way you would want your girl painted if Tintoretto were still around and, if he were not around, you settled for Velasquez. It was not the way either of them painted" (146). These are curious words. For one thing, Tintoretto is not really known as a painter of portraits in the same sense that Veláquez is. Tintoretto, in fact, did paint many portraits, most of which are at the Prado.[23] Of course, his votive pictures of various doges at the Ducal Palace are portraits in a sense. Particularly evident in these votive paintings, Tintoretto's portraits are highly idealized.

22 In the lower left center plane of Tintoretto's "Votive Portrait of Doge Francesco Donato" (1581–84; Ducal Palace) is a representation of Venice in which the buildings do, indeed, appear to be rising from the sea.

23 Twelve portraits by Tintoretto are at the Prado: e.g., "Portrait of a Venetian Senator" (1570–80) and the "So-Called Portrait of Sebastiano Venier" (ca. 1580). At the Accademia are "Portrait of Andrea Cappelo" (1555–60) and "Portrait of Doge Alvise Mocenigo" (1570–77).

Velázquez is more traditionally thought of as a painter of portraits, most of which are also at the Prado. He was, in many ways, more a realist than Tintoretto in that in his paintings people who are unattractive in reality are still unattractive in their portraits (e.g., his portraits of dwarfs or of Queen Mariana of Austria). Velázquez, however, was generally able to endow any sitter with some favorable quality, such as grace, or intelligence, or compassion. If the Colonel's analogy is valid, the portrait of Renata was probably idealized and revealed her most favorable qualities. Note especially that the Colonel, who himself looks at faces as Goya did (90), did not want Goya to paint Renata's picture. Perhaps Goya's interpretation would have been too harsh and too real.[24]

The portrait also serves another function structurally within the novel. In Chapter 17, for example, the portrait is used as a device to reveal the Colonel's consciousness when he is alone in his hotel room. He talks to the portrait as if it were another character. To a certain extent, this sort of response to a painting is indicative of the intimate association which the Colonel felt with all of art.

Cantwell's immersion in art is a powerful counterbalance to the memories of war which flood his mind and of which he must purge himself before death.[25] In a sense, therefore, the references

24 In his early days in Paris, Thomas Hudson once painted, at the request of a restaurant proprietor, a portrait which "was not a Manet that Manet would have signed, but it looked more like Manet than it did like Hudson and it looked exactly like the proprietor" (448). Although Manet's portraits were realistic for his day, to us they seem stiff and often shallow. He was more interested in technique than in character. The portraits before 1870 have a "mask-like impassivity" with "frozen, naturalistic poses and 'dead-pan' expressions"—undoubtedly the result of Manet's interest in photography. (See John Richardson, *Édouard Manet: Paintings and Drawings* [London, 1958], pp. 20ff.) Interestingly, Manet actually painted two portraits of restaurant proprietors: a father and son, "Chez le Père Lathuille" (1879; Musée de Beaux-Arts, Tournai), and "Portrait of the Fils Lathuille" (1879; New York, David M. Heyman). In some respects, it is surprising that Hemingway did not admire Manet more than he seemed to: Manet was greatly influenced by Goya, at times actually copying from "Tauromaquia," for example. There is also evidence to indicate that Manet gained courage to eliminate half-tones from his paintings because of his admiration for Goya's etchings.

25 Horst Oppel, "Hemingway's *Across the River and into the Trees*," trans. Joseph M. Bernstein, *Hemingway and His Critics: An International Anthology*, ed. Carlos Baker (New York, 1961), pp. 221–22.

to art, as well as the Colonel's romance with the young Renata, who is herself sensitive to art, are an affirmation of life—a participation in joy, so to speak, before death. In much the same way, especially at the end of *Islands in the Stream* as Hudson chases the Germans who will ultimately kill him, art offers a healthy and life-affirming contrast. In the early part of the novel, Hudson is an artist at work. At the end of the novel, he is an artist who has had to put aside his paints in order to chase Germans, but he is still an artist. Even as he scans beaches for Germans, he can respond to the beauty of flamingoes or to the artistic potential of a scene of men bathing in a storm. Hudson's artistic consciousness is continually present throughout the novel; his mind may be concentrating upon catching a German, but a bird or a tree can arouse his aesthetic sensitivity. Thus the development of Thomas Hudson's character does not depend so much on references to art or on his responses to works of art as Cantwell's does; Thomas Hudson's character *is* that of an artist, with aesthetic consciousness primary, references to art secondary. In one sense, Thomas Hudson is a reversal of Colonel Cantwell: Cantwell is a soldier, a fighting man, with an amateur's knowledge and understanding of art which approaches that of a practicing artist. Hudson, conversely, is an artist who becomes an amateur fighting man and who, at least in his one major naval operation, succeeds in his assignment.

With Thomas Hudson, life and art become blended. Throughout the novel, Hemingway is careful to balance physical activities with Hudson's aesthetic consciousness, with his painting, and with references to art. For example, in "Bimini," the first section of the novel, Hudson paints each morning, even when his sons are visiting. The rest of the day is to "enjoy life" (9), but in the enjoyment comes the experience for other pieces of art. It is at Bobby's that Hudson decides to paint the waterspouts. Only Colonel Cantwell's walk through the butcher market is comparable, in Hemingway's fiction, to the full realization of the juxtaposition and interrelation of life and art as experienced by Thomas Hudson.

For Hemingway to create the consciousness of a painter who is actually at work or contemplating work is rather bold. Why did he not let the reader see the consciousness of a writer at work? Certainly Hemingway would have been more familiar with the problems or vision of a writer. Perhaps such a portrait would have been too intimate, or perhaps Hemingway felt that the materials of Hudson's life so paralleled his own life that some artistic distance had to be maintained by making Hudson a painter. On the other hand, at least if Hudson can be viewed as speaking for Hemingway, Hemingway felt that painting is "easier": "'I don't know,' Thomas Hudson said. 'Maybe in painting the tradition and the line are clearer and there are more people helping you. Even when you break from the straight line of great painting, it is always there to help you'" (78). Thus, in a sense, if painting is easier, the consciousness of a painter is perhaps less complex and hence easier for Hemingway to create. Perhaps Hemingway's very intimacy with the consciousness of a writer might have caused the novel to flounder with the aesthetics, had Hudson been a writer.

But Hudson is a painter—and, clearly, a representational painter. In fact, at one point in the novel, he emphasizes that he does not paint abstract art (317). In the context of the actions (the early 1940's), such a statement is curious. Jackson Pollock's abstract expressionism, for example, did not develop until after World War II; Pollock's first "drip painting" was created in 1947. Picasso, Braque, Gris, Miró, and other artists whom Hudson mentions in affectionate reminiscences of his years in Paris must be termed abstract painters of sorts. Perhaps Hudson's rejection of abstract painting is a reflection of Hemingway's own disapproval of this art form, from the vantage point of the 1950's, when the novel was written.

Hudson appears to be a remarkably old-fashioned painter. His knowledge of and personal associations with other artists seem to have ended in Paris in the 1920's. His own paintings much more closely resemble those by nineteenth-century painters, such as Homer and the French impressionists. Only his sense of color indicates a positive awareness of twentieth-century techniques. Hudson closely parallels Hemingway's own interest in painting—an interest which, despite his friendships with Gattorno and Quintanilla, never really developed as new artists and new movements appeared after 1930.

Yet the portrait of Hudson is fascinating simply because it is an attempt on the part of a writer to create the consciousness of a painter—even as to aesthetic response to specific experience and to his re-creation of such material into art. Robert Cantwell may be the most intellectual of Hemingway's protagonists, but Hudson is the most artistic.

Thus far I have discussed character development in terms of personality rather than in terms of physical appearance. It is not difficult to find parallels between certain physical descriptions in Hemingway's fiction and the physical appearance of figures in paintings. With reference to the description of the banderillos examining the bulls in *Death in the Afternoon* (27), Carlos Baker states that "Goya would have fancied these people."[26] Hemingway himself associated the Spanish peasants and their villages with Velázquez. In *Death in the Afternoon*, he states that Aranjuez is "Velasquez to the edge" (40). With reference to, for example, Velázquez's "The Spinners" (Prado), Aranjuez must be a reasonably clean village with typical Spanish buildings and tiled roofs. The peasants were probably healthy and slightly rotund. From the edge of Aranjuez, however, the town is "straight Goya to the bullring." Obviously here reference can easily be made to Goya's "Tauromaquia" or to his bullring canvases. Furthermore, Velázquez's and Hemingway's Spanish peasants (as in *For Whom the Bell Tolls*) often exhibit the same qualities: pride, humility, and a certain cheerfulness. For example, the old man at right in "The Topers" (Prado) suggests Anselmo, while the central peasant, holding a bowl of wine, might describe Rafael the gypsy.

This sort of comparison, however, is not really what the Colonel was implying when he described the American writer in terms of Goya:

> They looked at the man at the third table. He had a strange face like an over-enlarged, disappointed weasel or ferret. It

26 Baker, *Hemingway: The Writer as Artist*, p. 69.

> looked as pock-marked and as blemished as the mountains of the moon seen through a cheap telescope. . . . Above this face, which was ceaselessly peering . . . there was black hair that seemed to have no connection with the human race. The man looked as though he had been scalped and then the hair replaced. . . . A little spit ran out of the corner of his mouth. . . . Has a wonderful face though, the Colonel thought. . . . "I was looking at him as at a drawing by Goya. Faces are pictures too" [87–90].

Apparently a person for whom the Colonel feels contempt should be drawn as Goya would have depicted him, but Renata must be painted by Tintoretto or Velázquez. The Colonel is indicating here the incredible honesty and extreme realism with which Goya depicted people he disliked, as in "The Family of Charles IV" (1800; Prado). Goya had learned the technique of psychological portraiture from Velázquez, but he was even more revealing. It is amazing that Goya did not lose favor (at the least) after he had painted Charles and his family: "Goya's eye pierced his models with a lucidity that verged on brutality, an impudence that often stung."[27] For Hemingway, Goya's portrait of "The Family of Charles IV" was "a masterpiece of loathing": "Look how he has painted his spittle into every face. Can you imagine that he had such genius that he could fulfill this commission and please the King, who, because of his fatuousness, could not see how Goya had stamped him for all the world to see."[28]

Cantwell's description of the American is not equal to Goya's portraits. The phrases of description are scattered throughout several pages of dialogue; the Colonel begins the description one way and then veers another. The pock marks on the man's cheeks, which might repel many, are obviously what fascinate Cantwell most. He compares them to the terrain of the moon and of Verdun. The man's face is a kind of map. His hair also—its color and texture—seems odd and therefore interesting to Cantwell. Finally, the saliva and the peering eyes are the qualities which complete

27 Jacques Lassaigne, *Goya,* trans. Rosamund Frost (New York, 1948), p. 36.
28 Quoted in Hotchner, *Papa Hemingway,* p. 187.

"Look how he has painted his spittle into every face. Can you imagine that he had such genius that he could fulfill this commission and please the King, who, because of his fatuousness, could not see how Goya had stamped him for all the world to see."

—ERNEST HEMINGWAY TO A. E. HOTCHNER (1950)

Francisco Goya, "The Family of Charles IV." 1800. Oil, 132 x 110 in. Prado.

the portrait. The man appears to be unattractive and stupid, but according to Cantwell, his face is "wonderful." If nothing else, this passage demonstrates the Colonel's propensity to see beauty in life, from carcasses in butcher markets to unattractive men.

In the sense that the Colonel saw beauty in the ugly, his vision of reality is certainly related to that of Goya. That is, "The Family of Charles IV" is beautiful in terms of organization and color. On the other hand, the brutal realism of Goya clearly displays the simple-mindedness of the King by means of a vacant stare, as well as the arrogance of the Queen, by her jutting chin and by the position of her head, which thrusts up and out. To a certain extent, therefore, Goya and the Colonel (and presumably Hemingway) saw beauty even in the midst of ugliness: the perception of a natural ugliness and the recognition of such ugliness for what it truly is represents a sense of beauty, or at least something "wonderful," to quote the Colonel.

Such a concept of beauty is in accordance with other types of beauty found in Hemingway's fiction: "With respect to the beautiful it appears to be a basic assumption in Hemingway's esthetic that what is true, in the sense of being natural and untinkered-with, is also beautiful. Ugliness in Hemingway is almost invariably associated with the abnormal and the unnatural."[29] The "wonderful" face of the American writer is worth the glance of an artist's eye because it is honest and conceals nothing. The artist, in turn, must also be honest in his interpretation and reproduction.

Descriptions of faces are not as important in the early fiction of Hemingway as in the later works, and there are practically no detailed descriptions of faces in the short stories. Before the late 1920's, Hemingway seldom describes faces; when he does, he does not dwell on them for long. For example, in *The Sun Also Rises*, bodies are slender or short, hair is dark or blond, and faces are white or tan. The group of Basques who ride the bus with Jake and Bill to Burguete would have been more specifically described by the Hemingway who wrote *For Whom the Bell Tolls*.

29 Baker, *Hemingway: The Writer as Artist*, p. 65.

Jake notes only that one has "wrinkles in his tanned neck" (104). Compare, for example, the attention to detail demanded by and expressed in this description of Count Greffi in *A Farewell to Arms*: "I thought he smiled sadly but I could not tell. He was so old and his face was very wrinkled, so that a smile used so many lines that all gradations were lost" (272). Or note this description of a very minor figure in *For Whom the Bell Tolls*, a guard at the bridge, as Robert Jordan views him through binoculars: "there was the face of the sentry so clear he could see the sunken cheekbones, the ash of the cigarette, and the greasy shine of the bayonet. It was a peasant's face, the cheeks hollow under the high cheekbones, the beard stubbled, the eyes shaded by heavy brows . . ." (36). It is generally true, I think, that Hemingway's description of physical features of his fictional characters shifted from a full-length view to a concentration upon the face as his fiction developed.

A curious feature of facial description in Hemingway's later fiction is his use of animal analogies, as in the Colonel's comparison of his subject to a weasel or ferret. In fact, descriptions of nearly any type of character often involve some reference to animals. *For Whom the Bell Tolls* abounds in such references: Golz has "hawk eyes" (8), and El Sordo's eyes are like a cat's or reptile's (141). Pablo is clearly a pig (9 and 193–94), and the face of one of his men is compared to a Serrano ham (51). In *Islands in the Stream*, the yachtsman with whom Roger fights has a face like "a really mean boar" (41), and Hudson's son David reminds him of an otter (52). Sometimes the allusions are simply to nature: Santiago's eyes are the color of the sea (10), and Maria's hair is "the golden brown of a grain field" (22).

Of the three painters of portraits whom Colonel Cantwell mentioned, Goya, Tintoretto, and Velázquez, none made faces which contained direct analogies with animals. On the other hand, in "The Disasters of War," Goya was not afraid to add the wings of a bat to the head of a priest (etching 71) or to place the head of a hawk on the body of a priest (etching 75). From these half-man–half-beast creations came the fantastic and allegorical beasts of the final etchings of this series and of such later works as "The Caprices." Hemingway seemed unable to imitate the technical qualities of the formal psychological portraits of Goya and Velázquez with words, except in the sense that he let the face express the inner reality of the character being described. He found that he could describe a face in such a way that it might foreshadow the character's action, or that such a delineation might act simply as a shorthand device for character development.

One must wonder why attention to facial detail or the psychological portrait came comparatively late in Hemingway's career. It is certainly a device other novelists used long before Hemingway.[30] I can only assume that he himself was simply unaware of its possibilities, or that he found himself unable to depict a face truly. (It is perhaps significant here that Thomas Hudson seemed to have painted only one portrait—a commissioned job in the style of Manet.) When Hemingway did become interested in such facial detail, he turned to analogies with animals especially to aid in the description—a device which is not always successful, but which Goya had used in the etchings and elsewhere. Perhaps, as the Colonel suggests, it was Goya's portraits that helped make Hemingway aware that "faces are pictures too."

Henry Strater painted three portraits of Hemingway—two on wood panels in the winter of 1922–23 in Rapello, and a canvas in 1930 in Key West. According to Strater, this was Hemingway's response to them:

> The first portrait, the profile, he said made him "look too literary, like H. G. Wells." He always rather repented that part of himself, the perfectionist artist, which made him a great writer. He wanted to be a real tough guy. His coloring was very handsome, dark hair and pink-and-white complexion; but the fair skin bothered him, so midway in the second portrait I said "O.K., I'll paint you the way you look

30 Note, for example, the great detail with which James Fenimore Cooper describes Natty Bumppo in his first appearance (Ch. 1 of *The Pioneers*). This passage establishes the general character of Natty for the entire Leatherstocking series.

"They looked at the man at the third table. He had a strange face like an over-enlarged, disappointed weasel or ferret."

—COLONEL CANTWELL IN *Across the River and into the Trees*

Francisco Goya, "The Disasters of War" #71. Etching. Courtesy of The Hispanic Society of America.

> boxing." The third portrait, done in 1930 when we were fishing at Key West, was a colorful one, as he was deeply tanned. With his usual verve, he took my brush after I had signed, and added his own name.[31]

Certainly Hemingway wanted himself painted psychologically—or at least in his own psychological image, even in 1922.

Yet it was not until the 1930's that Hemingway used the sort of facial description found in psychological portraits for development of fictional characters. At the same time, his protagonists themselves became more obviously self-conscious and self-revealing with references to their interests in art. These two developments, both important in themselves, are also evidence of Hemingway's own confidence in a unitary vision of the arts. It is easy enough to see the influence of Goya and Cézanne, especially in Hemingway's early work. It is not until the 1930's, however, that he was willing to indicate publicly that he was, indeed, moving toward a single art.

31 Henry Strater, "Hemingway," *Art in America* 49, no. 4 (1961):85.

VII

Architecture

Prose is architecture, not interior decoration, and the Baroque is over.[1]

"St. Mark's Square is where the pigeons are and where they have that big cathedral that looks sort of like a moving picture palace, isn't it?"[2]

"When are they going to tear that damned Cinema Palace down and put up a real cathedral?"[2]

Hemingway liked neither Byzantine nor Baroque architecture. Although as styles they were practiced at least 500 years apart, they have certain tendencies in common. To a certain extent, both depend upon the dramatic play of light and shadow for their effects. Both the exterior and the interior of "that damned Cinema Palace," St. Mark's Basilica in Venice, a Byzantine structure, are decorated with a variety of marbles, mosaics, glass, and other materials over which light plays in a sparkling fashion, if the day is sunny. Inside the cathedral, the recesses of the vast area, particularly the bottom half of the church, fall into heavy shadow, but the play of light continues over the surface decorations. In Baroque architecture, for example the sixteenth-century Il Gesu in Rome, the facade is not a union of design but combines rounded and straight forms, with movement the object and shadow a special interest. Apparently, although Hemingway liked chiaroscuro in paintings and in prose, he was not too fond of the same effect in Byzantine and Baroque structures.

1 *Death in the Afternoon*, p. 191.
2 *Across the River and into the Trees*, pp. 29 and 161.

More to the point, and perhaps Hemingway's chief objection to these two styles, is their artificial use of mosaics, statuary, and other decorative elements. Often, particularly in St. Mark's, the decoration was simply pasted on the wall. The decoration does not conform to the structure; it tends to reach out from the building and is not, as a whole, coordinated with the structure itself. The decoration is independent of the architecture; as a result, much of it seems superfluous. This surplus decoration is simply a part of Byzantine and Baroque art, because of, for one reason, its contribution to the play of light and shadow.

It is no surprise that Hemingway preferred the more simple and direct styles of Romanesque and Gothic architecture. From Jake Barnes' admiration of the cathedral of Pamplona to Colonel Cantwell's vigorous praises for the campanile of Burano, Hemingway's protagonists—and Hemingway himself—tend to find beauty in the windows, the interiors, and the decoration of Romanesque and Gothic structures. The only Byzantine church which receives any praise is the cathedral of Torcello. According to Colonel Cantwell, "This boy brought the remains of St. Mark to Venice, and he's their patron saint and they have a Cathedral there to him. But by that time, they were trading so far to the east that the architecture is pretty Byzantine for my taste. They never built any better than at the start there in Torcello" (29).

In one sense, Hemingway's knowledge of architectural history is a bit off. Both the cathedral of Torcello and the nearby Church of St. Fosca are Byzantine, "both in plan and detail."[3] On the other hand, it is true that the cathedral of Torcello antedates St. Mark's (but not by much[4]) and that it does not resemble a cinema palace. It is a basilica, a plan more common in Romanesque and Gothic structures than in Byzantine, which generally use the Greek-cross design. Its exterior decoration is minimal, and the

3 Thomas Graham Jackson, *Byzantine and Romanesque Architecture* I (Cambridge, 1920), p. 235.

4 The cathedral of Torcello was begun in the seventh century and was altered in 864 and again in 1001–8. The present St. Mark's Basilica was rebuilt in the tenth century (finished in 1085) after the ninth-century structure had been destroyed by fire. St. Fosca was built in the twelfth century.

interior mosaics tend to follow closely the lines of the structure. In defense of the Colonel's implication that the cathedral of Torcello is not Byzantine, or at least not very Byzantine, I can reflect from personal experience that visiting St. Mark's and then the cathedral of Torcello is very much like viewing Byzantine and then Romanesque, so unlike are the two cathedrals.

The cathedrals at Léon and at Pamplona are both Gothic, although neither is totally committed to the very heavy and dark design of the typical Spanish Gothic church. They are both more closely related to the soaring and light French Gothic.[5] It is the windows of both which seem to have interested Hemingway's protagonists: Jake Barnes speaks of "some wonderful big windows" in the cathedral of Pamplona, and Robert Jordan experiences an "authentic" feeling when he sees the light from the "great windows" of Chartres and Léon. In reality, there are no "wonderful big windows" in the cathedral of Pamplona. The small, heavily screened windows of this cathedral are notable, in fact, because they are the major element of Spanish Gothic style in the structure: "Although Pamplona Cathedral is largely French, certain features are typically Spanish. For instance, the trancepts are lit only by miniature rose-windows and throughout the church the windows are very small, while the tracery is so heavy that it occupies as much or more space than the glass."[6] One could with kindness presume, I suppose, that Jake is made to mention those "wonderful big windows" for artistic purposes within the context of the novel, and not because Hemingway had forgotten what sort of windows were in the cathedral.

Reality and art are correlated in *For Whom the Bell Tolls*, for there are "great windows" in the cathedrals at Chartres and Léon, and they are inspiring, as Robert Jordan indicates. Léon is a church totally French in design and intent, similar to Chartres. The interiors of both cathedrals are dominated by windows, notably the famous rose windows at Chartres and the clerestory

5 Bernard Bevan, *History of Spanish Architecture* (London, 1938), pp. 82 and 86.
6 Ibid., p. 86.

windows of Léon. The cathedral of Léon, in fact, has been called "a veritable lantern"[7] and is often compared to Chartres. Only the colors of the windows differ: those at Chartres are predominantly rose and blue, while golden yellows, greens, and purples dominate the windows at Léon.

The cathedral of Léon is more Gothic in design than the cathedral at Chartres. Its high vaulting shafts support the arches so that the mass of walls can be replaced with windows. The graceful and soaring arches, the cutting away of mass, the well-illuminated interior are all elements of middle Gothic. Chartres, on the other hand, is darker and displays more wall; its decoration conforms in some areas quite closely to the architecture (e.g., figures of the west facade are actually carved from the supporting columns). In fact, Chartres is an amazing blend of both Romanesque and early Gothic styles.

The only high or late Gothic structure mentioned in Hemingway's work is the cathedral of Milan, which was begun in 1385 and is the third largest in Europe. While recuperating in the hospital in Milan, Frederic Henry notices "the points of the cathedral" (109) from his room. Later, in the rain, he and Catherine walk by the cathedral: "It was white and wet in the mist. . . . There was a fog in the square and when we came close to the front of the cathedral it was very big and the stone was wet" (153). They also notice a soldier and his girl standing "in the shadow of one of the stone buttresses" (153). Actually, in view of Hemingway's general taste in architecture, it is odd that Frederic Henry would have thought the cathedral "fine."

Like St. Mark's, and except for size, the cathedral of Milan is like a cinema palace. It is topped by many slender marble spires, and its exterior is decorated by over 2,000 statues. The interior is ornate to the point of being Baroque. But then, Frederic Henry never went inside. This is the only cathedral described through a foggy atmosphere in Hemingway's work; its details cannot clearly be seen. Perhaps, by mentioning this cathedral in this context, Hemingway meant to suggest symbolically the beauty of

7 Ibid., p. 84.

the spiritual life which Frederic, Catherine, and Count Greffi can only sense dimly, as in a fog.

More Romanesque than Byzantine or Gothic is the "lovely" campanile of Burano which Colonel Cantwell points out to his driver and which the Colonel claims is leaning as much as the campanile at Pisa. Although the Venetian cathedrals and churches are chiefly Byzantine-influenced, their campaniles are more typically Italian Romanesque, primarily because of their solid towers reaching to a small gallery. In fact, the exterior surface of the campanile at Pisa is far more elaborately broken by arches and galleries than the campaniles of St. Mark's, Torcello, Burano, or Murano.

Hemingway's favorite cathedral seemed to be the cathedral of Santiago de Compostella. He clearly preferred it to Chartres and listed the cathedral among his "favorite things" in 1934.[8] A famous religious shrine, Santiago de Compostela was built in the eleventh and twelfth centuries as a Romanesque cathedral. A Baroque facade and other features were added in the eighteenth century, yet the west portico and the nave, which is almost entirely without decoration, still manifest its Romanesque structure. Unlike other Spanish Romanesque cathedrals, the interior is not particularly dark, although the windows are not especially notable. Exterior and interior express the substantial and orderly strength of the most traditional Romanesque architecture, despite the Baroque additions.

In general, then, Hemingway seemed to prefer the more simple and direct statements of Romanesque and Gothic architecture to the elaborate and often ornate decoration of Byzantine and Baroque. The relationship of his taste in architecture to his prose style is obvious. For Hemingway, "prose is architecture, not interior decoration, and the Baroque is over." Immediately preceding this statement, Hemingway had observed, "No matter how good a phrase or a simile [a writer] may have if he puts it in where it is not absolutely necessary and irreplaceable he is spoiling his work

8 Carlos Baker, *Ernest Hemingway: A Life Story* (New York, 1969), pp. 204–5 and 261.

for egotism."[9] Thus Hemingway demanded that prose be simple and direct, that its general plan and structure be apparent, and that any simile or phrase be subordinated to the whole. He later reaffirmed this statement in *A Moveable Feast*: "If I started to write elaborately . . . I found that I could cut that scrollwork or ornament out and throw it away and start with the first true declarative sentence I had written" (12).

Hemingway's definition of good prose sounds much like this description of Romanesque architecture: the Romanesque style exhibits "a sobriety and simplicity which distinguishes it from the Gothic art of the following period. The masses of its buildings are plain and solid, with plenty of bare-wall space, and none of that efflorescence into any pinnacles, niches, and canopies, open traceries and tabernacle work. . . . Not that Romanesque would not be splendid enough and indulge in ornament as well as Gothic . . . but the ornament is economised and used with discretion."[10] Furthermore, "the solidity of Romanesque buildings with their sturdy columns and massive proportion will often satisfy the artistic eye better than the more slender and ingenious construction of a later day."[11]

Hemingway's own analogy is valid. Carlos Baker terms Hemingway's prose "neoclassic" because of its restraint and sense of order.[12] Romanesque architecture is an immediate development from Roman or classical architecture and is also noted for its restraint and sense of order. Maxwell Geismar understands Hemingway's prose in terms of its "discipline," its "iron restraint" through which "the spirit's true visions" are allowed "to slip through" and "to emerge and create the wonderful tension of his work."[13] Again, the phrases of description might also be applied to Romanesque architecture. Harry Levin's emphasis upon

9 *Death in the Afternoon*, p. 191.
10 Jackson, *Byzantine and Romanesque Architecture* II, p. 260.
11 Ibid., p. 265.
12 Baker, *Hemingway: The Writer as Artist* (Princeton, N.J., 1963), pp. 51ff.
13 Maxwell Geismar, *Writers in Crisis: The American Novel 1925–1940* (Cambridge, Mass., 1942), pp. 39–40.

the factual, concrete nature of Hemingway's prose[14] corresponds with the directness and solidity associated with Romanesque structures. It is not really surprising that Hemingway's critics often speak of him in the same terms that art historians speak of Romanesque architecture.

I do not mean to imply that Hemingway actually learned to write prose from studying cathedrals in the same sense that he seems to have learned to depict landscapes from studying Cézanne. However, it is obvious that Hemingway himself recognized qualities of his own style in certain cathedrals; that is, he was able to understand that certain principles (such as restraint) can be expressed equally well with words and with stones. He was thus able to think of arrangements and meanings of words much as he thought of arrangements and meanings of stones. He was again expressing a unitary understanding of art.

Within the context of Hemingway's fiction, cathedrals play a rather interesting role. Jake Barnes enters a cathedral to pray; Frederic Henry hesitates in front of the cathedral of Milan, but does not enter. Both men express a certain admiration for the cathedrals as architectural entities. The windows of Chartres and Léon stimulate an "authentic" feeling in Robert Jordan. Colonel Cantwell admires the cathedral of Torcello and the campanile of Burano but dislikes St. Mark's and other high Byzantine architecture. If examined in order, these protagonists seem to indicate a lessening of religious feeling and a growing admiration of the architecture of the buildings. Jake is really the only one who tries to pray in a cathedral; the Colonel does not even consider entering any church.

In *The Sun Also Rises*, the cathedral represents a special and sacred place in which Jake can at least try to pray but in which the pagan Brett has no place. In *A Farewell to Arms*, Catherine's assertion to Frederic that "you're my religion" (120) negates even

14 Harry Levin, "Observations on the Style of Ernest Hemingway," *Hemingway and His Critics: An International Anthology*, ed. Carlos Baker (New York, 1961), pp. 95ff.

the slight religious sense that Jake had felt in *The Sun Also Rises.* Robert Jordan's assertion that the "great windows" at Chartres and Léon give him an "authentic" feeling is as much a tribute to the architects of the cathedrals as it is a praise of God. In short, as the Hemingway protagonists develop progressively, a cathedral is more a museum than a place of worship. Yet Hemingway is always careful to note the presence of the cathedrals and to express admiration for them. It is almost as if the cathedrals express a very special quality which the protagonists yearn for, but with which they cannot communicate, even when or if, like Jake, they try. As Carlos Baker has pointed out, "The consciousness of God is in his books,"[15] and Hemingway's references to cathedrals seem to support this contention. On the other hand, cathedrals in reality dominate any city, and if Hemingway wished to give the true texture of Venice, Pamplona, or Milan, he had to mention the cathedrals.

It is curious that Hemingway mentions only cathedrals—not churches, or chapels, or the roadside shrines which are so common in Europe. Nor does Hemingway mention any other special types of architecture, although Colonel Cantwell does point out the ruins of a "country house once built by Longhena" (13). A cathedral is, of course, the seat of a bishophric, where the highest local authority of the Roman Catholic Church rests. In the cathedrals, no matter what architectural style they exhibit, the discipline and tradition of the Church are manifest. The cathedral structure itself is the physical symbol of such power. It is perhaps the tradition and authority of the Church, as represented by the cathedrals (not, for example, by the humble and modest roadside shrines), that particularly attracted Hemingway and his protagonists.

Curious also is the fact that Hemingway has so totally overlooked the implications of the architecture of his own age. Had he not seen any of the work of Le Corbusier, who, with Ozenfant, had founded the purist group before World War I and had then published a magazine, *L'Esprit-Nouveau*, in Paris from 1920–25

15 Baker, *Hemingway: The Writer as Artist*, p. 328.

(a rather long life for such magazines)? Le Corbusier was first a cubist painter who followed Gris's style, but then he became an architect. His houses at Poissey and elsewhere in France, which were constructed during the 1920's, are landmarks of functional architecture. With cube-like white exteriors, these houses express that purity of line which Hemingway had noted so readily in the sculpture of Brancusi and in the form of good bullfighters.

Or had Hemingway noticed none of the architectural innovations closer to home, so to speak? Growing up as he did in the Chicago area and living there later as an adult (1920–21), why had he not been attracted to the prairie school of architects? Had he not seen, for example, Frank Lloyd Wright's Robie House (1909)? I would imagine that the synthesis of site and structure alone might have appealed to Hemingway. Or had he not noticed the more functionally designed office buildings in Chicago, such as the Liberty Mutual Insurance Building (1908) or the Dwight Building (1911)? There is simply no evidence that Hemingway was at all attracted to the purity of line and functionalism of modern architecture.

No, Hemingway's architectural interest was clearly dominated by the Romanesque and Gothic cathedrals of Italy, France, and Spain—a rather limited scope, admittedly. Yet there is a purity of line evident in these cathedrals; there is also, especially in the Romanesque style, a strong emphasis upon functional integration of all elements, as well as a synthesis of structure with site. Moreover, the cathedrals manifest two characteristics totally lacking in the structures of Wright and Le Corbusier—God and the Church. And it is obviously God and the Church which Jake Barnes was attempting to find, which Frederic Henry hesitantly passed by in the fog, which could inspire Robert Jordan, but which Colonel Cantwell rejected. It seems to me that, in Hemingway's fiction, the use of the cathedrals is almost wholly symbolic. On the other hand, Hemingway's statement with which this chapter opens is evidence that he himself is able to associate words and stones in a unitary sense.

VIII

Hemingway and the arts

"You really like to do this, what you do now, this silliness of kudu?"

"Just as much as I like to be in the Prado."

"One is not better than the other?"

"One is as necessary as the other. There are other things too."[1]

I was learning something from the painting of Cézanne that made writing simple true sentences far from enough to make the stories have the dimensions that I was trying to put in them.[2]

Even the most avid Hemingway buffs, especially those who are members of conservationist clubs and who are also friends of their local museums, must choke each time they are reminded of Hemingway's now-famous analogy between hunting kudu and visiting the Prado. Of course, Hemingway fans can take comfort in the passages following the analogy as Hemingway redeems himself with a rather long discussion of books (with perfectly respectable authors) which he enjoyed. The kudu-Prado analogy, however, was not written just for shock effect or for Hemingway's personal image-building. In so many words, Hemingway repeated the same concept fifteen years later, in *Across the River and into the Trees*, when Colonel Cantwell strolls through a butcher market and is reminded not only of the Prado, but also of the Accademia. Both passages, the one from a work of fiction

1 *Green Hills of Africa*, p. 25.
2 *A Moveable Feast*, p. 13.

and the other from a non-fictional book, reflect rather clearly what are for Hemingway three self-evident truths about life and art.

Art is, first of all for Hemingway, a part of life. The paintings at the Prado are as necessary to life as hunting kudu. Art is a part of all the experience which a writer must live (or, in Hemingway's case, sense) before he can create. Thus visiting the Prado is, indeed, like hunting kudu: both actions provide the experience from which the writer draws for his fiction. In order to create Colonel Cantwell, who could visit a butcher market much as he might visit the Accademia, Hemingway had to be able to hunt kudu as he hunted for a special Goya or El Greco in the Prado. Philip Young, in fact, has pointed out that Hemingway's response to hunting and paintings is identical—"aesthetic":

> it is at once clear on reading *By-Line* that taking the lives of fish and animals was for Hemingway an essentially aesthetic experience that brought emotions entirely comparable to those aroused by the experience of great painting or music. The "whirr of wings that moves you . . . more than any love of country," the beauty of a great marlin whose every jump was a sight to stop the heart, and at whose boating one is "purified," and welcome in the brotherhood of the "very elder gods," these things are not faked. The long broad gap between Hemingway the sportsman and Hemingway the writer has closed for at least one of his students.[3]

Indeed, Hemingway's portrait of Thomas Hudson clearly indicates that, for the artist, the relationship of the aesthetic and the physical is one of continual interaction and correspondences. The arts are as important to the consciousness of man as choosing meat for his dinner or participating in the ancient and honorable sport of hunting.

For Hemingway the arts are not superfluous; they are necessary. By comparing a visit to the Prado with hunting kudu,

3 Philip Young, "Hemingway by Moonlight," *Book Week, The Washington Post and Times Herald,* May 28, 1967, p. 6.

Hemingway intimates that art is a part of man's elemental consciousness. Such a concept is not in any way a denigration of art, at least for Hemingway. He sees art as an almost instinctive expression of man. This is not to say that producing art does not require a great deal of effort: what Hemingway learned from Cézanne was assimilated into his prose only with difficulty. The need to experience and then to express art is simply a part of man's psychological make-up. Putting art on this basis aligns Hemingway rather closely with the surrealists; then too, Hemingway's concept of art as instinctive is not really so far from the theories of aestheticians, such as Maritain, who must resort to labeling the source of art simply as "creative intuition."

Another "self-evident" truth reflected in this analogy is that man's response to art is basically instinctive and sensual, yet aesthetic. Obviously hunting kudu is a sensual and aesthetic experience. From any number of sources, such as Hemingway's interpretation of Goya in *Death in the Afternoon*, it is also certain that Hemingway's own response is primarily sensual. It is a sensuality which flows into an emotional heightening. Hemingway was ecstatic when he finally shot his kudus. When Robert Jordan views the great windows at Chartres and Léon, as well as the paintings at the Prado, the result is a feeling. Colonel Cantwell observes the textures and colors of lobsters in their baskets and on slippery floors and feels pleasure.

Hemingway himself responded in such a way to paintings—for example, Brueghel's "The Harvesters" (New York Metropolitan Museum): "It's the great one, of the harvesters. It is a lot of people cutting grain, but he uses the grain geometrically, to make an emotion so strong for me that I can hardly take it."[4] Hemingway's sentiments here sound ludicrous and have brought smiles to the faces of many; yet the grain fields are handled geometrically—and in a manner remarkably similar to Cézanne. Surely, given Cézanne's influence on Hemingway and the art of all moderns, Hemingway's response is not really as extravagant as it has often been interpreted to be. It is just such a handling of geomet-

4 Quoted in Lillian Ross, *Portrait of Hemingway* (New York, 1961), p. 58.

"It is a lot of people cutting grain, but he uses the grain geometrically, to make an emotion so strong for me that I can hardly take it."

—ERNEST HEMINGWAY TO LILLIAN ROSS (1950)

Pieter Brueghel the Elder, "The Harvesters." 1565. Oil on wood, 46½ x 63¼ in. The Metropolitan Museum of Art, Rogers Fund, 1919.

rical forms, combined with other elements such as color orchestration, which produces the synaesthetic quality of Cézanne's art. Thus the art itself must provide the sensual stimulation for the viewer to respond. Like the kudu and the land in which he lives, paintings at the Prado also demand that man see, hear, smell, and feel as totally as possible.

A third "self-evident" truth which Hemingway implied in this analogy is that there is beauty throughout life—the simple perception of beautiful physical forms. As has already been pointed out, Carlos Baker observed that Hemingway saw beauty in the honest, natural, and untainted. This is true, but such a statement does not really reveal how broad Hemingway's perception of beauty could be. Like Colonel Cantwell, who truly saw beauty in carcasses in a butcher market, Hemingway saw kudu as beautiful and clean. Beauty does not have to be something abstract or sublime or a quality apparent only through philosophical speculation. On a very factual level, quite similar to Emerson's first category of beauty (in simple forms), Hemingway found beauty in many things, whether natural (the kudu) or man-made (paintings at the Prado) or man himself (the American writer whose face Colonel Cantwell found "wonderful"). Despite the fact that we generally think of Hemingway, like Goya, as an artist of man's agony and *nada*, he often perceives beauty in unexpected places and in otherwise unglamorous or even ugly things, again like Goya or like those Dutch painters whose names Colonel Cantwell could not remember.

Other types of beauty are present in Hemingway's fiction, but now we must leave Hemingway's kudu and examine other passages—specifically his reference at the beginning of this chapter to the dimensions which he found in Cézanne's painting and which are beyond the simple declarative sentence of fact or, by implication, beyond perception of simple physical beauty. In physical form, some mountains are beautiful; this is one kind of beauty. Cézanne's mountains, however, showed Hemingway that he must add a dimension (i.e., the mountains as a symbol of order) to the physical truth of the simple fact that mountains are beautiful.

Such dimensions have already been pointed out in this book, but let me here define two specific types of beauty which are usually involved in those dimensions.

Context of an action or fact often provides a sense of beauty. Note, for example, this passage from *Death in the Afternoon*: "Without an ear for music the principle impression of an auditor at a symphony concert might be of the motions of the double bass, just as the spectator at a bullfight might remember only the obvious grotesqueness of a picador. The movements of a player of the double bass are grotesque and the sounds produced are many times, if heard by themselves, meaningless" (9). Within the context of the concert or the bullfight, however, the motions of the double bass player and the picador are beautiful. Conversely, when a beautiful act, such as Jordan's and Maria's love affair, occurs in an ugly context, the beauty of the act is enhanced. Other dimensions of beauty involve moral or ethical deeds and imply the search for order by man or his search for a code. What is intrinsically beautiful in the story of a semi-literate old fisherman who goes "out too far" and returns with nothing but a skeleton of a fish–except as Hemingway communicates that other dimension which makes Santiago's action beautiful?

Thus, to a great extent, Hemingway saw beauty in rather unexpected places; as a result, he opens the eye of the reader to such beauty. If we reexamine those painters whom Hemingway most liked, it is clear that they too found and revealed beauty in unexpected places: Goya's "The Third of May," Miró's "The Farm," El Greco's stormy "Toledo," Bosch's "Garden of Earthly Delights," Brueghel's "The Harvesters," and Mantegna's "Death of the [Pudgy] Virgin." And then there is Mont Sainte-Victoire. To be sure, Hemingway's beauty, which was apparently reinforced by these painters, is usually placed squarely in the context of overwhelming ugliness and *nada*, but the beauty is the more precious for that.

Ultimately there is a difference between hunting kudu and studying Cézanne. Hemingway hunted kudu and viewed paintings to gain experience, but he also studied paintings and architecture and other art forms in order to learn just how to write about hunting kudu and, in the process, to show truly "the shape of a country."[5] Hunting kudu did not teach Hemingway how to communicate the processes of the hunt or "the shape of the country." It did teach him how one hunts kudu and what that part of Africa looks like. It was Cézanne who helped Hemingway develop techniques by which he could indicate "the shape of the country."

It should be obvious by now that Hemingway was not a mere copyist of either techniques or images from other arts, the pictorial arts more specifically. There is a vast difference between copying and imitating. Hemingway himself pointed out that a great artist must learn from all other artists (in any category of art); the great artist, however, learns faster and better.[6] Yet despite the necessity to learn from others, all art is made only by the individual from that mysterious "well," as Hemingway told George Plimpton.[7] In fact, Hemingway's type of imitation is especially creative because he was dealing with two different media. He had to find ways to incorporate the methods and images from one art form into another. His kind of imitation is classical in the best and most original way.

Hemingway imitated a great many other artists—just as he says all great artists must do. The influence of other novelists and the imagist poets is well known. And surely, by now, it must be clear that he also imitated painters, both with respect to image and to technique. It seems to me that part of Hemingway's interest in the pictorial arts is directly the result of his desire to communicate sensual, empirical truth—what he could see, feel, hear and smell—more accurately and vividly. He was not the first American writer to seek a sensual heightening in the plastic media. In 1886, Henry Adams sought a "reawakening of sense" by making watercolors. For him, the pictorial arts were "the instrument of his sensuous

5 Foreword, *Green Hills of Africa.*
6 *Death in the Afternoon*, pp. 99–100.
7 George Plimpton, "An Interview with Ernest Hemingway," *Hemingway and His Critics: An International Anthology*, ed. Carlos Baker (New York, 1961), p. 25.

education,"[8] and this different kind of education is reflected in his later prose. Hemingway never painted,[9] but his response to art, as well as his own creation of art, involved a synaethesia. Carried to its extreme, obviously, an aesthetic of pure synaesthesia becomes the neo-Dada and neo-surrealist movements of today, in which Susan Sontag can demand a sensual expression which is "beyond interpretation" or the New York Museum of Contemporary Crafts can display in 1969 a show entitled, "Feel It."

Hemingway understood the dangers in such an aesthetic and thus sought the dimensions which were present in the paintings of Cézanne. In using techniques and images from the pictorial arts, Hemingway found that the word per se was of utmost importance. Even before Ludwig Wittgenstein had formulated his linguistic principles and long before the Cambridge positivists began their essentially linguistic literary criticism, Apollinaire and William Carlos Williams had made perfectly clear just what could be done with a word. For Hemingway, too, the burden of communicating both fact and dimension was placed upon the word.

Consider, for example, his use of the word "swamp" in "Big Two-Hearted River." On a simple, factual level, the word swamp indicates a thickly wooded area with water and undergrowth. "Swamp," however, can also indicate mystery or foreboding. Hence the fact that Nick refuses to enter the swamp is evidence of another dimension, whether in the mind of Nick or in the swamp itself. A swamp is also by nature dark and is thus juxtaposed to the light outside, along the river or on its lightly wooded banks. Thus part of the chiaroscuro effect is established by "swamp." Finally, "swamp" becomes more precisely associated with another dimension as Nick remarks that fishing in a swamp is "a tragic adventure." By introducing the swamp only in the

8 J. C. Levenson, *The Mind and Heart of Henry Adams* (Cambridge, Mass., 1957), p. 210.

9 According to Mary Hemingway, he sometimes illustrated signatures to his letters—as, for example, three triangular mountain peaks outlined above the signature "Your Mt. Man" (personal letter, October 6, 1969). Hemingway's mother was a successful painter for a time in the 1930's. See Marcelline Hemingway Sanford, *At the Hemingway's: A Family Portrait* (Boston, 1961), pp. 237–38.

final paragraphs of the story, Hemingway uses this word to provide the final tension and hence the reason for Nick's elaborate and self-conscious fishing ritual. Hemingway has made this word serve a variety of purposes and even concludes this short story, which is often judged to be one of his best, with "swamp."

The word, therefore, has been used to provide a series of dimensions and to serve functions beyond its actual physical definition. Clearly, this is precisely the sort of treatment a specific word might have received in the poetry of Williams or Eliot. Thus Hemingway has allowed the word, within the context of prose, to act as if it were part of a poem. But he also let the word act as if it were in the context of a painting or in a collage. His methods obviously were not those of Apollinaire or E. E. Cummings; that is, he did not vary type or traditional grammatical technique to break up and enrich the potentially dull visual surface of a page. He used other, original methods.

Except for three early, introductory mentions and the last word of "Big Two-Hearted River," the word swamp appears in only three other paragraphs (the fifth, sixth, and seventh from the end):

> Ahead the river narrowed and went into a *swamp*. The river became smooth and deep and the *swamp* looked solid with cedar trees, their trunks close together, their branches solid. It would not be possible to walk through a *swamp* like that. The branches grew so low. You would have to keep almost level with the ground to move at all. You could not crash through the branches. That must be why the animals that lived in *swamps* were built the way they were, Nick thought.
>
> He wished he had brought something to read. He felt like reading. He did not like going on into the *swamp*. He looked down the river. A big cedar slanted all the way across the stream. Beyond that the river went into the *swamp*.
>
> Nick did not want to go in there now. He felt a reaction against deep wading with the water deepening up under his armpits, to hook big trout in places impossible to land them. In the *swamp* the banks were bare, the big cedars came together overhead, the sun did not come through, except in

> patches; in the fast deep water, in the half light, the fishing would be tragic. In the *swamp* fishing was a tragic adventure. Nick did not want it. He did not want to go down the stream any further today [328–29, my italics].

Hemingway has consciously repeated "swamp." It is used eight times, with the pronoun "there" substituted once and "down the stream" allowed to stand for "swamp" once in order to provide continuity to the next paragraph, as well as to reinforce the symbolic dimension. In fact, there is a real danger that his repetition of "swamp" could have proved dully redundant, were it not for its context.

His repetition here of "swamp" could very well be related to the influence of musical repetition and counterpoint in his prose,[10] but the images seem far too visual and tactile to me to support this conclusion. Moreover, if read aloud, this passage does not rhythmically depend upon the word "swamp." Actually, in its visual context and tactile suggestions, "swamp" is used much as Gris or Braque might have used a word in a collage or a cubist painting. Often, as in Gris's "Bottle and Glass" (1914; Collection Marlborough Fine Art Limited, London) or Braque's "Young Girl with a Guitar" (1914; Musée National d'Art Moderne, Paris) or his collage "The Clarinet" (1913), a word or part of a word in some type face is situated somewhere near the center of the picture. The movement of line and plane arrangement is generally circular, around the word itself. Thus, as the eye follows the movement within the construct, the word itself is constantly kept within the range of the eye. Reference must be made continually to the word, not only for the visual texture which the type and design of the letters might offer but also for its significance as a word with a specific meaning.

In much the same way, Hemingway has written these paragraphs so that the eye must return continually to the word "swamp." Very carefully Hemingway has let the eye wander, in the first paragraph, into the swamp; then, in the second para-

10 Plimpton, "An Interview with Ernest Hemingway," pp. 27–28, and Ross, *Portrait of Hemingway*, p. 60.

graph, back to Nick; and, finally back to the swamp, but with Nick's projected image of himself fishing in the swamp. Again and again, "swamp" catches the eye and demands reinterpretation as the passages move along. There is a continual reiteration of the word as it is examined by Nick from different perspectives, much as Braque or Gris examined a clarinet or a bottle. And this is not a unique passage.

Another way in which Hemingway has let words approximate paint is in his use of color orchestration. Hemingway has been able to make a word of color description contribute or perhaps even dominate the color orchestration of an entire passage in a manner which is suggestive of the way in which a painter is able to use only a single brush stroke to define spatial position, describe edges, indicate volume, and add color. Hemingway's touch with such adjectives of color is so sure that he generally needs to mention the color itself only once. That is, he needs only the word itself, even in an extended passage, to accomplish these various ends. For example, in Jake's view of the plain of Burguete, the red of the roofs is mentioned only once; yet the sense of this color is strongly evident.[11] He has been able to use "red" much as Cézanne or Pissaro could employ only a single brush stroke of red to define the roofs of a distant village.

Hemingway has also demanded that words evoke sensual qualities. For me, this is one of the most significant ways in which he has imitated the techniques of the pictorial arts. Maria's "colorful" sexual climax, the tactile gray of the logs which Nick senses, the visual and audile "red black roar" as El Sordo's hill is bombed —all these and other passages suggest that color has become a thing, that the color word has become an object. In this use, it seems to me that Hemingway has most closely approached the pictorial arts, for the painter must depend to a great extent upon color to suggest the sensual connotations of the design or action which he has painted upon the flat canvas.

11 In this same passage, Hemingway has repeated the green of the plain (two mentions) because it is the overall color of the scene and because it is the only receding color in the vista. The whites he repeats because there are several whites: the road, the houses, and the clouds.

Hemingway has thus been able to reach beyond the word as used in the objective correlatives of the imagists and also has been able to avoid the radical experimentation of Apollinaire, James Joyce, and Gertrude Stein. The word, for him, was as important and basic as it was to these other writers, but he found special uses and dimensions for his words by using techniques adapted from the pictorial arts.

Such techniques are often inextricably bound up with specific images or symbols. For example, Hemingway's symbol of mountains as representative of order, stability, and occasionally peace are almost totally expressed with techniques taken from the pictorial arts, from the paintings of Cézanne especially. Hemingway continually describes mountains in geometrical analogies or adjectives (those same geometrical forms which thrilled him in Brueghel's "The Harvesters"). He also locates his mountains solidly in space; very seldom do they fade away. From these two specific techniques, which he seems to have learned from Cézanne, come the dimensions of the mountains as symbols. If Hemingway had wished to make the mountains or hills idyllic in only a factual, pragmatic manner, he could have done so easily enough by simply placing Jake and Bill or Catherine and Frederic or Maria and Robert in the mountains and showing them as happy. The reader is then left to assume that these people enjoy the privacy afforded them in a retreat away from the city and that they simply enjoy mountains. Hemingway wished to add a dimension, however; he wished to make mountains more significant than just mountains. By assimilating Cézanne's techniques into his description of mountains, he achieved the symbolic dimension he sought. The difference would be as evident if one were to read the simple, factual description of a snowstorm in William Cullen Bryant's "A Winter Piece" and then turn to Thoreau's "The Pond in Winter" (Ch. 16 of *Walden*). Hemingway could have used techniques other than Cézanne's, but these were the ones he chose. As he himself stated, it was Cézanne who had taught him the necessity of creating other dimensions within but beyond the factual statement.

Other images which seem to have been enriched by the pictorial arts do not depend as clearly upon specific technique and are thus more easily understood in an iconographic relationship. Thus, for example, Hemingway's numerous variations of the wounded soldier image, which centers upon Nick Adams but includes Jake Barnes, Frederic Henry, and Colonel Cantwell, is expressed with a variety of techniques in a variety of forms from the vignettes to the novels. As an image, it continues to expand and develop until the wounded soldier comes to stand for a wounded nation or generation and then, finally, to suggest the more universal concept of a wounded mankind. Whether the wound is mental or physical or whether or not the soldier has learned to accept it, these images naturally appear in the thematic context of violence or *nada*.

In many ways, it seems to me that Goya's "The Disasters of War" helped Hemingway define and enrich this image—not only with reference to actual scenes of wounding or violence or even specific technique, but also in terms of the general expansion of the image. "The Disasters of War" is composed of at least eighty specific scenes of violence and wounding, most of them handled in a very naturalistic manner. Goya transcends the occasional and the incidental—even the national—to make a statement concerning mankind's terrible condition in general. In fact, if one were to publish together those stories which deal with Nick Adams as a soldier, as well as other stories dealing with this theme and excerpts from the novels, the result would be Hemingway's own "Disasters of War"—a series quite similar to Goya's etchings in naturalistic treatment of the material, in specific techniques, and most especially in the thematic variation.

The repetition with variation of the same themes and the development of specific images, such as that of a wounded soldier, as done by Hemingway, is not really common in literature. Hemingway was not writing a series like the Forsyte Saga or the Leatherstocking Tales, nor was he handling the same material in different ways, like the classical dramatists. No, he was approximating more closely the type of thematic variation and image development found more often in painting and music. This is the method used by Goya in each of his five series of etchings and lithographs, or by Monet in his paintings of the cathedral of Rouen, or by Brahms in his variations upon the theme of Haydn. Hemingway's thematic repetition and single-image expansion is more constant that Twain's and more limited than Tolstoy's, both of whom Hemingway counted among his "literary forebears."[12]

Other images seem more expressive of the general philosophical or aesthetic beliefs of a particular artistic movement, as, for example, the concept of romantic love. It is rather striking, is it not, how very different Jake Barnes's true love Brett is from all the other Hemingway sweethearts in the novels? From the nymphomaniacal and alcoholic pagan Brett to the accommodating and saintly Renata, there is a series of mistresses and wives—all tending more toward Renata than Brett. The child-woman quality, the total devotion to the man, the man's great satisfaction and happiness (albeit short-lived), the association of some of these women with the Virgin Mary—all these characteristics suggest the *amour fou* of Breton and the surrealists. In no other Hemingway novel is this surrealistic love more evident than in *For Whom the Bell Tolls*—a novel in which the male protagonist also exhibits certain surrealistic traits.[13] Indeed, those rather baroque passages describing Jordan's sexual experience—passages which are unique in Hemingway's fiction and with which certain critics find fault—are closely related to the poems of Éluard or even to de Chirico's paintings of tunnels and womb-like buildings. The surrealists viewed art as unitary; hence their images were expressed in much the same manner in any of their artistic creations. Surrealist images and their illusionist techniques are more evident in the few passages of dreams or introspective fantasy which Hemingway allows his protagonists. The generally static images, in their pure and bright contrasting colors, of which Santiago dreams certainly sug-

12 Plimpton, "An Interview with Ernest Hemingway," p. 27.

13 It is really no coincidence that in 1937 Hemingway "was often in the apartment of the leftist poet Robert Desnos" during a ten-day visit in Paris. (Carlos Baker, *Ernest Hemingway: A Life Story* [New York, 1969], p. 301). More important than his being a "leftist poet," however, is the fact that Desnos was also one of the major surrealist poets.

gest that Hemingway might have found something else worth imitating among the surrealists.

Perhaps the most outstanding example of the enrichment of Hemingway's images by the pictorial arts is the theme of *nada* with all its various expressions. With reference to Goya alone, it is clear just how Hemingway might have used the word-image *nada* of Goya's famed etching and extended it in various ways. Nowhere in Hemingway's fiction is Goya's specter of the etching repeated, but the haunting message of *nada* permeated Hemingway's prose. Within the context of "The Disasters of War," the specter's *nada* suggests several meanings—from the senseless tragedy of war to the generally desperate condition of man to the absolute despair of nothingness even beyond the grave. For Hemingway, the sense of *nada* was generally limited to the facts of man's empirical position, such as the suicide of "Indian Camp" or the death of Catherine Barkley in childbirth in *A Farewell to Arms*. The *nada* of the present and immediate situation is so overwhelming for Nick and Frederic Henry that they dare not speculate beyond—to the grave, for example. In other stories, however, such as "A Clean, Well-Lighted Place," the implications of *nada* reach beyond man's empirical condition as the old waiter prays, "Our nada who art in nada."

A sense of despair, if not the sense of *nada*, is remarkably expressed in the works of many of Hemingway's favorite painters: Masson, Goya, Brueghel, and Bosch. How can the terrors of human agony be more explicitly depicted than in Masson's paintings of children eating raw fish, or Goya's "The Disasters of War" and "The Caprices," or Brueghel's portrait of a sickle-bearing Death, or Bosch's "Hell" panel of the "Garden of Earthly Delights" triptych? Bad dreams, scenes of human suffering and brutality, or symbolic statements of man's tragic condition—all of these images which Hemingway found in the pictorial arts contributed to the development and extension of his own images of despair.

Numerically, Hemingway preferred more painters who affirmed the existence of some sort of order or code in the universe than he did painters who expressed despair. Cézanne, Klee, Gris, Miró, Velázquez, Goya's "Tauromaquia," Brueghel's "The Harvesters," El Greco, Tintoretto, Mantegna, Degas—the list could be continued; all of them sensed some sort of order and transcendental beauty and expressed these in their paintings. At this point, I have returned to Hemingway's concept of beauty with which I began this chapter: that is, the simple perception of beauty in physical form (Miró's "The Farm" or Brueghel's fields), the sense of beauty within a specific context (Goya's bullfighters or Tintoretto's votive portraits of certain plain-looking old men who became handsome doges), or the beauty of a moral or heroic action (El Greco's saints or Cézanne's personal vision of mountains). Beauty thus becomes associated with a code.

In fact, all of these painters who affirm some sort of order in the universe express the kinds of codes for which the Hemingway protagonists are searching: Goya, in the bravery of men and women at war and in the "purity of line" of good bullfighters; Miró and Cézanne, in the transcendental order of nature which they expressed in geometrical forms; El Greco's and Mantegna's suffering but ecstatic saints; the stoicism and health of Velázquez's peasants—again, the list could be continued. Hemingway did not develop identical images, except perhaps in the case of certain of Goya's bullfight scenes and in his use of Cézanne's and Miró's geometrical forms; yet the sense of order, the affirmation of something more permanent than man, and the value of certain of man's actions are all common to these painters and Hemingway. Perhaps each painter, in his own way, reinforced Hemingway's own sense of order and helped him to form the essentially visual images which embody both reality and dimensions.

Many of these painters also are known for an economy of means in their styles, not only with respect to technique but also with reference to images. There is no baroque extravagance and ornateness in the works of most of these painters. Goya's etchings most clearly represent this economy of form and theme: the simplicity of lines, planes, and tones are paralleled by the clarity of the action of the few figures in any scene and by the single-theme variations. Cézanne and Miró represent a different kind of economy: the geometrical forms which they repeat not only simplify technique but also enhance the symbolic dimensions of their paintings. Hemingway's preferences in other art forms also reflect his general desire for economy and simplicity of expression: the musician whom he mentions most often is Bach; he disliked the ornate extravagances of both Byzantine and Baroque architecture; the only sculptor he mentions in a favorable way is Brancusi.

Hemingway thus preferred those painters who were capable of producing a "true simple declarative sentence," so to speak—with dimensions, but without scrollwork. His own style is economic in the extreme. As he explained to George Plimpton, "*The Old Man and the Sea* could have been a thousand pages longer and had every character in the village in it. . . . This is done excellently and well by other writers."[14] Hemingway sought to eliminate what was for him the unnecessary scrollwork and to create only the "true simple declarative sentence" (with dimensions) in order to create the old man and the boy, much as Miró concentrated upon the hunter or Goya upon a few figures in each etching. In this sense, the economy of style reflects clearly the economy of expression for both Hemingway and his favorite painters.

Hemingway's understanding of art was one of depth rather than breadth. He seems to have been attracted to only a relatively few artists, but these he knew well and understood thoroughly. The types of painters he liked were those who, like Goya and Cézanne, shared many of the same beliefs about life and art with him. These painters, it seems to me, indicated to Hemingway various ways in which he could develop images and techniques. Most of the artists who interested Hemingway were ones who were especially popular and influential among Hemingway's friends in the 1920's.

Obviously, the artists who most helped Hemingway shape his prose were painters. He does seem knowledgable enough about architecture—but again in depth, not in breadth. It is surprising to me that, at least until *Islands in the Stream*, he practically ig-

14 Plimpton, "An Interview with Ernest Hemingway," p. 34.

nores sculpture. Frederic Henry's observation that sculpture reminds him of cemeteries must be taken into account here: perhaps Hemingway really did connect cemeteries and sculpture in an adverse association. Even though Thomas Hudson responds in a more favorable way to sculpture, he too mentions funerary sculpture—and his favorite sculpted art seems to be driftwood, works formed by nature, not man. On the other hand, it seems to me that the static stillness of a sculpted human form might have disturbed Hemingway. The art he preferred was dynamic and vibrant, whether by means of color orchestration in Cézanne or simply by the actions of figures in Goya. Even Goya's majas lie poised alluringly. The one sculptor whom Hemingway did praise is Brancusi, who abstracted human and other natural forms to geometrical shapes without losing the actual representational quality of the figure—in short, a Cézanne who turned to sculpture.

No, it was with the makers of the pictorial arts with whom Hemingway most fully associated. Of all the artists who were working toward a single art before World War I and in the 1920's, the painters and writers were the most innovative and creative in the unitary sense. In philosophy they believed that all art is one; in practice, they shared images, themes, and techniques. As Piet Mondrian pointed out, "the expressive means are used in common."[15] In his own way, Hemingway advanced toward a single art, with the help of contemporaries, such as Masson and Miró; with the help of favorites of his contemporaries, such as Cézanne and El Greco; and with the influence of other painters with whom Hemingway himself had some affinity, such as Goya and Mantegna.

At least in the 1920's, this unitary sense of art seems based upon the sensual and pragmatic expression of truth, whether of mental or physical reality. The reasons why such a phenomenon occurred are not entirely clear even today. McLuhan feels that the impulse was the new electronics. No matter what the reasons, however,

15 Piet Mondrian, "Towards the True Vision of Reality," *Plastic Art and Pure Plastic Art, 1937, and Other Essays, 1941–1943, Documents of Modern Art* (New York, 1945), p. 14.

the unitary sense is not even avant-garde in the 1970's, when Roy McMullen discusses "painters-sculptors, painters-musicians, painter-dancers, and painter-architects (along with the painter-painters)."[16] He sees in the arts a "blurring of frontiers" and notes, "The blurring, it seems to me, has become more noticeable in recent years."[17] The "blurring" may be "more noticeable" today, but it has been going on for some time. For Hemingway to have lived in Paris in the 1920's, where he could experience the reality and know the formulators of a unitary sense of art, was indeed fortunate. That he himself was artist enough to be able to incorporate elements of other art forms into his prose attests to his own sensitivity and ability in the attempt to create a single art.

16 Roy McMullen, *Art, Affluence, and Alienation: The Fine Arts Today* (New York, 1968), p. 154.
17 Ibid., pp. 154 and 261.

An index of references to the arts in the works of Ernest Hemingway and of his biographies and critics

Several valuable general bibliographies of Hemingway are available, the most useful being *Ernest Hemingway: A Comprehensive Bibliography* (1967) by Audre Hanneman. My index concentrates upon two types of references: first, those specific mentions of or allusions to the arts which Hemingway himself made in his published writings; second, a selection of studies in which his biographers and critics have quoted or associated Hemingway in some way with the arts. This list does not pretend to be all-inclusive, but it is offered as a guide for scholars as well as for the general reader. Works which contain several references are abbreviated in the following manner:

PUBLISHED WORKS OF HEMINGWAY

Across the River and into the Trees (New York, 1950)=ARAIT
By-Line: Ernest Hemingway, ed. William White (New York, 1967)=B-L
Death in the Afternoon (New York, 1932)=DIA
A Farewell to Arms (New York, 1953)=FTA
For Whom the Bell Tolls (New York, 1953)=FWBT
Green Hills of Africa (New York, 1935)=GHA
Islands in the Stream (New York, 1970)=IITS

A Moveable Feast (New York, 1964)=MF
The Short Stories of Ernest Hemingway (New York: Modern Library, n.d.)=SS
The Sun Also Rises (New York, 1954)=SAR
Torrents of Spring, in *The Hemingway Reader* (New York, 1953)=TS

A Selection of Works in Which Hemingway Is Quoted Concerning the Arts or Associated with Them:

Baker, Carlos. *Ernest Hemingway: A Life Story* (New York, 1969)=EHLS
———. *Hemingway: The Writer As Artist* (Princeton, N.J., 1963)=WAA
Fenton, Charles A. *The Apprenticeship of Ernest Hemingway: The Early Years* (New York, 1965)=Fenton
Hotchner, A. E. *Papa Hemingway* (New York, 1966)=Hotchner
Joost, Nicholas. *Ernest Hemingway and the Little Magazines: The Paris Years* (Barre, Mass., 1968)=Joost
Plimpton, George. "An Interview with Ernest Hemingway," reprinted in *Hemingway and His Critics: An International Anthology*, ed. Carlos Baker (New York, 1961), pp. 19–37=Plimpton
Ross, Lillian. *Portrait of Hemingway* (New York, 1961)=Ross

I. ARTISTS, ARCHITECTS, SCULPTORS, ARTISTIC MOVEMENTS, AND OBJETS D'ART

"Abstract Painter," IITS, 317.
Andrea del Sarto (Italian, 1486–1531), "Portrait of a Woman," EHLS, 513; Hotchner, 187–88.
Anthiel, George (American, 1900–59), his "sketchbook," Joost, 90–91.
Bosch, Hieronymous (Dutch, ca. 1450–1516), ARAIT, 254; IITS, 21; EHLS, 513; Hotchner, 187; Plimpton, 27–28.

II. CAMPANILES AND CATHEDRALS

A. *Campaniles*

B. *Cathedrals*

III. MUSEUMS

Index